THE HISTORIC GARDENS *of* ENGLAND

OXFORDSHIRE

A Map of OXFORDSHIRE North West from London
Humbly inscrib'd to his Grace ÿ. Duke of Marlboro' Lord Lieut. of ÿ County.

From Henley to Watlington 8 - 1 to Oxford 11 - to Islip 8 - 3 to Banbury
17 - 1 in all 44 - 5 from London to Oxford 55 - 6

According to Act of Parliam.ᵗ G. Bickham 1751

THE HISTORIC GARDENS *of* ENGLAND
OXFORDSHIRE

Timothy Mowl

TEMPUS

For Paul Stamper

The publication of this volume has been made possible by a grant from

THE LEVERHULME TRUST

to cover all the necessary research work

Frontispiece: George Bickham's 1751 Map of Oxfordshire. *Bodleian Library, MS. Top Oxon a 37, f.4*

First published 2007

Tempus Publishing Limited
The Mill, Brimscombe Port,
Stroud, Gloucestershire, GL5 2QG
www.tempus-publishing.com

British Library Cataloguing in Publication Data.
A catalogue record for this book is available from the British Library.

ISBN 978 0 7524 4086 6

Typesetting and origination by Tempus Publishing Limited
Printed in Great Britain

CONTENTS

= The old boundary with Berkshire

ACKNOWLEDGEMENTS

As with the last three books in this series, my first thanks go to Professor Sir Richard Brook and his Trustees at the Leverhulme Trust whose generous funding of the research has made the Oxfordshire travelling and garden visiting a pleasure rather than a financial worry. I should like to acknowledge the warm and enthusiastic support for the series of Paul Stamper, to whom this book is dedicated. His continued encouragement and generous reviews of the earlier books have made this, often arduous, but always stimulating, academic and topographical journey worthwhile. I am indebted to Joanna Matthews of the Oxfordshire Gardens Trust who has sent me off to visit gardens that were not, initially, on my radar.

Other owners, archivists, friends, colleagues and Bristol University MA Garden History students and PhD researchers who have been particularly helpful include: Charles & Angela Cottrell-Dormer, Mavis Batey, David Lambert, Hal Moggridge, Chris Carter, Trish Gibson, Francesca Fraser-Darling, Sheila Ottway, Kate Felus, Clare Hickman, Helen Langley, Paige Johnson, Stephen Morris, Geoffrey Tyack, Alan Powers, Michael Cousins, Lord & Lady Camoys, Lord Rotherwick, Lady Neidpath, Sir Beville Stanier, Lady Wills, Robin Darwall-Smith, David Clark, Raymond Blanc, Leanda Pearman, Michie & John Herbert, Peter Warren, Iain Davies, Sally Rowlands, Rosie Pearson, Jon Edgar, Valerie Ferguson, Christine Martin, Carol Clark, Jennifer Meir, Helene Gammack, Caroline Dalton, Inara Gipsle, Pru Leith, Peter Ward, Stewart MacDonald, Alan Webb, Jeremy Wall, Simon Bing, Nick Warboys, Sir Anthony & Lady Bamford, Stephen Hepburn, Barbara Hester, Sheila Tofts, Jean Robinson, Nigel Phillips, Cecilia Akerman-Kressner, Tom Stuart-Smith, Rosie Pearson, Robin Whalley, Rosalind Ingrams, Hannah Gardener, Piers Newth, John Weaver, Christopher Galloway, Bernard Saunders, David & Trudy Yates, Richard Bellamy, Manda Patel, Joanna Matthews, Helen Hall, Mrs & Mrs Jobling, Sally Jeffery, Pete Smith, Denney Wickham, John & Waveney Luke, Sofka Zinovieff & Vassilis Papadimitriou, Jeremy Hulme, Andy Smith, Sandy & Diana Gray, Chloe & Maurice Robson, Miles & Mary Tuely, Michael Haynes, Mr & Mrs John Loudon, Leonard Rwodzi, Karen Irving, Brian & Reinhild Lloyd, Arpad Turmezei, Michael Peagram, Milton Grundy, Rodney Wilkinson, Camilla Costello, Dominic Walters, Anna Betts, Ruth Power, Anthony & Rita Gallagher, Stan Garbett, James Waterfield, Andrew Woodall, Simon Horwood.

I would like to make special mention of Olivia Harrison who allowed me access to her private grounds at Friar Park for one of the most visually memorable visits of the series to date.

Sue Grice and Anne Leaver of Bristol University's Department of Archaeology & Anthropology have photographed and scanned most professionally the archival images from my own university's Special Collections. I must thank Michael Richardson yet again for bringing many important texts to my notice. Peter Kemmis Betty and Thomas Vivian have been as efficient and enthusiastic as ever at Tempus, and Douglas Matthews has produced yet another definitive index. My agent, Sara Menguc, has supported the project with her typical drive and determination and encouraged me at the right time as I was writing a parallel book on the social and architectural edginess of Bristol.

As with all the books in the series, *The Historic Gardens of England: Oxfordshire* has been researched alongside my teaching of Bristol University's MA in Garden History, so I must thank my Co-Director, Michael Liversidge, for his advice on matters of aesthetics and Mark Horton and Joshua Pollard on matters archaeological. My friend and collaborator on architectural studies, Brian Earnshaw, has accompanied me on all the garden visits, undertaken several areas of the research and done his usual intellectually combative job of editing the text at manuscript stage. My wife, Sarah, and daughter, Olivia, joined me on an early visit to Buscot and have been as understanding and accommodating as ever as I have been absent during most of the summer, and my son, Adam, has been a lively and stimulating lunch companion in Oxford after long hours spent poring over documents in Duke Humphrey's library at the Bodleian.

This is the last book in the first phase of Leverhulme funding for the series; with the Trust's continued generous funding I now embark, together with my consultants, upon the next five years, starting with Lord Leverhulme's home county of soft sandstone hills and lush river valleys, bling and WAGs: Cheshire.

Timothy Mowl
Bristol, Winter 2006

INTRODUCTION

One of the richest and most influential of garden counties, especially after it pillaged most of Berkshire's best estates, Oxfordshire has not always been the easiest to visit. Coming from the welcoming warmth of garden owners in Worcestershire and Cornwall, an Oxfordshire response has often been: 'We are very private', which explains some notable gaps in this book.[1] London or foreign new money tends to treat an estate like an urban back garden or private oasis, not realising that the English aristocracy has survived as a popular and potent institution by leaving its parks and gardens conditionally open as places of public entertainment and show. Wealth creates great gardens, but it should not lock them away like a miser's hoard.

Before the rape of Berkshire, the one-time 'Royal County' of Oxfordshire was a narrow belt running north–south in the same relationship to gardens that Dorset's jurassic coast had to geology. In the north is the brooding ironstone country around Banbury, then a generous chunk of Cotswold limestone, followed by a clay country of warm red bricks, ending in the south with the soft chalk and hard flints of the Chilterns. Oxford city used to be literally a stone's throw from the Berkshire border, but now it stands centrally, as a county town should, with star-ranking gardens at Buscot, Buckland, Pusey and Faringdon wrapping it round on the west. It just so happens that Faringdon House has the most imaginative twentieth-century garden building of any of the six counties covered in this series to date: Robert Heber Percy's swimming pool guarded by two giant stone wyverns and a Gothick tower on top of a ziggurat. Swimming pools, symptoms of the frustration of an inland county, have been an Oxfordshire speciality, one feature the Medici never thought to patronise, though the murals on Buscot's east pavilion enclosing its inviting pool would grace any Florentine villa.

So Oxfordshire is the new royal county. Henry II laid out a Siculo-Norman garden for his mistress at Woodstock. King Alfred gifted Beckley Park to a kinsman; Edward II gave the place to his lover, Piers Gaveston, and the Chaucer family handled it for the Black Prince. Beckley has ended up as an amazing palimpsest of a garden, a haunted maze of ditches on the edge of a marsh, with topiary by an early twentieth-century Buddhist. Possibly because of the royal connection and the University, the county has been at the forefront of garden design. Blenheim, a miniature county in itself, nudged neighbouring parks in a military direction. Rousham is the most intensely personal and atmospheric of all English Arcadias, miraculously preserved with all its attendant erotic artworks, by the wise guardianship of the Cotrell-Dormer family: a national treasure. Unhappily not a wrack remains of the trick jets and rainbow fountain of the Henrietta Garden, Thomas Bushell's Caroline grotto at Neat Enstone, but something equally, or even more important, survives nearby at Heythrop.

Some forty years ago, when the Jesuits owned Heythrop, the patrol I led won the Archbishop's Flag for its scouting activities there, but I did not appreciate that in the marshy ruin of the Duke of Shrewsbury's park, where I was camping, lay the fount and origin of all subsequent Arcadias. It is a cluster of forlorn Cold Bath, Nymphaeum and water courses which urged the garden writer, Stephen Switzer, to hail it as a unique invention, the prototype for the *Jardin Anglais* that would sweep western Europe and Russia later in the century. It is still there, hidden in dark woodland, waiting to be hunted down and made as famous as it deserves.

The county has at least three more five-star gardens, so far only half acknowledged for their significance. At Sandford Park there is a Regency double-faced Chinese Temple (*1*) as exotically charming as anything sketched out by William Kent.[2] Stylistically linked, but of the 1960s, is the Japanese Garden at New House, Shipton-under-Wychwood. A house of angular shafts of stone is set within an exotic landscape of moss and pools: a green

1 The rare Janus-faced Chinoiserie Temple has alcove seats which command two eighteenth-century lakes at Sandford Park

gloom of delicate adjustments with no open vistas and scarcely a glimpse of the sky. By my reckoning it is the most moving garden in the county. But then, what about Friar Park? Oxfordshire does make a demand on superlatives. Little known and little visited, but saved by a generous and inspired campaign of restoration by the current owners, it is, beyond question, the greatest, the most ambitious Victorian garden in Britain: Sir Frank Crisp's creation of wit, scepticism, eclecticism and poetry, as humane and personal as Rousham. It is difficult to believe that in all the gardens of counties still untravelled for this series there will ever be a garden quite as astonishing as the underground lakes, ice caves and enchanted Matterhorn of Friar Park.

Perhaps the best way to conclude the experience of such a cluster of major gardens would be to walk Joseph Addison's paths around Magdalen College's fritillary meadow, somewhere near the first week of April and then to dine at Raymond Blanc's Manoir aux Quat' Saisons, cleverly sited at Great Milton near the M40, to tempt greedy Oxford dons and their most important London visitors. Dinner could end, not with a fine dessert wine, but with a walk in the garden to savour the whimsical bronze statues luring guests from seventeenth-century pool to Japanese Tea House to sumptuous Potager in M. Blanc's updating of a raunchy Arcadia. The shame of it – a Frenchman teaching us how to make an entertaining and original garden!

NOTES

1   Other sites, such as Coleshill House and its spectacular 1792 eye-catcher, Strattenborough Castle Farmhouse, have been purposely omitted to find their places in a proposed later volume based on the historic boundaries of Berkshire.

2   It was built as part of a landscape campaign by Mary Heywood who bought the property in 1774 and died in 1797; see Christopher Hussey, 'Sandford Park, Oxfordshire', *Country Life*, 11 May 1940.

1

MAZES AND WATER IN THE MEDIEVAL GARDENS OF THE COUNTY

It is hardly surprising that, in the defence-conscious insecurities of medieval England, gardens should be closely associated with the water of moats. What was surprising, coming from the gardens of Worcestershire to those of Oxfordshire, was to find Oxfordshire's water gardens so much less defensive, so much more imaginative, functional, even sometimes lyrical, than those of its western neighbour. In Worcestershire virtually every older aristocratic seat, and even most major farms and squire's houses, have a precise, square moat, 12–20ft across, usually encircling not only the house itself but a garden or a farmyard of modest size, the walls of the house often dipping directly into deep water.[1]

This emphasises, of course, the danger of making country-wide rather than county-wide claims about English garden history. Worcestershire, for all the narrow, protective belt of north Herefordshire, was a border county, sometimes the royal base for excursions against the Welsh. Its farms were moated to protect livestock from cattle raids. In contrast, Oxfordshire was secure and sophisticated. There was the cultural lure of its university and, close to Oxford, the favourite royal seat of Woodstock Palace, which was as much visited by Plantagenet courts as Clarendon Palace in Wiltshire. Neither palace was heavily fortified like Windsor. In their walks and gardens, kings were more intent upon courtly love, reading, administering and hunting than on martial matters. Where kings retire for pleasure courtiers are inclined to cluster, but entangled with the theme of water in these gardens is the more puzzling theme of the maze.

At Woodstock, Fair Rosamond, the lover of King Henry II, lived hidden, according to legend, in a garden maze of waters probably designed by Islamic master gardeners from the Norman royal court of Sicily. The dangerously over-confident male lover of King Edward II, Piers Gaveston, was given a hunting and hawking seat at Beckley, close again, like Woodstock, to Oxford town, and Beckley's later Tudor lodge stands in an older garden maze of water channels, dated 1375 and in parts even earlier. The castles of Broughton and Hanwell both have strong water associations, in neither case entirely defensive. For, despite that memorable Norman keep in the heart of Oxford itself, this is not a county of great fortresses. Even Shirburn Castle, which lies in its moat like an ideal version of the Middle Ages, is largely an early eighteenth-century toy, a round-arched preliminary to the Gothic Revival set in an eclectic garden, like the ultimate garden pavilion.[2]

2 The Maze at Troy Farm – a sixteenth-century enclosure for contemplation or the site of local fertility rituals?

Medieval gardens are an area for speculation and scholarly uncertainties. Sources are usually vague, actual remains are often scanty.[3] As a county, Oxfordshire seems to offer more information on the medieval garden than any of the previous counties in this series, but it is still necessary to tread carefully, suggesting possibilities rather than launching confident theories. This is particularly true with one of the most mysterious gardens in north Oxfordshire: the Maze at Troy Farm in Somerton parish. But with such a theme of lost or putative garden mazes in the county it is most satisfying to find one of the only seven surviving pre-Tudor mazes in England lying intact and in perfect preservation just off a country road; but then, is it really pre-Tudor?

The Troy Farm Maze is both a pleasure and a disappointment (2). Sherwood and Pevsner describe it as sixteenth-century in date[4], which is arbitrary and hard to prove when all we are dealing with is a pattern of turf banks about a couple of feet wide and a few inches high with yellow gravel filling the winding paths between the banks. The evidence of well-preserved tiled mazes in medieval cathedrals like Ely or Chartres might suggest that an outdoor maze is just as likely to be a medieval, as it is to be a sixteenth-century, garden feature. The naïve confusion between the city of Troy and the maze of the Minator at Knossos in Crete is not likely to have been made in the Renaissance sixteenth century, whereas medieval garden designers could well have been confused about the geography of the Theseus story. Whatever its true date, Troy Farm's Maze has its place in this early chapter of garden experiments in the county.

The Farm, which looks to have been at one time a row of cottages, lies on the north side of the road. On the south side is a little wilderness of long grass and bushes with a faintly indented path. This leads 50 yards further on into a big yew bush, part of a masking yew hedge. On the far side of this, backed by more tall yew hedges, is the Maze, filling a round clearing. A notice before it reads: 'Please do not walk on the Maze' when, of course, the whole point of a maze is to walk it, either to contemplate life and the soul, or to gain some feeling of life with an ultimate goal and purpose; or simply to dance and have fun.[5] Those, at least, are Sir Roy Strong's theories as to the purposes of these structures.[6]

It is, therefore, disappointing, on entering this yew circle, to have the whole swirling pattern of the Maze paths immediately laid out as on the pages of a book. Later mazes tend to high hedges and claustrophobia, but on this Maze the paths can be absorbed in a moment, so it becomes quite clear that this is a maze with no goal, no centre, merely circular progressions. It could still have functioned as a dance floor, with the dancers strung together hand-to-hand in a chain, working their way around and about. Male Greek dancers link together by holding handkerchiefs and footing out linear patterns. But it would require nimble footwork as the gravel paths are only a foot wide. Its extraordinary survival over the centuries indicates that this was a place of local recreation and valued as such. Could it have served some musical fertility ritual?

It stands across the road from the cottages, and the villagers seem to have been interested enough in their hidden Maze to want to preserve its intricacies. Shakespeare relates that in an unfavourable season, 'The nine man's morris [a dance floor] is filled up with mud', and 'the quaint mazes in the wanton green/For lack of tread are undistinguishable'.[7] If those 'greens' were 'wanton', it suggests that they were used for cheerful, courting dances, certainly not for thoughtful contemplation by philosophically minded cottage dwellers. The privacy of this Troy Farm Maze is another indication of a quite lively ritual; why else should it be sited away from the houses and not linked to their gardens? Another question, however, relates to that small wilderness of rough ground through which the Troy Maze is approached. Has it always been so isolated? Does that ground cover the foundations of 'Somertons', a lost manor house, which the *Victoria County History* (hereafter *VCH*) mentions as having been the principal house in the parish.[8] There remains the oddity of the Maze being preserved when all the rest of the garden has gone under grass and bushes. Certainly the idea of a maze, like that of a secret underground passage linked to a convent, has a strong hold on the popular imagination. The pattern of the Troy Farm Maze is very similar to mazes illustrated in the background of two Tudor portraits: that of Lord Edward Russell (1573) and of Sir George Delves (1577).[9] But in any round maze the paths are as likely to run in roughly the same swirling patterns, as do the much earlier cathedral floor mazes. Whatever its real date it is useful to have experienced the modest realities of Troy Farm before passing judgement on the maze associations of Oxfordshire's two very different royal love nests, where a hedge or a wall or a ditch transformed a dance floor.

According to the *Historia Anglorum*, the Conqueror's youngest son, King Henry I, made the park at Woodstock a 'celebrated place ... for the habitation of men and beasts'[10], and not just for deer, as the *Gesta Regum* records a porcupine given to the king by William

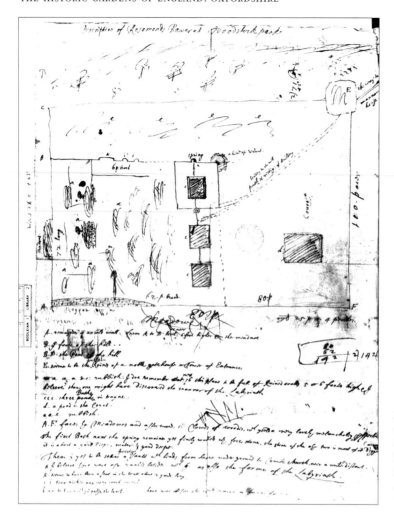

3 John Aubrey's
annotated sketch
of the remains of
Rosamond's Bower
in Woodstock Park.
*Bodleian Library, MS.
Wood 276b, f.43v*

of Montpellier.[11] There was a menagerie here at Woodstock six centuries before the neat little menagerie pavilion was built in the woods at neighbouring Ditchley Park. Rosamond Clifford's garden, with her cloistered retreat among its stepped-down pools of flowing water, has gone, though the unfailing and supposedly medicinal waters of the Everswell still run prosaically out of a steep bank framed by great cedars running down to the lakeside at Blenheim across from the Palace's overwhelmingly stately north entrance front. The water once ran through a twelfth-century sequence of pools, but now it falls into a rectangular tank of faintly municipal appearance. In compensation for the loss of garden poetry we have rich medieval records of its construction, hints as to its Sicilian-Islamic designers and a detailed mid-seventeenth-century sketch of it (*3*) by the antiquary John Aubrey.[12]

Woodstock Manor overlooked Rosamond's Bower and a visiting Norwich army officer reported in 1634 that King Henry II's wife, the jealous and formidable Eleanor of Aquitaine, found her way into 'the labirynth where the fayre lady and great monarch's concubine was surprised by a clew of silk'[13] as in the Cretan labyrinth of classical legend.

Once at the labyrinth's heart the Queen presented the terrified girl with a choice of death by dagger or by poisoned cup. Rosamund chose the cup and 'her obsequies were celebrated in a solemne manner'.[14] The officer described the bower surviving in substantial ruins, which he interpreted as being the walls of a maze:

> I found nothing in this bower but ruines, but many strong and strange winding walls and turnings, and a dainty, cleare, square paved well, knee deep, wherein this beautifull creature sometime did wash and bathe her self.[15]

The officer gives an overview, not just of Rosamond's Bower, but also of the whole park as it existed in the 1630s:

> I had a full prospect of that great and spacious walled parke, ye brave lawnes and waters, the neat and finely built lodge [High Lodge] for his majestie's chief ranger to inhabit, sweetly seated on a hill, near to this sumptuous Court, and many other handsome lodges, wherein many gentlemen keepers of quality doe reside.[16]

As if the melodrama of Queen and mistress were not legendary enough, Woodstock Manor was later the prison where Bloody Mary kept the future Queen Elizabeth out of harm's way from plotting aristocrats, and the young princess must often have walked in Rosamond's Bower, just below the Manor. So the manor-palace with its adjacent Bower was a truly mythic site.

Howard Colvin, the doyen of English architectural historians, himself something of a legend for his strict dependence upon proven documentary material for any attribution, becomes gently credulous, almost lyrical, when writing about that lost garden by the lake in Blenheim park. He relates how the legend of Tristan and Isolde, with all its courtly love and restraint, had been rewritten for King Henry's enjoyment and speculates that, as Tristan communicated with Isolde, arranging trysts by floating twigs down the stream that ran through her cloister, so Henry may have played Tristan by sending twigs down the pools of Everswell. When Aubrey drew his plan of the ruined Bower and garden much of its charm still survived.[17] Cut into the hillside was a wall with three seating alcoves. The spring of the Everswell gushed out from this wall into 'the first Bath next the Spring [which] remaines yet finely walled with free stone'. It then brimmed down a spout into two successive pools: 'three Baths in trayne'. Next to these on the right of Aubrey's sketch was a fourth pool, with ruins on the left. Aubrey recalled these in better preservation on an earlier visit: 'I doe remember that in anno 16- this place to be full of ruined walls 5 or 6 foote high and I beleeve that then, one might have discovered the manner of the Labyrinth'. He clearly believed in the maze story and was as eager for poetry as Colvin, reporting that the garden 'faces the Meadowes and afterwards into Clowds of Woodes, which yield a very lovely melancholy prospect'. A little enchantment still clings to the garden site, despite that municipal-type pool. The great cedars of Lebanon shade the hillside and the waters of Lancelot Brown's new lake lap up quite close to the pool's iron railings.

Intertwined with the literary Tristan explanation for the water garden are the historical links between Henry's court and the gardens of the Norman kings of Sicily. The royal pleasure grounds in the suburbs of Palermo were created by Islamic gardeners of that multi-racial kingdom and featured connecting pools of water, cloister walks and garden pavilions. In their prime they are supposed to have resembled the exquisite Moorish water gardens of the Alhambra at Granada. Records prove that larger and smaller pools, the former within the 'magnam claustrum'[18], were built at the Everswell in Rosamond Clifford's lifetime, so there was real cultural transference. King Henry's almoner, Thomas Brown, had come from Sicily where he had served King Roger II, the island's Norman ruler; and Henry's daughter, Joanna, was married in 1177 to the next king, William II, of Sicily. The links were, therefore, not merely plausible, but probable. By way of exchange, several Englishmen were appointed to Sicilian bishoprics.

Without Aubrey's sketch plan and his speculative annotations about a lost maze and an underground passage to Coombe church, we would have little or no guide to what may have been the most exotic and imaginative garden in medieval England, a courtyard space alive with the tinkle of falling water. At Beckley the situation is completely reversed; there the garden survives in a bewildering intricacy of channels and pools, the medieval sub-structure overlaid with twentieth-century topiary work and twenty-first-century flower gardening by the present, inspired owner. Today, Rosamond's pool is a mere interval in the smooth green lawns of Blenheim park; Beckley Park in contrast has a fair claim to be considered the most atmospheric and rewarding garden in the whole of a county richly endowed with historic gardens.

It is, for a start, extraordinarily remote in feeling for a place only a few miles from Oxford city. A long, rough track, which could never be described as a drive, leads across the fields below Beckley village to a gauntly beautiful house that looks and reads like a construct for one of Iris Murdoch's wilder novels (*colour plate 1*). That a place touched by a perverse and tragic love affair from that most doomed reign of the Middle Ages, Edward II's twenty strife-torn years from 1307-27, should also have an even earlier Saxon association, seems almost too much to ask from an historic garden. But it was the Saxon 'Beccaule' which King Alfred bequeathed to his kinsman Osferth in his last will and testament, thus setting a pattern of passage, not from father to son in the usual manner, but of gifting from friend to friend as a rare treasure.[19] After the Norman Conquest, Beckley became the capital seat of the so-called Honour of St Valery. Robert d'Oilly gave it to his friend Roger d'Ivry, a luxury toy for the pleasure of a favourite. The lodge has its feet in the last solid, or semi-solid, ground at the edge of Otmoor, a fenland which would at that time have teemed with marsh fowl for hawking and eels and fish for profit.

Roger d'Ivry died in 1112 and another owner, Bernard St Valery, died on crusade at the siege of Acre in 1190 putting the property back in the royal gift. In 1230 King Henry III gave it to his brother, the ambitious Earl Richard of Cornwall – who would be crowned King of the Romans in Aachen Cathedral in 1257, though he never quite became Holy Roman Emperor. Edward II gave Beckley to Gaveston and in his 1591-2 play, *Edward II*, Christopher Marlowe may be recording a folk memory of that episode when he has Gaveston stride onto the stage telling the audience that, now he has returned from exile, he will stage garden parties for the susceptible King Edward with masques in which water plays a significant role:

> And in the day, when he shall walk abroad,
> Like sylvan nymphs my pages shall be clad;
> My men, like satyrs grazing on the lawns,
> Shall with their goat-feet dance the antic hay.
> Sometime a lovely boy in Dian's shape,
> With hair that gilds the water as it glides,
> Crownets of pearl about his naked arms,
> And in his sportful hands an olive-tree,
> To hide those parts which men delight to see
> Shall bathe him in a spring....
> Such things as these best please his majesty.[20]

This is literary speculation, but certainly there are springs enough at Beckley for any number of water-borne masques.

When the outraged barons captured Gaveston at Deddington and had him murdered at Kenilworth Castle, King Edward gave Beckley to another favourite, Hugh le Despencer. In the next reign the property went to the Black Prince with the poet Geoffrey Chaucer's kinsman, Thomas Chaucer, as its steward. The role of famous names is some indication of how much Beckley was valued, but what is most satisfying is that records stating which of all these owners dug out the three moats on the Otmoor, garden side of the house and the two moats on the entrance side survive in the royal accounts. In 1373 the Black Prince gave the manor of Beckley, together with the hunting lodge, to Edward III and it was rebuilt in 1375.[21] Huge buttresses were constructed in the ditch surrounding the inner court of the lodge to support the new great hall. This moat had to be drained during the works, but a new outer moat, 'le utmest dych'[22], was dug and a new entrance to the complex was created. In 1376 a hedge was planted around the outer moat and the park walls were repaired. Unaware of this documentary evidence, Christopher Hussey speculated that it was Richard, Earl of Cornwall, who had the multiple ditches dug. This was a fair assumption as the Earl was something of a garden creator judging by his enclosures on the rock of Tintagel.[23] But what is obvious about the triple garden-side moats is that they were never meant to defend a 'castle' as they can quite easily be jumped or even stepped over. They must be functional features like the double moats around so many Worcestershire houses. A moat is more likely to be a medieval damp course than a medieval defensive earthwork; Beckley is a dry house in a wet marsh. Whether the moats also served as larders for eels and fish is another possibility.

The most confusing factor at Beckley is the present house itself, which is not medieval but Tudor in date, a work of about 1540 for Lord Williams of Thame, built upon the triple-moated medieval site. There are other distractions at Beckley. The south, or entrance, front is reached over a solid, stone-arched bridge across a moat as green as a lawn with waterweed. Valerian pours out of the crumbling grey lias of the moat walls

4 The north garden at Beckley Park is defended with a necklace of triple moats, the outer one dug out in the 1370s

and there is one pyramidal-roofed pavilion rising out of the water at the right-hand corner. Restored by the Victorians, it is probably the survivor of a Tudor twin pair. Clouds of pink roses billow out from the narrow garden strip between the moat and the plum-coloured brick house walls.

Lady Amanda Neidpath, the present owner and thoughtful gardener of Beckley, works not from the house, which for all its towering height is narrow-waisted and surprisingly small in its interior rooms, but from a barn to the side, festooned in white roses, ornamented with richly carved Indian panels and liberally decorated with Buddhist and Tibetan images and drawings. It is a place apart, drenched in its owner's personality and set in its own lawn. From the barn, paths lead past miniature garden enclosures, again Eastern in their ornaments, to turn a corner of the house, and there, beyond a deep pit of water with gunnera, foxgloves and rampageous flowers, is the remarkable north garden with its triple moats, which hang below the house like three strands of a necklace (*4*). Between the stone terrace of the house and these moats are two lozenge-shaped garden rooms, one with a tall tulip tree, and round these lozenges topiary passages spread out in a delicious but bewildering green maze, curiously dry above so much still, green water. What crowns these mazes of box and visually overwhelms everything else, floral or green, are the box pyramids, not two or three of them, but an uncountable multitude of 20-30 green spires all kept neat and geometric by the cowman.

The impact of this area is overpowering and difficult to convey. The north wall of the house, with its three projecting towers, rises up sheer from the narrow terrace, and at every few yards off the terrace there are entry points into the moat and topiary maze. Lady Amanda has created routes into the confusion by bridging the moats with clustered telegraph poles; but because the water is greener even than the lawns there is a perilous uncertainty as to where a foot can be placed. Yellow irises flourish in the green water; wild strawberries grow temptingly brilliant upon surprisingly dry banks. Lilies and roses, these last pale pink and wine dark, almost purple, enliven, together with red hot pokers, every small patch of open ground except for the lawns in those two intimate twin garden rooms.

Between the first and second moats runs the Ladies' Walk, a rare straight garden feature, tree shaded and reached by one of the causeway bridges. Out at the narrow north-west end of the house is the third and most impressive of the three garden rooms, the Yew Garden (5), in dark contrast to the cheerful, light green of the prevailing box-hedged walls. Fourteeen bushes, each cut into an abstract shape, fill the rectangular area and it seems reasonable, given the general chronological uncertainty of the site, to call this the Privy Garden and date it to at least as early as 1540 because a Tudor-arched doorway and steps lead down into it from the Privy Chamber at the top end of the house's modest hall. This wonderfully intimate, event-crowded complex of garden rooms was planned in 1919 by Bertie Moore, a Buddhist monk and a friend of Amanda's relative, Percy Feilding. So there are spiritual meanings behind the evident horticultural success. It is Moore's triumph that the intensely characterful house does not overwhelm the garden so closely gathered around it.

From this west end of the Yew Garden stepping stones set giddily in dark water lead out to the great Fishpond and the blank open spaces of Otmoor. This is a relatively treeless area of the grounds, still under development. Interlocking spaces, gauged to the roots of three and five, make sacred Tibetan geometries. The island in the Fishpond is for the swans, which come over, not gliding elegantly, but battering with their wings like noisy motor bikes, to protect their young cygnets. A Chinese temple or a Buddhist stupa is intended eventually for a mound near the water's edge, as there is a notable lack of horizontal features at this point.

The contrast between Beckley's atmospheric disorder and the crisp geometries of Rosamond's Bower at Woodstock, as Aubrey recorded them, underlines the danger of making generalisations about Plantagenet gardens. At Beckley there is little or no fall of the land on which to project waterfalls and step-set pools. Topography is the master and the director of any garden. Whoever originally planned Beckley's moist garden simply intended to impose an island of order upon a fen, and succeeded brilliantly. It is a timely reminder of the basic garden problems faced by our ancestors: first drain, then garden.

That Fishpond at Beckley does, however, bring two additional elements into the medieval garden equation: one is the larder, the other is visual beauty. Any great house, manor or palace had to be self-sustaining. Eels can only be invited, but fish can be cultivated. Swans too were the medieval equivalents of the Christmas turkey, the most relished and, therefore, jealously guarded roasts on feast days. On my last visit to Beckley the foxes had just taken a

5 Spiritualism underpins horticulture in Beckley's Yew Garden, laid out after 1919 by Bertie Moore, a Buddhist monk

cygnet, so an island refuge for a swannery was an essential that could, by degrees, become a visual pleasure. At Hanwell Castle and Broughton Castle, both up in the Midland north of the county near Banbury, the exact functions of the moats are becoming an equivocation between the defensive, the larder and the pleasance.

A few dates may help to trace the rise of the aesthetic element in water at these sites. While few gardens can be fixed down to one precise year of creation, a rough guide would be 1170 for Woodstock, 1320 for Broughton Castle, with its crenellation much later in 1406.[24] Beckley was begun in the Saxon Dark Ages, but 1375 will serve for much of the ditching and hedging, while Henry VII's Cofferer, William Cope, set to work seriously at Hanwell Castle in 1498[25] when it was safe to predict that the turbulence of the Wars of the Roses was a thing of the past and garden roses could be cultivated again. While that ends the medieval period, it is worth considering that in the next chapter the water theme will again feature prominently with Sir Anthony Cope's spectacular seventeenth-century waterworks with their 'House of *diversion*' at Hanwell, and also the geometrical garden at Tackley, which is an ambitious Jacobean water garden entirely, yet playfully, themed upon the defensive works of war. Old garden habits live on a long while after circumstances have changed.

Neither Broughton nor Hanwell has ever been short of water. Broughton was sited at the confluence of three streams and Hanwell stands above a narrow valley that oozes with springs. A source, which looks to be chalybeate, bubbles out of what must have been the Privy Garden, hence the 'Han' well. Park Farm a little to the north of the village was originally Spring Farm, which supplied the village with water and fills the Castle's impressive Fishpond, but water seems from the start to have been a garden luxury at Hanwell. Broughton, being 100 years earlier in its foundation by Sir John de Broughton, utilised its waters more defensively, with a wide, lake-like moat later commanded by a battlemented curtain wall, which defended some ranges of the Castle, while others were left open to the moat, thereby creating a wide space for ornamental gardens and utilitarian areas.[26] The signs are that Broughton has always been a courtier's sophisticated manor house rather than defensive castle, with an extensive inner court to contain fruit, vegetables, chickens and pigs and a moat to harvest fish: in short, a typical polite Oxfordshire home anticipating the security of the Tudors.

If a foreign visitor had to see one perfect English historic garden then Broughton would be a likely contender for that distinction. Perfectly ordered today and brilliant with tasteful blue symphonies of flowers, the Castle is the seat of the octogenarian 21st Lord Saye and Sele. The 1st Lord Saye and Sele had, like William Cope at Hanwell, been a royal treasurer, so it is unlikely to be a coincidence that two wealthy civil servants both played down the defensive elements of their homes and emphasised the utilitarian or aesthetic role of water in their gardens.

Broughton's moat is so wide, so shimmering, and so neatly lawned to its low banks as to urge that it was always valued for its looks. With water, not trees or walls, for its outer boundaries, the Castle's gardens are now unusually open to the gently rising slopes of the western hills. On the approach from Broughton village and church the way, after an 1840 Tudor-style lodge and short wooded drive, leads dramatically over a bridge and under the Gatehouse into a notably treeless, widely spaced area of vast lawns and little horticulture. These lawns are so uninterrupted and perfectly mown that it is difficult to imagine the original medieval chaos, but the long, dull lodgings range to the left of the Gatehouse suggests a lost squalor of stables and servants' quarters.

Today the former kitchens range to the south-west is defended by a long terrace of flowers, with aliums and honeysuckle making a riotous show and wisteria draped on most of the walls (*6*). Apart from this once utilitarian area, there are two gardens tied closely to the south ranges of the Castle. The first of these, to the south-east, lies in the same intimate relationship to the splendidly crafted Gothick private apartments as

6 The south-west terrace at Broughton Castle gives on to a wide expanse of lawn before the defensive waters of the moat – space for vegetables or an ornamental garden?

that Yew Garden at Beckley lay to the Privy Chamber at the top end of its Great Hall. It has a sunken lawn with blockish, geometrically clipped topiary. Where gardens are concerned there does seem in this medieval period to have been more concern for privacy than for display. At the south-west corner is the Ladies' Garden (*colour plate 2*), much larger and laid out with fleur-de-lys beds in the 1880s within the walls of the sixteenth-century kitchens.[27]

What gives the handsome grounds an air of unreality is probably the fact that Lancelot 'Capability' Brown and his followers were kept at a distance. A 1781 'Plan of the Intended Improvement' by John Davenport hanging in the house would have altered the banks of a much narrower moat with sinuous river-like extensions to north, south and west, all tree planted. On the south edge of the park Davenport intended a Brownian sector of carriage road leading to an extensive wooded park on the high ground to the east. He would also have clumped those open slopes that lilt away so beautifully to the west. Sanderson Miller is said to have advised on the landscaping of the grounds earlier in the 1760s, but its appearance today is of pasture with a few single trees – oak, beech, lime and sycamore – and small plantations towards the west boundary.[28] To drape trees each and everywhere about open parkland is an eighteenth-century fashion. Most noble medieval and Tudor houses were once surrounded by relatively tree-less pasture, common ground and enclosed park areas for livestock and game. The English Heritage Register entry states that 'the present park [at Broughton] occupies the site of several rectangular enclosures known as park areas during the late C17 and early C18', as shown on estate maps of 1685 and 1724, and that from the seventeenth to the nineteenth century an area to the south-east was known as 'The Warren'. The Warren had been licensed as early as 1301[29], and it must have encouraged William of Wykeham, who was later to found New College, Oxford, and who bought the Castle in 1377, to have 'a most unusual belvedere built upon a loggia of two tall arches' from which he could 'look over the battlements of the outer walls at the moat and at the game in "The Warren" on the hillside opposite'.[30] We are probably closer to the Middle Ages at Broughton, despite its neatness, than in most country house landscapes. Only on the east side across the moat are there the usual pockets of deciduous woodland with a few stark Scots pine. Around the Castle all is airy, windy and sun-filled, and that may well be what, despite our impressions of untrimmed forests, the gardens and grounds of the Middle Ages were like.

NOTES

1   For an account of these see Timothy Mowl, *Historic Gardens of Worcestershire* (Stroud, 2006), Chapter One.

2   See Timothy Mowl & Brian Earnshaw, 'The Origins of the Gothic Revival in a Georgian Norman Castle', *Journal of the Society of Architectural Historians of the United States*, vol.xl, no.4 (December, 1981), pp.289-94.

3   This is particularly so at one of the county's most impressive medieval secular buildings, Stanton Harcourt Manor, with its Great Kitchen and 'Pope's Tower'. No medieval garden features survive except the Lady's Pool, which must once have been fishponds acting as a larder for the house. The grounds of the Manor were senstively restored and replanted by Lord Harcourt and his wife after they decided to settle at Stanton Harcourt in 1947; see Lanning Roper, 'Romantic Oxfordshire Garden', *Country Life*, 3 May 1962.

4   Jennifer Sherwood & Nikolaus Pevsner, *The Buildings of England: Oxfordshire*, 1974, p.768.

5   This notice has been set up by the present owner, Ruth Power, to protect the structure, which she tends carefully and without financial support from the heritage agencies. It is to be hoped that this book will alert scholars and enthusiasts alike to its existence and that grant aid for its continued maintenance can be secured.

6   Roy Strong, *The Renaissance Garden in England*, 1979, pp.39-43.

7   *A Mid-Summer Night's Dream*, Act 2, scene 1, lines 98-9.

8   *Victoria County History* (hereafter *VCH*), vol.6, 1959, p.291.

9   Roy Strong, *The Artist & the Garden*, 2000, pp.90-3 and plates 100, 101 & 104.

10 Howard Colvin (ed.), *The History of the King's Works, Volume II: The Middle Ages*, 1963, p.1009.

11 Ibid., p.1010, footnote 1.

12 For Rosamond's Well see Colvin, *King's Works, II*, pp.1013-16; Howard Colvin, 'Royal Gardens in Medieval England', in *Medieval Gardens* (Dumbarton Oaks Research Library and Collection, Washington DC, 1986), pp.9-22; pp.18-20; David Green, *Blenheim Palace*, 1951, pp.23-5; James Bond & Kate Tiller (eds.), *Blenheim: Landscape for a Palace* (Stroud, 1997), pp.46-8; Paula Henderson, *The Tudor House and Garden*, 2005, pp.74-6.

13 From 'An Account of Woodstock Manor in 1634 by a Gentleman of the Army at Norwich', British Museum, Lansdowne MS. 313, pp.319-48; quoted in Green, *Blenheim Palace*, Appendix II, p.296.

14   Ibid.

15   Ibid.

16   Ibid.

17   The following quotations are taken from Aubrey's annotations to the sketch plan. These are given in full in Colvin's Dumbarton Oaks article, Appendix, p.22.

18   Colvin, *King's Works*, p.1014, citing Pipe Roll 19 Henry III: 'magnam claustrum maioris fontis apud Everswelle'.

19   See Christopher Hussey, 'Beckley Park, Oxfordshire', *Country Life*, 23 March 1929; also Colvin, *King's Works*, II, pp.899-900 and the *VCH*, vol.5, 1957, pp.56-63.

20   Act 1, scene 1. Marlowe was obviously writing in terms of Elizabethan rather than Edwardian masques, but he was 250 years nearer to the events of that unhappy reign than we are, and the King's gift to Gaveston does suggest royal meetings and rural revels in private.

21   Colvin, *King's Works*, II, p.899.

22   Ibid.

23   For Tintagel see Timothy Mowl, *Historic Gardens of Cornwall* (Stroud, 2005), pp.20-23.

24   See *VCH*, vol.9, 1969, pp.89-92; also Marcus Binney, 'Broughton Castle, Oxfordshire I, II & III', *Country Life*, 2, 9 & 16 December 1976.

25   *VCH*, vol.9, 1969, pp.112-15.

26   This is shown clearly in Buck's 1729 view of the Castle: Binney, *Country Life*, 2 December 1976, plate 2.

27   The existing planting here was based on advice given by Lanning Roper in 1970 and developed in the 1980s by Randal Anderson. See 'Design Guide: Broughton Castle', *The English Garden*, July 2006, pp.66-71.

28   English Heritage Register of Parks and Gardens (hereafter EH Register).

29   Binney, *Country Life*, 2 Decmber 1976.

30   Geoffrey & Susan Jellicoe (eds.), *The Oxford Companion to Gardens* (Oxford, 1986), p.441. I owe this reference to Helene Gammack.

2

WALLED ENCLOSURES, HYDRAULICS AND GEOMETRY – TUDOR TO STUART

In a book of this kind, dedicated to the tracing of county, as opposed to national, garden styles, it is always satisfying to find surprises, variants or even contradictions to broad national trends. The gardens of Oxfordshire's sixteenth and seventeenth centuries offer such variants. From the supposedly glorious cultural reign of Elizabeth the county's gardens are lacklustre, recyclings of the huddle of walled enclosures found around most large houses of the later fifteenth century. But from the reigns of the first two Stuarts: James I and Charles I, came far more adventurous, thoughtful, experimental and scientific proving grounds. It may not have been a coincidence that Shakespeare's silliest and least inventive play, *The Merry Wives of Windsor*, was written to please Queen Elizabeth, at her express request to see Sir John Falstaff in love, whereas two of his greatest and most exploratory tragedies – *Macbeth* and *Hamlet* – with their respective Scottish and Danish themes, were obviously written to catch the interest of a Scottish King James and his wife, Queen Anne of Denmark, two serious intellectuals.

National legends are a long time dying. Elizabeth spent little on palaces or gardens, relying for accommodation on what she had inherited from her father; while the Court festivals on her Accession Day each 17 November were merely colourful revamps of medieval tournaments.[1] In the following reign of James and Anne the Court witnessed richly conceived masques with moral messages, complex symbolism and theatrical staging, at least one of which was themed upon gardens and flowers. The *Masque of Flowers*, presented in 1614 to celebrate the marriage of an infamous couple, the King's favourite Robert Carr, Earl of Somerset, and Lady Frances Howard, is particularly interesting, as it is believed to have been inspired by the hermetic philosophy of the Attorney General, Sir Francis Bacon.[2] As will be seen later, Bacon's hermeticism resulted in his acolyte Thomas Bushell's construction of the Enstone Marvels in north Oxfordshire. The idea behind the grossly flattering *Masque of Flowers* was that James, as a Sun King, could command the seasons by his magical royal power and turn men into flower-creatures, creating Spring in the midst of Winter. Bacon's celebrated essay 'Of Gardens' would not be published until 1625, but he was already brewing up his symbolic theories. Probably as a result of Bacon's influence, King James became fascinated by gardens and parks; not just by their soft fruit, the cherries and the plums that he relished, but by their forms, their conceits and their self-advertising grandeur.

7 The homely, utilitarian enclosures of Wytham Abbey as depicted in *Britannia Illustrata. Bristol University, Special Collections*

It was noted in the previous chapter that while Sir Anthony Cope kept great state at Hanwell Castle in the hope of a visit from Queen Elizabeth, she never came; but in the next reign James came and was entertained twice, in 1605 and 1612, to enjoy the hydraulic marvels in Cope's 'House of *diversion*'.[3] Geography and royal progresses do much to explain Oxfordshire's poor Elizabethan showing of gardens. The Queen visited Oxford University at length, in order to demonstrate her own fluency in Latin, but the aristocracy of Oxfordshire did not produce Elizabethan royal favourites to rival those of Warwickshire or Northamptonshire. The Queen paid no less than four visits to Kenilworth alone after 1563, once for a whole sensational week. James, because of a weakness in his legs, was an ardent rider and hunter. He travelled much, being eager to meet any influential gentry and secure his initially precarious position.

By good fortune Oxfordshire has two gardens exactly recorded in Kip and Knyff's *Britannia Illustrata*, both owned by the same man, the Earl of Abingdon, Baron Norreys of Rycote. The two gardens are those of Wytham Abbey, which was in Berkshire at that time, though within two miles of Oxford, and now, after the usual bureaucratic vandalism, officially absorbed into the county and a valued possession of the University. The other is Rycote itself, the Earl's principal seat with its gardens consequently set out in the height of late seventeenth-century fashion. Wytham, however, as one of the Earl's lesser seats, retained its homely Elizabethan, or more precisely, sixteenth-century garden styling and a comparison of the two is a useful preparation for all the county's seventeenth-century gardens.

Wytham (7) was only called Wytham Abbey as a Gothic device in the nineteenth century.[4] It was a knight's fee of Abingdon Abbey, a fairly modest huddle of two tightly linked courtyards with crow-stepped gables. A few simple gables and one embattled gatehouse sufficed to demonstrate its owner's consequence and its gardens presented a similar image. Most informal and utilitarian is the approach route. Visitors came along a rough lane by a notably humble, un-towered church, with a kitchen garden, farmyard and haystacks across the way, to end in a stable yard between two service ranges. No attempt was made to conceal manure and mess at the side. Then came a walk across the bridge over a moat which, rectangular like that at Broughton Castle, enclosed three sides of the ornamental grounds as well as the house, but was a demarcation line, not a defensive feature. On the right, within the rectangle, was that Tudor essential: a Bowling Green with a few flowerbeds behind it. Left of the house and still within the moat were two plain lawns bordered by alternate round and pyramidal clipped shrubs. A raised terrace looked across the moat to an ordinary hayfield, so there was clearly no interest in landscape or any park as such. Beyond the moat all was utility: vegetable beds, four short arbours trained over with fruit, and a big orchard flanked by straight walls and cornered by little arbour towers. That was all.

At Rycote (8) grandeur, pattern and pretension have taken over. To the front and rear of the main house long avenues, clearly inspired by John Evelyn's *Sylva* of 1664, predominate. Double lines of trees in front of the house enclose two deer parks. To the left of the house, but entirely screened from it by a neat, formal square garden and stables, is a farmyard with vegetable beds and barns. To the right of the house all is geometric formality. First there are two lawns enclosed on three sides by a wide moat. This water is bridged to reach two flamboyant Union Jack-pathed gardens celebrating King James' new supra-national unity. Further to the right is a long terrace raised above an Orangery: steps climb it to a central Pavilion behind which woods rise up with a viewing tower at the far end. Beyond all this order are two or three more deer parks, three solid blocks of woodland and three badly sited rectangular lakes, with one more relaxed pool complete with an island yet forming no obvious area of a deliberate landscape; that kind of visual sophistication is still far ahead.

That was late seventeenth-century Rycote where patriotism, memories of moated defence works and timber for investment were the main sources for the design. To control those grounds the house itself is crudely magnificent, it is still basically a medieval courtyard structure but dramatised at the corners by ogee-capped towers that answered the garden tower and thus created a visual unity. The moats have now been filled in, some of the tree blocks have been cropped and the formal garden has disappeared. Most of the house has been demolished and only the stables remain intact with some twentieth-century additions. The grounds preserve some of their bucolic wildness, but a thick hedge of pale green laurel has been planted to ensure that no paying visitor to the church shall have anything but the merest glimpse of the now largely lawned gardens down in the hollow.[5] It is not easy to gain access to Rycote church today. English Heritage has taken over the administration of the church, which is only open for limited periods, and electronically controlled, Artisan Mannerist-style gates and gate piers have

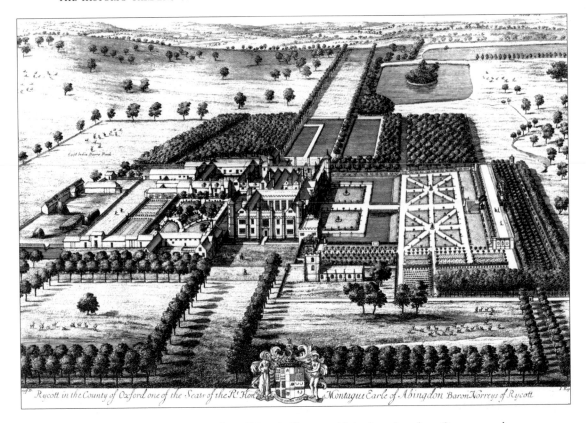

Rycott in the County of Oxford one of the Seats of the Rt. Hon. ... Montague Earle of Abingdon Baron Norreys of Rycott

8 Geometric formality at Rycote from *Britannia Illustrata* with its formal gardens, Orangery and raised terrace with viewing pavilion. *Bristol University, Special Collections*

been erected to guard the entrance. But the church still conveys something of the crude gusto of those lost grounds. Otherwise we would only have Kip and Knyff to thank for their remembrance. Rather more, however, of the feeling for Jacobean and early seventeenth-century garden design can still, after a most rewarding effort of exploration rather than simple garden viewing, be recovered at another site closer to Oxford.

Anyone frustrated by English Heritage's guardianship of Rycote should take heart and investigate the haunted garden remains of Ascott Park, once home to the great Oxfordshire family of the Dormers, in Stadhampton and Great Milton parishes. This is how gardens should be allowed to decay. Not trussed up in regulations, electronic gates and intrusive privacy hedges, but left unkempt, half-hidden and atmospheric in brambles and dark waters, a place for exploration and conjecture, where lines of dry grass suggest a lost wall and quaint garden houses have been half-abandoned to the rats and the swallows.

The house had an unfortunate history. Sir Michael Dormer acquired the property in 1518 and his son Ambrose's widow, Jane, re-married a rich Muscovy company merchant, William Hawtrey.[6] Her son by her first husband, another Sir Michael Dormer, had a moderately grand house with a long gallery and 12 bedchambers, but this was damaged by John Hampden's raid in the Civil War. Sir Michael's son, Sir William, rebuilt it in the 1660s, but the house was damaged by fire in 1662 before it was completed. Either it was rebuilt again or some of it was left because the frontispiece to Plot's 1677 *Oxfordshire* illustrates the house and there was a chapel and an enclosed formal garden as late as 1797. What happened next is never quite clear and even Sherwood and Pevsner skirt cautiously over the date of the surviving buildings. So garden enthusiasts have an excellent opportunity to pursue their own researches and make their own estimates. It is the most rewarding site in the county because it has been spared restoration.

A side lane leads to Ascott Park Farm and, unlike at Rycote, there is a whole fan of public rights-of-way leading off through fields into the woods. Even before that, on the main road, two handsome sets of gate piers, oddly set next to each other, front a mature avenue of limes focusing on that best of garden destinations: a nowhere region of trenches and grassy banks.[7] A cottage, part modern and part suggestive of old garden walls and half-absorbed structures, stands against the woods. The *VCH* speaks of a Piccadilly Cottage with the remains of a summerhouse and this may be the cottage, re-christened. Most encouragingly, in the middle of a dry field there are two 'Tudor' buildings of harsh red brick (*9*). Puzzlingly, yet understandably, the *VCH* describes these as seventeenth-century in date, conservative hangovers.[8]

9 The dovecote and granary are survivors of a large complex originally laid out with formal terraced gardens and geometric lakes at Ascott Park, Stadhampton

One is a dovecote with diamond, chevron and chequer patterns of darker brick and a cusped eaves cornice like a church corbel table. The other is an octagonal 'granary'[9], a tall building with a massive cellar, a stone, four-centred arched doorframe and stone window frames. Might the cellar have been an ice-house? The two brashly textured, unweathered buildings flank a wide declivity, which marks the cellars of the lost manor house, and the high bank of its garden terrace; but they do not match each other stylistically and the bond of their brickwork is Flemish. If they are of Tudor date, as their style suggests, then their bond should be English. Flemish bond is supposed, on somewhat uncertain grounds, to have been first introduced in the Dutch House or Kew Palace, built in 1631.[10] So if these characterful but gnomic structures were part of Sir William Dormer's rebuilding of the 1660s, which escaped the 1662 fire, then a trendy Flemish bond would be plausible. What still bewilders is their Tudor-style detail, but that could just be due to provincial bricklayers.

Beyond these structures the woods close in with a whole mesh of sinister-looking fishponds. To reconstruct the site in the mind's eye the woods probably need to be removed. That high terrace by the house must have overlooked a geometry of semi-formal waters, partly acting, like those at Tackley on the far side of the county, as a larder for the house. Today the woods have taken them over, but there seems to have been one large fishpond and a series of ornamental lakelets to the west of it. Of the chapel, which had medieval wall paintings of Christ's Passion, nothing remains. It was ruined in 1805, but there are drawings of it in both intact and roofless condition.[11] The whole site is an intense pleasure to walk and a perfect illustration of how attractive an historic area can be when it has not been taken into the officious but well-meaning care of an historic agency or a trust, but simply allowed to moulder away.

If we put together the confident geometry of Rycote, as Kip and Knyff recorded it, and these richly chaotic, obstinately conservative garden relics in the scruffy fields of Ascott, we have a fair impression of what grew naively and organically out of the relative aesthetic poverty of late sixteenth-century Oxfordshire gardens. Those buildings, so solid that they seem almost carved out of their brickwork, are still vernacular with no classical grace notes, but the tree avenues at Rycote, quaintly doubled and over-emphasised at Ascott, are obviously intended to assert some formal emphasis and some territorial claim. At both houses the water is beginning to be organised into squares or rectangles, but with no feeling for grand canal vistas; so there is some movement from the basically functional medieval garden divisions which lesser sixteenth-century Tudor and Elizabethan houses generally were happy to retain.

It is not often easy to find that unimaginative system of walled enclosures because those homely yards of stone terraces have usually been transformed by imaginative modern planting, statuary and new garden pavilions. Those Elizabethan dry bones were a gift to later Edwardian gardeners who usually relished hard garden features as a frame for their velvet lawns: yew hedges, fountain pools, garden houses, steps and balustrades. These later additions will find their proper places in the later chapters; but garden enthusiasts with the ability to mentally cut out modern enrichments and focus on the structural walls, stripped of exotic flowers and planted instead with simple vegetables, herbs and fruit trees, can reconstruct in their minds gardens of the county that at least suggest their sixteenth-century condition. These are Greys Court, of 1520 and after, Garsington Manor of the sixteenth century with some seventeenth-century remodelling and Asthall Manor of 1620 on an earlier base. But clearest of all in its stony essence is Kelmscott Manor of 1570 with a later, seventeenth-century wing. The Manor House at Shipton-under-Wychwood, begun by the Laceys in 1603, is another instance of an early Jacobean garden overlaid by the Edwardians. Chastleton House, also of 1603, was probably, as legend suggests and the subtle design of the House tends to confirm, the work of the great Robert Smythson, designer of Hardwick Hall in Derbyshire. So a Smythson garden is a thing of great interest. As the House is a Chinese box of cleverly interlocking rooms and stairs, so are its gardens. First comes the forecourt (*colour plate 3*), as at Garsington, leading with dignity, but no undue pomp, directly from the lane to the hidden front door, tucked away in an angle to avoid draughts and give access to the still essential screens passage. The forecourt originally had a stepped division to mark exactly how far a horseman could come with his steed. Such demarcations, usually by a light, paled fence, were commonplace at this time as owners were trying to achieve a civilised entrance point, while carriages were still rare and most travelled on horseback.[12] The way from the forecourt into the eastern or Best Garden was not opened until early in the nineteenth century. When the house was built for another successful Welsh lawyer, Walter Jones, each of Chastleton's gardens was cut off from the other and approached from within the house, so, in a sense, preserving the older tradition of walled enclosures but without the walls. Accessibility and parade were not valued as yet, or at least not by a provincial lawyer and MP for Worcestershire.

The Best Garden was accessed down steps from the Inner Hall of the Great Parlour. These steps led to a terrace from which the garden could be enjoyed, with an even better view indoors from the windows of the Great Chamber on the first floor: an instance of Smythson's ingenuity of design. But the *clairvoyée* at the far end of the Best Garden is a modification of about 1700; all the original *hortus conclusus* effect was destroyed when the wall of the *clairvoyée* was lowered in about 1800 to accord with the fashion for views and openness, making Jacobean insistence on privacy seem old-fashioned. There was originally no parkland to afford views, only the ridge-and-furrow of the village fields. As for the 24 fabulously distorted and suggestive yew shapes (*10*) in the central circle of the Best Garden, they are Chastleton's big conundrum: they are as likely as any other topiary feature in England to be four centuries old. But they are a problem.

First it is not clear what they were intended to represent: zodiac signs, chess pieces, symbols of the seasons. Early photographs owned by the National Trust suggest a cake stand, a teapot, a peacock, a ship in full sail, a crown, a sheep, a chicken, a squirrel and a horse. But yew shapes are at the mercy of every gardener assigned to trim them. What matters is that Francis Inigo Thomas, Reginald Blomfield and other garden designers have been inspired by the whimsically abstract qualities of this circle around its sundial. There have, however, been other times when topiary was fashionable, particularly in the early eighteenth century and the later Victorian and Edwardian periods. House records suggest that Anne Jones may have replanted the circle in 1713 and Dorothy Whitmore Jones in

10 The yews of the Best Garden at Chastleton House could symbolise chess pieces, the signs of the zodiac or just animal shapes

1833.[13] The glorious luck of the Jones dynasty, which only ended in 1991, was that they were never rich enough to make radical changes to their gardens.[14] Jacobite gestures like the Scots pines on the side of the house and the 'Boscobel' oak[15] out in the later small park only cost a cone or an acorn. But those early twentieth-century photographs do record quite a clutter of rose arbours and flowerbeds around the yew circle.[16]

North of the house the ground falls steeply in 'Renaissance' style, down the three traditional terraces to the Wild Garden. One of the terraces became a Croquet Lawn. Walter Jones Whitmore codified the rules of croquet, that most aggressive of games, in an 1865 edition of *The Field*, and went on to win its first championship: a melancholy distinction. Curiously there was never a kitchen garden until he created one in the angle between Wild and Best Gardens. Apparently the village supplied the vegetables. Last and least attractive of these Chastleton gardens, the Base Court lies low to the west, accessed from the kitchens and servants' areas, with a Drying Green, Wash House and Stables. The solid yew hedges down there were plantings of the 1930s when greenhouses and cold frames were demolished. To the enormous credit of the National Trust this perfect survival of house and garden has not been spoilt by a restaurant; the restraint is most laudable.

Tackley represents almost as miraculous a survival as Chastleton, but of the garden only. By buying not one but two houses, John Harborne complicated the garden history of the parish. A merchant with a legal background, as he was 'of the Middle Temple', he settled in Tackley in 1612.[17] Thomas Ayleworth had sold him both houses for £5800.

John's remote cousin William Harborne was English Ambassador to Turkey and John's steward, Rowley Ward, married his sister Joane. In 1632 John was High Sheriff of the county, but his son, another John, was a drunkard who in 1653 sold both the Tackley houses: Hill Court above the village and Base Court down by the water gardens. Hill Court was demolished, but left a handsome dovecote, a manorial barn and an archway dated 1615. The Base Court, a plain vernacular building now called Court Farm, stands intact. The upper house may have been the more pretentious, but the Base Court must have been John Harborne's favourite as he was a devoted fisherman. His fishing garden was celebrated in its time, recorded with a plan in Gervase Markham's third edition of his *Cheape and Good Husbandry* of 1623, and appearing again in his *A way to get wealth* (1631) and his *The Country Husbandman* (1638). It was one of the best-known gardens in Stuart England in the age of Isaac Walton and the fad for fly fishing. Markham's plan is annotated: 'A Platforme for Ponds, which the Printer hath added to this ensuing discourse, for the better satisfaction and delight of such as having a convenient plot of ground for the same purpose shall be desirous to make any Ponds for the increase and store of Fish'. A further annotation at the foot of the plan gives some indication as to how the walks were planted up: 'The Walkes about the Ponds may be planted with Fruite-trees or Willowes'.

Because St John's College, Oxford, owned a parcel of village land, which it refused to sell, Harborne never quite completed the symmetrical layout of the ponds (*11*) based upon military defence works, with ravelin islands and arrowhead-shaped pennisulas. They were never intended to defend anything, but to create separate ponds for different fish and to provide anglers with long banks on which to stand and cast their lines. What is to be celebrated is that everything which he did construct, three-quarters of the projected plan, survives evocatively untouched in an idyllic water world under mature trees. When I visited the garden in mild Spring rain the grass was alive with primroses, anemones and a decent rash of daffodils. The little ravelin islets sat like small Edens in the dark waters. Sir Harold Peake, Court Farm's owner in the 1960s, cleared and restored these military pools and geometric causeways to revive a garden that can, with honesty, be declared unique.

A ceremonial approach from an arbitrary western point unrelated to Court Farm leads up a broad causeway, overwhelmed by towering leylandia, to a formal stone gateway dated 1620 and inscribed in Latin with Harborne's motto — 'God blesses industry' — apparently in this case, fishing. Then the trees and flowers close in, creating an intense pleasure in a garden so entirely preserved and so strange. To sit there damply reading Walton's *Compleat Angler* among the primroses would be a perfect time trip back to that pre-Civil War idyll of aristocratic content and natural appreciation. It is fair to suggest that this is one of the 10 most important gardens in Oxfordshire, but one little known: a pastiche of militarism adapted to one man's hobby. A public path from Nethercott affords oblique views of everything except the wooded mound at the back of it, where St John's College spoils the symmetry. Only Bindon Abbey in Dorset, some 50 years earlier, can rival it as a survivng water garden of the period.[18] It is of particular interest to anyone wishing to evoke the great, lost gardens of James I's England.

11 A watery enclosure of military precision – John Harborne's fishing garden at Tackley. *University of Cambridge, Unit for Landscape Modelling*

Chronologically after Tackley comes another, but far more concentrated, water world and one that has vanished as absolutely as Tackley has survived. This is Thomas Bushell's Enstone Marvels, a triumph of applied hydraulic engineering as set forth in Salomon de Caus' *Les Raisons des forces mouvantes* of 1615 and Isaac de Caus' shamelessly plagiaristic *Nouvelle Invention* of 1644.[19] The Marvels was a grotto that Bushell had constructed on what he claimed to have found on the property he held in Enstone when 'clearing the Spring then called *Goldwell*, though quite over-grown with bryars and bushes, to place a *Cistern* for his own drinking'.[20] Upon stripping away the undergrowth he 'met with a *Rock* so wonderfully contrived by *Nature* her self, that he thought it worthy of all imaginable advancement by *Art*'.[21]

Within a year or two of this dubious discovery Bushell had built on top of the Rock a Hermitage (*12*) with mullioned openings and a Gothick-arched six-light traceried window. This last lit a banqueting room and there was a bedroom above. All this, though a notionally famous link between science and applied science, must be treated cautiously. Bushell was a highly successful showman.[22] King Charles and Queen Henrietta Maria paid the Enstone Marvels a state visit when it was completed in 1636. Technically the '*Rock, Grove, Walks,* and all other the appurtenances' were presented to the Queen, not the King, and she graciously consented that in future the Marvels should be called 'HENRIETTA'.[23] As the couple approached 'there rose a *Hermite* out of the ground, and entertain'd them with a *Speech*; returning again in the close down to his peaceful

12 Thomas Bushell's Hermitage at Neat Enstone had a banqueting house above a grotto inspired by the hermetic philosophy of Francis Bacon. *Bristol University, Special Collections*

Urn'.[24] There followed music: 'a *Song* answer'd by an *Echo*', then 'a *banquet* presented also in a *Sonnet*, within the Pillar of the Table; with some other songs, all set by *Symon Ive*'.[25] What came next must, for Bushell, have been the tricky bit, as he had to show royalty the grotto, where the whole point of a visit was that one ended up very wet. Plot does not relate whether Henrietta's legs got wet or whether it was all taken as good fun; one wonders if Charles I ever had a strong sense of humour.

In Plot's illustration (*13*) the Grotto looks to be an artificial construction framing the natural Rock, to which Bushell added elaborate waterworks. Bushell was a self-taught, or Bacon-instructed, hermetic philosopher, not an easy term to define, but relating to Christianity rather as the Kabbalah relates to Jewish faith: a kind of mystical pseudo-science, magic with religious underpinnings. Physics was being applied to create elaborate parlour tricks.[26] But before elaborating further on the Marvels it should be noted that Plot, who was a near contemporary figure, puts Sir Anthony Cope's rival waterworks at Hanwell Castle before Bushell at Enstone, though allowing Enstone's prodigies to be superior.[27] He writes:

> There are some other *Water-works* at the same Sir *Anthony Copes*, in a House of *diversion* built in a small *Island* in one of the *Fish-ponds*, Eastward of his house, where a *ball* is tost by a *column* of *water*, and artificial *showers* descend at pleasure; within which they can yet so place a *candle*, that though one would think it must needs be overwhelmed with *water*, it shall not be extinguisht.[28]

We know much more from Plot about the Enstone Marvels than we do about Hanwell. It seems likely that Bushell had not only learnt from the two de Caus books, but actually visited Isaac de Caus' Grotto in Wilton Garden to get wet, see the rainbow fountain and hear the 'magical' sounds. He seems to have been less interested in Wilton Garden's moving automata, but near the entrance to the Hermitage he did create 'a Cistern *of stone, with five spouts of* water *issuing out of a ball of brass, in which a small* Spaniel *hunts a* Duck, *both diving after one another, and having their motion from the water*'.[29] That served as an appetiser for greater delights to come down in the Grotto, 'out of which flows *water* perpetually night and day, dashing against the *Rocks* below, and that in great plenty in the dryest Seasons'.[30] Water jets rose in a low fence in front of the rough rocks and in three very tall jets behind them. Also, more disturbingly, jets could rise to close the only exit from the chamber. Further streams poured down from the roof. Amidst all this chaos of splashing water came the sound 'near resembling the *notes* of a *Nightingale*' followed by the noise 'somwhat like the sound of a *drum*, performed by the rushing in of *air* into the hollow of the *pipe*, which is large, and of *copper*'.[31] The nightingale's song was produced when the water level in a hidden cistern rose 'and having a *mouth* and *Languet* just above its surface, the *air* being forced into it by the approaches of the *water*'[32], made the nightingale sounds. There were further pleasures and perils to negotiate. Climbing upstairs, when the water door shut off, the royals were given food and music in the Hermitage. The banqueting room was painted with biblical stories concerning water and it may be here that Bushell contrived his own rainbow effect to rival that at Wilton Garden:

13 The Grotto at Bushell's Enstone Marvels had automata and trick jets to delight and to wet its royal visitors. *Bristol University, Special Collections*

In this Chamber is a naturall Rocke, like unto the Head of a Beare; on the top thereof, the water rises and spouts forth, falling in the Rocke … from about the middle of this Chamber, they make a canopy of Raine, which … with the reflection of the Sunn at high Noone, makes appeare to our fancies Rainbowes and flashing like Lightening.[33]

The royal couple were spared the perils which would face later visitors on the 'Island', which was added in 1674 by the Earl of Lichfield following a restoration programme after the Marvels had fallen into decay during the Civil War. The Island was round and moated, sited just outside the Hermitage. Once visitors had stood on it an assistant pressed a cock and water jets came up to make any exit a soaking experience, to which was added a very tall central jet, the grand climax of the visit.

It may all sound rather childish, but some elaborate water management, clever timing and specific knowledge of physics must have gone into making the Enstone Marvels. Bushell's reward was to be made the King's farmer of Welsh minerals, and it does seem that, by his pumping of water to clear the Cardiganshire silver mines and through his managing of the Royal Mint at Aberystwyth, he did much to keep the royal army in the field for several desperate years of the Civil War while Queen Henrietta was pawning the royal jewels in Holland to stave off bankruptcy. Bushell simply coined silver money from raw Welsh ore. He was undoubtedly a crank, but a successful showman and probably sincere in his belief that a hermetical regime of pure food, pure living and austerity could discipline the mind to achieve great things. By his works and those of Sir Anthony Cope, Oxfordshire gardens were, for a time, at the cutting edge of experiment. This would lead, via the marvels of Wadham College gardens, to the founding of the Royal Society in the next reign, to Newton and to Britain's head start over the rest of Europe in the Industrial Revolution, which was only science applied to making money fast. Whether Bushell's devices owed much to Oxford University, to his apprenticeship to Sir Francis Bacon or to his years of self-imposed austerity and exile on the Island of Lundy is an interesting question. What matters is that the Caroline and Carolean periods were a time when the symbolism of gardens and the ability of an imaginative garden to bolster the image of its owner-creator were becoming widely appreciated. The age of the Gentleman Garden was dawning.

Whether the *convivia philosophicum*, the sessions of poets that Lucius Cary, Viscount Falkland, was holding at Great Tew in the first golden years of the reign of Charles I, had any direct influence upon Caroline garden design is one of the mysteries of Oxfordshire's garden history. Great Tew has not been a fortunate house, so little survives of its Caroline gardens, but Lord Clarendon, remembering it all in the Restoration, saw it as a magical time of gathered talent, 'a college situated in purer air; so that his house was a university bound in a lesser volume whither they came not so much for repose as study'.[34] Prelates and wits mingled: Dr Morley, Dr Sheldon, Sir John Suckling, Will Davenant, Endymion Porter and the great Ben Jonson: 'Who told them plainly he deserv'd the bays,/For his were call'd works, where others' were but plays.'[35] Yet for all the good will, good wine and collected talent, that college air remains as legendary and insubstantial, because it produced no accurate recording of genius, as the gardens of Great Tew themselves. There is a walled enclosure of the period, whether in its original state or not is uncertain. A wonderfully rich and hoary stone gateway of about 1630 fronts the lane outside the parish church. It has all the air of being a Nicholas Stone design like those gateways at Oxford's Physic Garden, with niches for busts above and statues below. Lucius Cary, like an earlier Rupert Brooke, flung himself loyally into the first fighting of the Civil War, fought in 1642 at Edgehill and was found a year later, a battered corpse, on the field of Newbury; he was 33.

Which leaves Cornbury Park, the last garden in an epic chapter that has swept from near-medieval, homely simplicities to the great formalities of the Restoration. At Cornbury it is never possible to forget that we are in the wreck of the Royal Forest of Wychwood, wide tracts of which still lie gloomily down to the south-west of the consciously noble fronts, one by Nicholas Stone, one by Hugh May, of Cornbury Park. Slicing the park and the forest terrain is a web of long, straight rides (14), called locally 'lights', where we can experience the John Evelyn effect and the impact of his *Sylva*: trees upon trees, rarely in any relaxed, natural disposition, always in geometrical avenues or clearings.

As a favourite royal seat, Cornbury was usually granted to favoured courtiers only, which was why Earl Danby, founder of Oxford's Physic Garden, who had occupied it since 1615, was given it 'forever' by Charles I in 1642, and the ultimate Royalist, Edward Hyde, 1st Earl of Clarendon and Viscount Cornbury, was made Ranger of Wychwood after the Restoration. John Evelyn visited in 1664 and again in 1680 to advise on the tree planting. Consequently a truly vast axis cuts north-east to south-west across the park, starting up the long triple chestnut-lined north drive, following the earliest ha-ha in Britain across the front of the house and then on down the Grand Vista with a kink around Maple Hill to the village lodge. Almost as assertive, another avenue cuts down across it from the Ranger's Lodge to Lake Superior on the chain of naturalised fishponds.

Cornbury can be seen as the natural conclusion to those bold avenues at Rycote, or the final negation of Wytham with its farmyard entry or the tight enclosures of Kelmscott and Greys. By its vastness and by the avenues with their straight lengths, the park asserts the confident territorial power of the landowning oligarchy. Most interesting and most typical is that ingenious paved terrace with its ha-ha wall that Hugh May seems to have devised in 1665-6 in order that the family could have uninterrupted views of the park and across the whole sweep of Wychwood from the east front of the house. That in itself was a profound garden statement of extraversion, with an underlying aesthetic motivation; marking a growing appreciation of fine landscapes. Lining it on the house side is an interesting sequence of modern and nineteenth-century inner gardens, which must be kept for later. But John Talman's overstated five-arched bridge of 1689, which carries that main drive in across a trivial rivulet, can be mentioned as it actually continues the 'Vista Light' drive.

The truth about the design of Cornbury's park is that a whole system of laying long straight lines arbitrarily across a landscape, with an occasional pause for a circular or star-shaped clearing, was ill-conceived. An elaborate formal garden of parterres and statuary can create its own sense of interest and get away with the ruthless application of Art to

14 The legacy of John Evelyn's *Sylva* – a network of tree avenues and rides, know locally as 'lights', criss-crosses the park at Cornbury. *University of Cambridge, Unit for Landscape Modelling*

Nature, but by merely laying down lines of trees, regardless of the natural rise and fall of a landscape, which is what Evelyn advised the Clarendons, father and son, to do at Cornbury, a mere discord is achieved. There is another truth too behind this park. It is all very hopeful to create a stone walled ha-ha that lays a wide view open to the windows of a façade, but what if that wide view has not been sensitively adjusted by planting, or given focus points to hold the eye? Not all wide landscapes are inherently beautiful or satisfying. That was the lesson which formal gardeners, trained in the late seventeenth century, had still to learn in the wiser eighteenth century.

NOTES

1   See Roy Strong, *The English Renaissance Miniature*, 1983, pp.93-9; see also Timothy Mowl, *Elizabethan and Jacobean Style*, 1993, pp.10-17.
2   I am indebted to Christine Martin for bringing this masque to my attention and to her Bristol MA dissertation on Jacobean masques and their symbolism. The staging of the Masque of Flowers was paid for by Bacon.
3   Robert Plot, *The Natural History of Oxfordshire*, 1677, p.235.
4   See Wytham: *A Record issued by the Oxford Preservation Trust on the Acquisition of Wytham Abbey and Estate by the University of Oxford*, 1943.
5   I could not gain access as the owners were away when I visited, but Joanna Matthews reports that Mr & Mrs Bernard Taylor have done much restoration on the site and now live in what was the stable block to the main house. They commissioned a survey of the site before beginning, have made a new garden in front of their house and have installed a new glasshouse in the old walled Kitchen Garden.
6   *VCH*, vol.7, 1962, pp.121-2.
7   The *VCH* records (p.122) that stone gate piers and eighteenth-century wrought iron gates from here are now preserved in the Victoria & Albert Musuem.
8   Ibid., p.122.
9   Ibid.
10   See R.W. Brunskill, *Brick Building in Britain*, 1990, pp.49-56 for bonding.
11   Bodleian Library, MS. Top. Oxon. b165, f.211.
12   See Timothy Mowl, 'John Drapentier's Views of the Gentry Gardens of Hertfordshire', *Garden History*, vol.29, no.2 (Winter, 2001), pp.152-70.
13   *Chastleton House*, The National Trust, 2001, p.37.
14   They were fined heavily for their loyalty in the Civil War.
15   Planted in 1852.
16   See Anon, 'Chastleton House', *Country Life*, 19 July 1902.
17   Elisabeth Whittle & Christopher Taylor, 'The early-seventeenth-century gardens of Tackley, Oxfordshire', *Garden History*, vol.22, no.1 (Spring,1994), pp.37-63.
18   See Timothy Mowl, *Historic Gardens of Dorset* (Stroud, 2003), pp.15-24.
19   *Les Raisons* came out in two enlarged editions in 1624. For full accounts of these writings see Timothy Mowl & Brian Earnshaw, *Architecture Without Kings: The rise of puritan classicism under Cromwell* (Manchester, 1995), pp.44-5, and Strong, *Renaissance Garden*, pp.127-34.
20   Plot, *Oxfordshire*, p.236.
21   Ibid.
22   See J.W. Gough, *The Superlative Prodigall: A Life of Thomas Bushell*, 1932.
23   Plot, *Oxfordshire*, p.236.
24   Ibid.
25   Ibid.
26   See Strong, *Renaissance Garden*, pp.130-34.
27   The fact, noted earlier, that King James visited Hanwell in 1605 and 1612, long before King Charles' 1636 visit to Enstone, suggests that Plot was correct in seeing Hanwell as the leading garden in this pursuit of applied physics.
28   Plot, *Oxfordshire*, pp.235-6.
29   Ibid., p.237.
30   Ibid.
31   Ibid.
32   Ibid., p.238.
33   A 1635 visitor's account quoted in Strong, *Renaissance Garden*, p.132.
34   Quoted by Christopher Hussey, 'Great Tew, Oxfordshire – I', *Country Life*, 22 July 1949.
35   Ibid.

3

MILITARY FORMALISM IN THE SHADOWS OF A PRODIGY PALACE

And so, to Blenheim; not so much a park as a county within a county: 2119 acres, with a 77 acre walled pleasure garden approached between two parterres, each 250 yards long, and a Great Avenue to the north 2466 yards long.[1] How did the gardens of the shire react when the masterwork of John Vanbrugh, Charles Bridgeman and Henry Wise was created in their midst, with the great Churchill Duke himself demanding perverse oddities from the obedient professionals? That question is worth considering, for the only other county in Britain to have had a house and a garden of Blenheim's imperial scale imposed upon it was Yorkshire, which had the Earl of Carlisle and Vanbrugh's Castle Howard. Blenheim was begun in 1705; Castle Howard was commissioned in 1699, but Yorkshire is more a province than a county, wide enough to take several imperial palaces. Oxfordshire was initially a pinch-waisted affair, limited in area and its families inter-related. Consequently when Blenheim was cast down upon it several garden-quakes were caused in the neighbourhood.

For England, 1705 was a vulnerable year in garden styling, and notably so for Oxfordshire. Neither Dutch formal canals nor an Evelyn-inspired web of avenues would have been the obvious response to what Vanbrugh was planning to raise at Blenheim in 1705. It was, however, usual to plan the new garden at the same time as beginning a new house, and the eminent semi-royal gardener, Henry Wise[2], then a confident 52 years old, was actually at hand to supervise the huge task of digging out the foundations of the palace and saving the precious topsoil. Rather less likely to be influential was Charles Bridgeman[3], dextrous at drawing plans on paper, but inclined to conceive in harsh geometries of shape, imposing lines, amphitheatres and squares wherever the natural topography offered even a hint of these shapes. John Vanbrugh, of course, was an amateur, a gifted man who thought theatrically, had been given the job on the reputation of designing Castle Howard, and widened his design experience amazingly during a stay of several years in India, something no other contemporary architect had ever enjoyed. Travel, and in this case the East India Company, which had employed him, was making the world smaller and the flow of eclectic influences easier.[4]

In addition to these three men – Wise, Bridgeman and Vanbrugh – there was a fourth whose influence upon Blenheim's garden design tends to be underplayed. This was John Churchill himself, 1st Duke of Marlborough and the greatest Englishman of his age. Joseph Addison, who always had a strong feeling for a soldier, referred to him as 'that God-like man', and Churchill had indeed, by diplomacy and military genius, made Great Britain the leading power in Europe, a position which it would hold, sometimes precariously, for the next 200 years. Long the master of the seas, Britain had now, by an Austrian alliance, out-pointed France as a military power on land. The nation was grateful, Queen Anne hero-worshipped her Duke and, most importantly, did not feel threatened by him. Marlborough had potential political influence but little inclination to use it. He had been a brilliant general, now all he wanted was to retire in comfortable glory and eat peaches; like King James I, he adored soft fruit.

These factors explain the unique character of Blenheim. Stuck with a plump, uninteresting Queen Anne, the nation gave its generous respect and affection to a modest, manly soldier and cheerfully passed him the money and the land for the imperial palace that it would never give to its monarchs. Blenheim 'Castle', as it was originally styled, and its extraordinary park were the seal upon a nation's confidence in its aristocracy, that oligarchy of titled and landed families which would evolve, effortlessly, over the years, into a parliamentary democracy and a global empire. One of the underlying sources of that popularity and that trust was the aristocracy's willingness to stage horse races and sports events and to open its grounds for public pleasure and to gratify public curiosity. It should not be forgotten that at the heart of Blenheim's park was a large racecourse (15) marked out with mile posts, and that the tall Column of Victory in the middle of it, erected in 1723 for her Duke by the Duchess Sarah as a 'lasting monument of his glory and her affection to him'[5], served also as a perfect vantage point for following the horses all round the circuit. Blenheim works in many ways, not all of them obvious. Some of the ways, however, work very badly, but it is hard to apportion the blame because in essence, garden and park were evolved by a committee. Henry Wise and Vanbrugh's architectural partner, Nicholas Hawksmoor[6], were the two sensible professionals who went around correcting other men's errors. The two major flaws were the hexagonal stone-walled State or Bastion Garden, enclosing a Great Parterre with a wilderness section known as the 'Woodwork'. The second was the lengthy, entirely dysfunctional, Great Avenue to the north.

The Duke was probably to blame for the Bastion Garden; but Bridgeman and Vanbrugh himself must share some of the blame, and to an extent the credit, for the Great Avenue and that outrageously picturesque, imperial-scaled viaduct which it needed to cross 'the Chasm', the steep-sided valley of the Glyme. This was an unimpressive but hard-working stream, which had already serviced three parks and collected the waters of the Enstone Marvels before coming to embarrass Blenheim by its manifest, marshy inadequacy. Vanbrugh had sited his new Palace quite close to Woodstock village and looking across the Glyme valley to the towered and romantic structure, still just habitable, of Henry II's Woodstock Manor set on its hill above Rosamond's Well. But the presence of the Manor meant that the only terrain on which the seriously grand approach drive could be laid out was to the north. In all other directions the park walls were quite close. This is where Henry Wise, or his assistant, Charles Bridgeman, may have insisted on having an impressive, largely useless, elm-lined avenue.

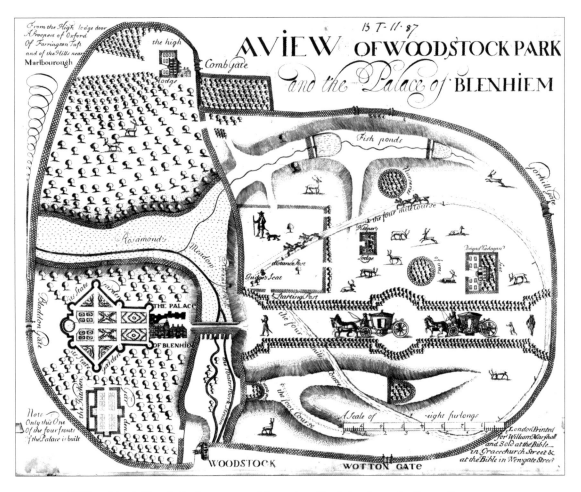

15 William Marshall's naïvely drawn map of the park at Blenheim shows the four-mile racecourse, the State Garden and the High Lodge before it was re-designed by Lancelot Brown. *Bodleian Library, MS. Gough Maps 26, f.50B*

The Great Avenue would have two major disadvantages. First there was no significant town to the north. Oxford, the obvious neighbour, was a few miles away to the south-east. Secondly, the north approach drive would have to cross the Glyme Chasm, promising trouble for horse-drawn carriages. Perversely, that would have seemed an advantage to Sir John. His surname Vanbrugh translates as 'of the bridge', so the chance to design the ultimate bridge, and thereby put his signature on the park, attracted him. Irresponsibly, therefore, he supported the dysfunctional and wildly expensive north approach, designing the superb Grand Bridge (*16*) for it and leaving Wise to construct the massive earthwork embankments required to reach it and to offer a level carriage way. The Grand Bridge would seem, from the house, to be supporting visually the half-ruined Woodstock Manor on the hill behind it, creating a truly picturesque composition.

47

16 Perhaps the greatest park building in the country – Vanbrugh's imperial viaduct crossing the waters of the Glyme at Blenheim

The Glyme remained a problem. It was far too small to justify a Roman imperial arch with all its empty rooms looming above it[7], but those rooms were for house pumping machinery to bring the supposedly medicinal waters of Rosamond's Well to Blenheim's kitchens.[8] Obviously the Glyme needed to be dammed to create a lake, and here there is a mystery. As all garden history aficionados know, Capability Brown would come to Blenheim in the mid-1760s and achieve a coup by damming the Glyme and creating that obvious waterscape flattery for Vanbrugh's pet bridge. Yet there are two early drawings of the park[9]; both of them show the approximate outlines of the hexagonal Bastion Garden brutally dominating the new Palace by its aggressive geometry. One of the drawings shows what was initially proposed for the Glyme. A straight, very narrow canal passes under the arch of the Grand Bridge, performs a few geometric turns, sidles along the Chasm in a more informal manner and then, in a stretch of awkward straight sections, fiddles its way around the bulge of the land below the Bastion Garden. Several later views, including Boydell's 1752 'North West View'[10] of the park (*17*), prove that it was a much enlarged version of this that was the solution taken before Brown came on the scene. This canalising scheme was devised in 1719 by Colonel Armstrong, who had been Marlborough's chief engineer, and it was executed in the mid-1720s by the masons William Townesend and Bartholomew Paisley.[11] It did, however, result in two generous sheets of water, one above, one below the Grand Bridge, each large enough for trawling for fish.

A North West View of Blenheim House and Park, in the County of Oxford, with Woodstock in the Distance.

17 Boydell's 1752 north-west view of the park shows Colonel Armstrong's misguided 1720s canalising of the Glyme. *Bodleian Library, MS Gough Maps 26, fol. 55B*

The mystery lies in the earlier of these two drawings. This shows the Glyme widened out into a lake winding around Blenheim Palace as in the Bridgeman plan of 1709, and very much as it does today, with long islets probing back into the park. On the drawing, Woodstock Manor has been encircled by a bastioned wall and stands splendidly right on the edge of the new lake. Most interestingly, there is no Grand Bridge carrying the North Avenue; the only approach to the Palace seems to be from the east. The mystery is who anticipated Brown and who rejected common sense? The naturalised version of the Glyme, as shown on the earlier drawing, had been anticipated by two other plans, one by Wise, possibly of 1705, and one by Bridgeman of 1709. This indicates that common sense had always assumed that the whole valley would be flooded as Brown eventually managed to do. In a letter to the Duke of Somerset the Duchess confirmed this: 'Sir John formerly set his heart in turning that [valley] into a lake'.[12] Armstrong's narrow canals were a foolish improvisation. Did the Duke, eager for some pomp, insist on bringing the Bridge back into the design and building the warm brick walls of the Kitchen Garden, also absent on the earlier drawing, to cultivate his beloved peaches?

It was left to Henry Wise to design a compromise plan, followed in virtually every detail by another of 1709, drawn by Bridgeman and subsequently published in *Vitruivus Britannicus* (*18*).[13] That was the year when the celebrated wrangle between Vanbrugh and Duchess Sarah over preserving or demolishing the historic and visually dramatic wreck

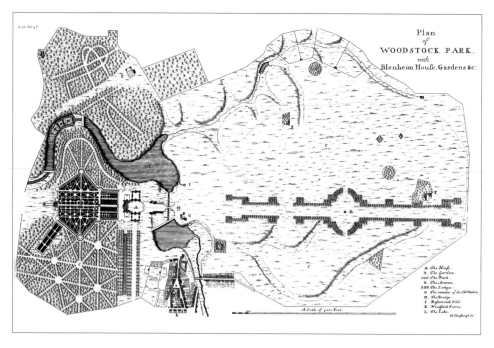

18 Charles Bridgeman's 1709 plan for the park at Blenheim, based on one drawn up by Henry Wise, from the third, 1725, volume of *Vitruvius Britannicus. Bristol University, Special Collections*

of Woodstock Manor was at its height. Significantly, Wise did not indicate even a trace of the Manor on his plan, but Bridgeman's has the faintest outline of it to the north of the Grand Bridge suggesting 'that he was party to the dispute about it'.[14] An illustration made in 1677 for Plot's *Oxfordshire* shows the Manor intact and lowering impressively over the valley of what Plot calls 'the Rivulet'.[15] It explains both the Duchess' determination to demolish it and Vanbrugh's serious struggle to preserve it:

> That Part of the Park which is Seen from the North Front of the New Building, has Little Variety of Objects, Nor does the Country beyond it Afford any of Vallue, It therefore Stands in Need of all the helps that can be given, which are only Two; Buildings and Plantations. These rightly dispos'd will indeed Supply all the wants of Nature in that Place. And the Most Agreable Disposition is to Mix them: in which this Old Manour *gives so happy an Occasion for*, that were the inclosure filld with Trees (principally Fine Yews and Hollys) Promiscuously Set to grow up in a Wild Thicket; So that all the Building left … might Appear in Two Rising amongst 'em, it wou'd make One of the Most Agreable Objects that the best of Landskip Painters can invent.[16]

Undoubtedly the Manor did intrude visually and was wildly picturesque. Left intact, and Vanbrugh was actually rebuilding parts of it furtively to live in[17], it would have challenged even a structure like Blenheim by its position, its profile and its contrasting style. How could Blenheim call itself a 'Castle', as it did in its first decades, with a real medieval castle staring down its sight lines? On the other hand, Vanbrugh was visually intelligent, far in advance of his times, in appreciating its Gothic picturesque and revelling in its Romantic associations with the murdered Rosamond.

What seems now so paradoxical is that the Duchess demolished a real castle to the north of her new Palace but, obedient to her husband's military whim, allowed a fake modern fortification, something that would have been more at home around a town on the flat lands of Holland, to be put up immediately south of the Palace and in the eye of the view from her own private apartments. No engraving survives to record the impact the Bastion Garden must have made on the grounds, but the *Vitruvius Britannicus* plan shows its vast extent.[18] It had been swept away before Brown came in 1764 and only the lesser bastion walls of the Kitchen Garden give some impression of it.[19] Woodland cloaked it on its east and west. The Woodwork or wilderness with its six fountains, geometrical clearings and straight, strictly formal and unnatural connecting ways makes one question whether Vanbrugh's much praised contemporary Wray Wood at Castle Howard can ever have anticipated Rococo liveliness and invention very convincingly. The actual planting within the Great Parterre was intensely conventional, a maze of low box. Most of the flowers ordered from the Brompton Park Nurseries may have gone into the long, sinuous cut-work parterres linking the south front to the hexagon. 'Brompton Stocks (Purple and Strip'd), Rose Campions, Poppey Emmonyes, Imperiall Honeysuckles, Italian Starworts, Narcissus Polianthus, 18,500 Dutch Yellow Crocus (at 1s 6d a hundred), Double Junquills, Persian Iris, 4,600 Tulips, 5,100 Hyacinths, 5,600 Double White Narcissus, Ranunculus, Carnations, Violett, Marigolds and 100 Damask Roses'[20] were piled into beds between shady lime walks, and it takes an effort of the imagination to see them against Blenheim's overwhelming façades and distances.

If the Great Avenue was a tactical disaster the Duchess Sarah had a more fortunate access problem closer to the Palace. Wise had always seen that the obvious way into the Palace via the East Gate was from the Woodstock–Oxford Road and he had planted trees to command it but, in a surprising and refreshing episode of legal democracy, the old gardener, whose cottage blocked that drive's exit to the main road, refused to sell his property even when he was visited personally by the Duchess.[21] By that obstinacy a far superior entrance and Triumphal Arch (*colour plate 4*) was built in 1723 at the edge of Woodstock, obliging carriages to navigate busy streets before arriving at a blank wall about a small square with the Arch still blocking even a hint of the breathtaking prospect beyond. It resulted in the purest garden theatre and thousands enjoy its visual drama today. To demonstrate his command of every possible style Hawksmoor devised a satisfying three-dimensional Palladian box. It contains a real porter's lodge and at one time housed a family of five in its single room. The Latin inscription carved upon it is the first of several in the park intended to impress the memory of the 1st Duke. On the inside face to the park it is repeated in English:

> This gate was built the year after the death of the most illustrious John Duke of Marlborough by order of Sarah his most beloved wife, to whom he left the sole direction of the many things that remained unfinished of this fabrick. The services of this great man to his country the pillar will tell you which the Duchess has erected for a lasting monument of his glory and her affection to him. MDCCXXIII.[22]

Accounts of Blenheim can rely perhaps too heavily upon Duchess Sarah's tantrums rather than on the inspired designers who imposed their visions upon her will, but she faced strange administrative decisions and the creation of a complex unprecedented in English architectural history. In retrospect she was right to demolish the old Woodstock Manor. It was just her bad luck to be seen as a philistine opposing an innovative new mood of Romanticism.

There, in this chapter on formal gardening, Blenheim must be left a little raw and incomplete, despite all those flowers from the Brompton Park Nurseries. But if that incomplete visual image can be recreated in the mind's eye: those thin, straight reaches of the Glyme scrabbling along the broad valley, the Bastion Garden rearing its curtain walls in front of the Palace in an entirely unsympathetic style, the petty geometry of those quincunxes in the Woodwork, then Blenheim's grounds can be seen as crying out, louder probably than any other park in England, for a new, more relaxed and natural garden styling. By the very scale of its visual errors and by the prestige invested in it by a proud nation, it deserved better and, in a later phase, it would get better. With the Hanoverian succession in 1714 the nation's garden styling would shift from rigid formalism to a more informal planting in accord with simple Palladian elegance. Blenheim's best years were ahead of it; meanwhile its giant formal features were not the only strand working in Oxfordshire's gardens at this disciplined and military triumphalist period.

What is remarkable about this phase of formal gardening in Oxfordshire is how closely packed together in date are the county's disciplined gardens. We are also missing, no doubt, some unrecorded formal layouts. Plot's *Oxfordshire* was published in 1677, a few years too early to catch the crest of Franco-Dutch formal garden fashion; but taking Blenheim's projection as about 1705, the tight clustering that followed includes Heythrop (1707-10), Ditchley House (from 1720), Shotover Park (begun 1718), Kingston House, Kingston Bagpuize (from 1720), Shirburn Castle (begun 1718) and Britwell House, Britwell Salome (1727-8). Of these only Heythrop approaches Blenheim in scale.

Ditchley was more overtly awed by Blenheim, its near neighbour, and has one of its many tree avenues pointing straight down to the Palace. The grounds of Kingston House (until recently a Berkshire layout) are formal in an entirely different bourgeois mood to those of Blenheim. A trim, brick doll's house façade looks out on to a square lawn, which once had a parterre. On the left a high terrace walk juts out at right-angles for parterre viewing with garden storage vaults beneath it and a simple brick Pavilion at the end of it. The original paths complex in the Wilderness behind the high terrace is not reliably recorded, but the feeling of these grounds is geometric and controlled. In its first state the similar neat, brick house at Britwell Salome was equally balanced and symmetrical in its gardens. Its strictly formal entrance court has survived, but behind the imaginative garden reshapings of the twentieth century the symmetries of its garden front have almost been lost.

Shirburn Castle just outside Watlington (*19*) is the fascinating oddity in this group. That George I's corrupt Lord Chancellor, Thomas Parker, created Earl Macclesfield in 1721 and disgraced for his briberies in 1725, should, in that brief period of his fortune, have bought a dilapidated moated castle of 1377 and entirely refurbished it as his country seat, can only be seen as an indirect reference to Blenheim 'Castle'.[23] The round-arched

19 Thomas Parker's Shirburn Castle at Watlington – an early-Georgian Norman rebuilding of a genuine fourteenth-century castle. *Country Life Picture Library*

medievalising gesture may seem prematurely Romantic, but Parker's garden responses were strictly formal. An early eighteenth-century map (*20*) by William Burgess of 1736[24] shows the Castle moat extended into a long, rectangular canal to the west leading to the kennels and a further canal striking out north through the village. To the north-west of the Castle is a formal garden with a cross pattern of paths. This is flanked on the left by a Wilderness of trees with two formal avenues, marked on a later 1807 map as the Clare Walk and the Terrace Walk. At the end of the Clare Walk is a circular temple. A contemporary Temple, which survives in a decayed condition today, is in a different position and clearly shown on its present site on the later map.[25] To the south of the Castle the Home Field has been criss-crossed by tree avenues, but as yet there is no sign of a landscaped park and the village still encroaches into the private areas of the Castle.

There is, then, no clear pattern to the gardens of this little formal group. Not one of them owes a direct debt to Blenheim because the Palace-Castle was always seen as unique in its scale and status. The next step forward towards Arcadian informality would seem to be William Kent's softening of the formal geometries at Shotover, devised after 1730, which led naturally to his reshaping of Rousham after 1738. There is, however, an Oxfordshire precursor to the Rousham Arcadia, one that has gone unnoticed by most

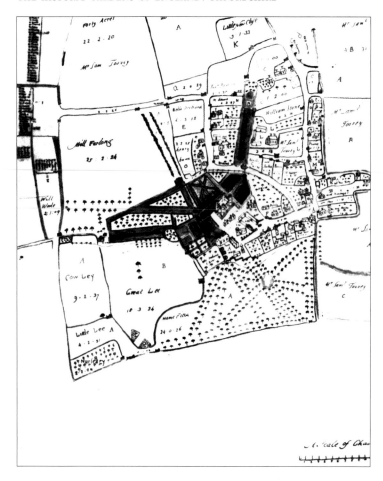

20 William Burgess' 1736 map of the grounds of Shirburn Castle with its formal water gardens and the village still encroaching upon the park. *Bodleian Library, (E) C17.49 (264)*

garden historians and by its contemporary commentators, all except for Stephen Switzer (1682-1745)[26], that most urbane and literary of gardeners who, working for George London and Henry Wise at their Brompton Park Nurseries in west London, would have had a wider knowledge of new garden ventures and stylistic innovations than most practising gardeners of the period. Heythrop, seat of the 1st Duke of Shrewsbury, had achieved a full-blown classical garden before 1710, when Switzer visited it. That would put Heythrop almost 30 years ahead of Rousham.

In its present forlorn and ivy-mantled condition the Heythrop Classical Grove cannot hold a candle to Rousham's Arcadia for photogenic charm. But it still retains all the classical elements, roughly composed in wild woodland, and offering any determined garden enthusiast the most exciting and rewarding exploration in the county. Not even the dense thickets and sinister pools of Ascott Park at Stadhampton can equal the garden surprises lurking on the waterlogged banks of Heythrop. Long before the formal garden had given way nationally to innovation and Arcadias, someone, either the 1st Duke or his Italian trained architect, Thomas Archer, had conceived, planted and built a model or prototype of the 'English Garden', which was to become standard in England for more than 40 years and go on to be copied all over western Europe and even Russia. A garden of such significance merits far more attention than it has so far been given.

The main difference between these two rival classical gardens, Heythrop and Rousham, is that at Rousham, Kent was working to soften an already firmly structured composition of Bridgeman's previous devising. At Heythrop the Classical Grove lies isolated as just one sector of a much bigger Switzer-style garden-park. Heythrop House, Thomas Archer's first complete country house, has had an unfortunate history. Charles Talbot, the 12th Earl and 1st (and only) Duke of Shrewsbury, who had it built between 1707 and 1710, lived in the immense shadow of Blenheim, which was going up at the same time. Talbot was a handsome apostate from the Church of Rome, a prime mover in the 1688 Glorious Revolution. He had his ducal title to live up to as well as being Lord High Treasurer, Lord Chamberlain and Lord Lieutenant of Ireland. Unlike Marlborough, however, he was no gallant soldier who could depend upon an admiring sovereign to finance his building ventures. Nevertheless, with its height and the lively Baroque flourish of short, domed wings, Heythrop was, in its prime, more palace than country house.[27]

Charles Talbot died childless in 1718, thereby ending the dukedom. He was succeeded by a cousin, Gilbert, the 13th Earl, who was a Roman Catholic priest; he in turn was followed by a nephew, George, the 14th Earl and the only Talbot to live, between 1743 and 1787, for any length of time in the great house. His nephew, the 15th Earl, retreated to Alton Towers, where the Talbots then settled. This meant that the grounds around the house, more a vast garden than a conventional park, are, in their gently dilapidated condition, a rare and fascinating survival of an early eighteenth-century layout that was never given a treatment by Kent or, more importantly, a Brownian minimalist make-over with its attendant draining, clumping, carriage drives and generous lakes. It was shaped very early by, presumably, Archer, who definitely designed that cascade-bridge at the head of a long sequence of linear cascades and little pools.

The vital evidence as to what else was done comes from Stephen Switzer's casual claim, in his 1718 *Inchnographia Rustica*, that, as early as 1710, when he, as a self-proclaimed 'Servant to Mr *London* and Mr *Wise*'[28], visited the place, advising for the Brompton Park Nurseries. Heythrop was 'the first attempt of this kind, I ever saw'[29] at one of the new, relaxed natural gardens, which Switzer was trying to make his special offering to prospective garden patrons. Switzer was an educated man, fond of quoting the poets – Milton, Cowley or Pope – to support his notions of the ideal visual presentation for a country house landscape. He was a very early Romantic who believed that gardens should respond actively to emotions: 'In truth, in all the beautiful Scenes of a Country Seat, one passes thro' the several Gradations of Joy, Love, Fear, Contrition and Repentence'.[30] Therefore, his ideal garden functioned somewhere between a religion and a psychiatrist:

> There seems to be a much more inexpressible Entertainment to a Virtuous and Thoughtful Mind, in Desolate Prospects, Cool murmuring Streams, and Grots, and in several other Cheap and Natural Embellishments, than in what many of our modern Designers have recommended, in themselves very expensive.[31]

Here Switzer had hit upon what would make Arcadias so popular across the Continent: not only did they respond well to melancholy or depressive natures, they cost far less in upkeep than formal gardens with all their elaborate bedding, weeding and hydraulic engineering. An Arcadia virtually looked after itself, and moving on by many garden exemplars to the rather dubious point that Christ was buried in a garden, Switzer described exactly the lure of a scatter of eclectic garden buildings: 'Thus to Noble and Ingenious Natures, a Piece of *Ruin* is more entertaining than the most beautiful Edifice; and the sorrowful Reflexions they draw, are of the softest Temperament imaginable'.[32] He captured that element of surprise, which is the essence of Rococo eclecticism, in his writing long before the Rococo garden was accepted in this country: 'How surprizing would it be to a Stranger to fall accidentally on the Ruins of *Rome*, (tho' 'twas in Epitome) at the End of a Noble Walk!'[33] If it was so early and so much has survived, why has Heythrop been given so little scholarly attention compared with Rousham, which appears in every book on the period? The reason lies in a drive.

No walk of exploration at Heythrop park should be undertaken without the guidance of Alun Jones' map (21).[34] The early eighteenth-century layout survived a 40 year desolation between 1831, when Archer's elegant nightmare of a house was gutted by a disastrous fire, and 1869 when the railway 'King', Thomas Brassey, bought the roofless wreck as a wedding present for his son, Albert. There followed a prosperous interlude when Alfred Waterhouse made extensive additions to the gardens after repairing the house. The Brassey family sold up in 1920 and from 1922-69 Heythrop was a Jesuit seminary with halls of residence sprouting up in the grounds. The Natwest Bank followed the Jesuits, but now Heythrop is a luxury golfing hotel. It has never become a popular place for garden history enthusiasts.

So in all those years since its building in 1706 only two men – George, the 14th Earl, and Thomas Brassey – have done much to shape the grounds. It seems, though this is only speculation, that the 12th Earl and 1st Duke had been as much influenced by his four years (1701-5) in Rome, where he married a rich Italian widow, as William Kent would be influenced by his nine years (1709-19), in the same city. Both men would appear to have picked up, from the picturesque scatter of garden buildings around Roman palaces like the Borghese, the notion of classical Arcadias: miniature classical buildings working informally, not trapped on an axis.

We must expect nothing sensational immediately around the house, but Heythrop has the oddest drive in Oxfordshire. The house lies midway between Heythrop and Enstone villages with Little Tew, a slight cluster of farms and cottages, nearer to the north-east. Enstone is a sizeable village on two main roads: the obvious place for a main drive with entrance lodges. Yet it was not until Albert Brassey took over that an Enstone drive was constructed. Instead, Archer was made to lay out two pale counter attractions to Blenheim's sensational Great Avenue with Vanbrugh's Grand Bridge. Archer's Bridge on the dam with its vista drive runs down to the house from insignificant Little Tew. A second drive was begun, heading out to Norton Common and directed from Heythrop's lost forecourt. This drive was straight, apart from a kink as it bypassed Heythrop village. At its northern end a few of the original flanking platoons of trees, some round, some square, survive.

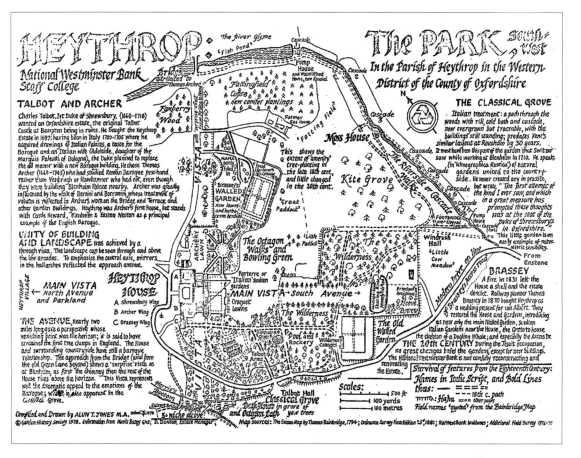

21 Alun Jones' map of Heythrop makes sense of the Duke of Shrewsbury's proto-Arcadian layout, which was later severed in two by Albert Brassey's south drive from Enstone. *By kind permission of the Garden History Society*

Albert Brassey's 1886 drive to Enstone is delightfully different. As if leading to some Devonshire resort hotel, it winds up a picturesque wooded valley with an enchantingly lively stream rushing along beside it. This feeder of the Glyme then branches out into two sub-streams both of which feature strongly in Heythrop's Classical Grove. Unfortunately this Brassey drive cuts the Grove into two distinct halves and ravages its original unity. One of its seats, the Alcove Bower[35], set up on a bluff to the right to command an outward view, is a reminder of what Brassey ignored and under-played, the Arcadian landscape which Switzer so much admired. Switzer had also praised the contemporary and much better known Wray Wood:

> That beautiful Wood belonging to the Earl of *Carlisle*, at *Castle-Howard*, where Mr. *London* design'd a Star, which would have spoil'd the Wood; but that his Lordship's superlative Genius prevented it, and to the great Advancement of the Design, has given it that Labyrinth diverting Model we now see it.[36]

22 The Moss House in the Classical Grove at Heythrop – one of a cluster of garden buildings within water-threaded woodland hailed by Stephen Switzer as the first attempt at informal gardening

Oddly enough, Switzer's praise has been something of a blight to its object. Most garden histories cite Castle Howard's Wray Wood as the earliest Arcadia of wandering paths and classical statues, but no illustrations of its supposedly innovative delights survive, and its prime garden building, the Temple of Venus, was not added to an angle of the retaining wall until the early 1730s.[37] But the abstract for masons' work in the 'New Gardin in Wray Wood' between October 1706 and December 1710 gives some idea of what it contained:

> Building of Wray wood wall, More seats, Fountaine att ye Summerhouse, The Pedestall of Flora Backus and Steps and Seat att ye Rock, Pedestall of ye Satyir and Venus, Pedestall of ye Shepard Diana Venus and ffoott of ye term and Steps in Seaverall Places.[38]

Later visitors praised the beauties of the Wood, but it was not deemed to be unusual for its time and consisted mainly of fountains, statuary, at least one summerhouse at its inception and gravel walks.[39] Without contemporary illustrations it is not possible to gauge the visual aesthetics, but Switzer's verdict was that the Earl of Carlisle had achieved 'the highest pitch that Natural and Polite Gard'ning can possibly arrive to: 'Tis There that Nature is truly imitated, if not excell'd, and from which the Ingenious may draw the best of their Schemes in natural and Rural Gardening'.[40] The same failure of visual record has fallen on the Heythrop Classical Grove.

Due to its division by the Brassey drive two separate explorations are required and the most logical sequence is to begin at Archer's Bridge on the dam and work downstream. The cataract spouting out under the Bridge's central arch is impressive but visually almost inaccessible. Archer gave no thought to how his theatrical effects should have been enjoyed except by looking down over the parapet. Downstream a sequence of small fishponds sets in, each one with its pretty little cataract, until the stream passes that rare survival, a Moss House (22). Still green and mossy, the octagonal walls composed entirely of logs set upright, it stands unsupported by any bank in a thin grove of trees. Until recently its floor was composed of horse's teeth, but they have all been taken away as souvenirs. However, it still retains its Gothic windows, which suggest a Regency remodelling.

Then comes what must once have been a pretty walk through woodland, down a shallow valley where the stream falls from cataract after cataract, none of them more than two feet high. This is where the absence of Capability Brown is most felt. Because the valley is not drained the path is often impassable, a marsh with its banks a muddy quagmire of horse-tail grasses. The only way to track the Grove is to climb out into the fields and follow its course on a parallel line until the stream cuts under the Brassey drive by that Alcove Bower and joins its other branch. So far then, there has only been a chain of cataracts, one of them substantial but almost inaccessible, and one Moss House of a later date.

The other sector of the Heythrop Classical Grove is more impressive, though even wetter. Describing his ideal classical grove (he never uses the term 'Arcadia'), Switzer writes:

> On each Side are several little Rooms or Cabinets of Retirement, one within another; and, as all of them are furnish'd with Niches for Statues, Urns and other Vases, and in the Middle some little Grass-Plat or Fountain of Water, I cannot but hope it will be thought extreamly pretty and diverting.[41]

This is, more or less, a description of what survives in the wet woodland on the west side of the Brassey drive. To understand Kent's visual and intellectual genius it would be instructive to travel directly from this Heythrop set of 'little Rooms or Cabinets of Retirement' to Rousham to see how Kent created a real Arcadia.

Switzer was not so much concerned with compositions as with surprises. His three volumes of the *Ichnographia Rustica* have impressive fold-out plans for vast garden-parks (23). Deer are ignored; instead, a sinuous web of walks, eight feet wide, hedged on both sides, paved in gravel, sand or cockle shells, weave in and out of woodland. Privet is to be used to line them or else 'Parsley looks very well, and will be very good food for your Hares'.[42] His mood is deliberately anti-formal: 'These Hedge-Rows being mix'd with Primroses, Violets, and such natural sweet, and pleasant Flowers; the Walks that lead through afford as much Pleasure as (nay I venture to say more than) the most elaborate, fine Garden'.[43] This was an economy that the Duke may well have welcomed. Switzer is precise about his inspiration for this pre-Wordsworthian delight in simple Nature woven around modest classical pavilions and events:

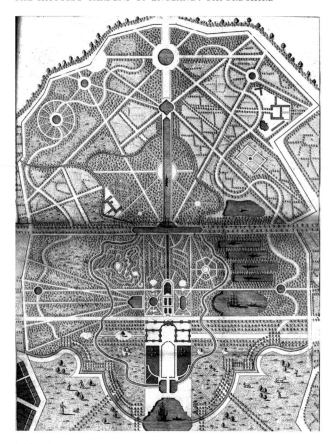

23 A plan for a garden–park from Switzer's 1718 *Ichnographia Rustica. Bristol University, Special Collections*

The first attempt of this kind, I ever saw, and which has in a great measure prompted on these rural thoughts, was at the Seat of a very great Person of this Age; I mean his Grace the Duke of *Shrewsbury's* which in *Oxfordshire*; is truly delightful, rural, easy, and pleasant; for, whatever some may think of Magnificence, there is an inexpressible Pleasure in these Natural, Twinings, and private Walks, to a quiet, thoughtful, studious Mind.[44]

So often in this *Ichnographia* a reader has to remind him or herself that it was published in 1718, 70 years before Wordsworth found his clear Romantic voice expressing the supporting harmony between a sensitive traveller and a wild landscape. Switzer has all Wordsworth's feeling for Pantheism:

'Twas under a Tree, Mr. *Evelyn* observes, that St *Austin's* solemn Conversion was wrought … And we may reasonably suppose (from that Example) that the Air of such retired Places may be assistant and influential for the Incitement of Penitential Expressions and Affections, especially when thereto is added solitary Grotts, murmuring Streams, and desolate Prospects.[45]

The difference between such feelings at the beginning of the century and at its end is that Switzer's thoughts take flight from a small cluster of relatively simple buildings and waters in a wood, while Wordsworth needed a frowning cliff towering over a full-blown river or lake.

On the west side of the Brassey drive the six-foot walk, muddy as ever, dives down towards the stream again. First comes the Bath House (*24*), heavy-handed with its two porthole windows, surely signs of Archer trying to design a small building but using his favourite chunky mouldings. Mud and debris have filled its bath, but there are two niches, perhaps for statues. Steps may still lead down into the square mud-filled bath and water trickles into it from a little octagonal pool in the wood above it, and out to the stream. Next, down the hill and cloaked in ivy, is a Nymphaeum wall (*25*) with three alcoves, each beset with niches for busts. 'I need but just mention', Switzer wrote,

> that at all the Intersections of the Walks shou'd be made a Fountain, or a little Garden, of such a Figure as you will find, in this or any other Book, or any Gardener can contrive; and should be set round with little Nitches, Seats, and Benches … and these little Gardens will look as well a Mile or two off, as just by the House (wherever there is such an extent) and will, in truth, be much more surprizing, the farther they are from the Place where one would expect to find Gardens.[46]

This is a passage that pre-empts precisely the spirit of the English Rococo gardens of the 1730s and 1740s, when Kent perfected Switzer's pattern. This Classical Grove at Heythrop is, as Switzer urges, remote, a full half mile from the great house, reached by

24 The Duke of Shrewsbury's Bath House, fed by a natural spring, in the Classical Grove at Heythrop

25 Heythrop's Nymphaeum, with its niches for statues and seating alcove, reflects perfectly Switzer's requirement for 'Cabinets of Retirement' in his ideal grove

a walk branching sideways from the formal Main Vista of the South Avenue which runs down from the terraces of the house, between two Wildernesses to an oval pond. Those Wildernesses contain other garden events: a pool or two, a Rockery, a Rosary and one of Heythrop's two walled Kitchen Gardens.[47] Heythrop never quite develops the usual open park, for all the size of the estate, because the planning is based on Switzer's notion of a big garden of events with walks swirling around an axis, that of the South Avenue, but never quite opening up into predictable Brownian views.

This Classical Grove above its 'murmuring Stream' in that damp wood of ivy-draped trees and buildings, was the inspiration for Switzer (we have his word for it that it was) and Switzer's writing, loaded with sophisticated literary references, theological solemnities and sly hints of possible economies, was the actual launch vehicle for the so-called English Garden. When the stylistic importance of Heythrop's classical Arcadia has been widely appreciated its buildings will be restored, the ivy stripped and the drainage moles laid; but something memorably melancholy and time-touched will inevitably be lost. Heythrop is the place where a duke, who was a prime mover in the Glorious Revolution of 1688, found time to realise those fanciful, over-ambitious plans in Switzer's *Inchnographia Rustica* and, thereby, project another revolution, this time in English garden design rather than in English constitutional history.

NOTES

1   The best account of the palace and grounds remains David Green, *Gardener to Queen Anne: Henry Wise (1653-1738) and the Formal Garden* (Oxford, 1956), and the same author's *Blenheim Palace*, 1951; but see also James Bond & Kate Tiller (eds.), *Blenheim: Landscape for a Palace* (Stroud, 1987) and Christopher Ridgway & Robert Williams (eds.), *Sir John Vanbrugh and Landscape Architecture in Baroque England 1690-1730* (Stroud, 2000).

2   See Green, *Gardener to Queen Anne*.

3   See Peter Willis, *Charles Bridgeman and the English Landscape Garden* (2nd edition, Newcastle-upon-Tyne, 2002).

4   For the background to Vanbrugh's cultural and literary pursuits see Laurence Whistler, *The Imagination of Vanbrugh and his Fellow Artists*, 1954 and F. McCormick, *Sir John Vanbrugh, The Playwright as Architect* (Pennsylvania, 1991); for his architectural works see Kerry Downes, *Vanbrugh*, 1977 and for a full biography see Kerry Downes, *Sir John Vanbrugh*, 1987. For Vanbrugh's Indian episode see Robert Williams, 'Vanbrugh's India and his Mausolea for England', Ridgway & Williams, *Vanbrugh and Landscape Architecture*, chapter 7.

5   Taken from the inscription on the Woodstock Lodge.

6   See Kerry Downes, *Hawksmoor*, 1959 (2nd ed., 1969) and Vaughan Hart, *Nicholas Hawksmoor: Building Ancient Wonders*, 2002.

7   See Howard Colvin & Alistair Rowan, 'The Grand Bridge in Blenheim Park' in John Bold & Edward Chaney (eds.), *English Architecture, Public & Private*, 1993, pp.159-75.

8   There is still a notice in the palace kitchens which reads: 'Remember to fetch from the kitchen the beautiful Rosamond's Well water'.

9   They are illustrated in Green, *Henry Wise*, plates 30 & 31. He gives a Bodleian reference of MS. Top. Oxon, a.37 for both, but this is inaccurate. I have been unable to track them down.

10 Bodleian Library, MS Gough Maps 26, fol.55B.

11 The 1719 plan for this scheme is illustrated in Bond & Tiller, *Blenheim*, plate 70.

12 Ibid., p.82.

13 It has 'Bridgman Discrip' in very small characters. David Green, in his *Gardener to Queen Anne*, is not convinced of its authenticity (pp.102-4), but Willis, *Bridgeman* takes it to be by Bridgeman and quotes (pp.46-7) later letters between the Duchess and Bridgeman's widow, Sarah, which mention Bridgeman 'Performing his articles', supervising earth moving and planting trees, hedges and laying out gravel walks.

14 Willis, *Bridgeman*, p.46.

15 Plot, *Oxfordshire*, p.16.

16 Green, *Blenheim*, Appendix VII: 'Reasons Offer'd For Preserving Some Part of the Old Manor', 11 June 1709.

17 He even built a round penthouse, which the Duchess called a closet 'as if he had been to study the Planets' (Green, *Henry Wise*, p.117).

18 *Vitruvius Britannicus*, vol.3 (1725), plates 71-2.

19 For the Walled Garden see Green, *Blenheim*, plate 27 on p.66.

20 Green, *Gardener to Queen Anne*, p.11.

21 Green, *Blenheim*, p.158.

22 Ibid., pp.158-9.

23 Timothy Mowl & Brian Earnshaw, 'The Origins of the Gothic Revival in a Georgian Norman Castle', *Journal of the Society of Architectural Historians of the United States*, vol.xl, no.4 (December, 1981), pp.289-94.

24 Bodleian Library, (E) C17.49 (264): 'A Survey of the Castle and Manour of Shirburn, in Oxfordshire'. This survey is almost identical in its details to another contemporary survey in the estate office at Shirburn, but this has a Bridgemanesque treatment to the Wilderness with rectangular and octagonal canals and ponds linked by a serpentine rill, in the manner of that at Rousham.

25   Bodleian Library, (R) C17 49 (193) Box 4A: 'A Map of the Parish and Manor of Shirburn in the County of Oxford', 1807, 'Surveyed by Wm. Rutt'. The Temple was designed for the 2nd Earl in 1741 by Westby Gill.

26   There is very little written on Switzer, but see William Alvis Brogden, "Stephen Switzer: 'La Grand Manier'" in Peter Willis (ed.), *Furor Hortensis: Essays on the history of the English Landscape Garden in memory of H F Clark* (Edinburgh, 1974), pp.21-30; James Turner, 'Stephen Switzer and the Political Fallacy in the Landscape Garden History' in *Eighteenth-Century Studies*, vol.11 (1977-8), no.4 (1978), pp.489-97; Judith Roberts, 'Stephen Switzer and Water Gardens', in Ridgway & Williams (eds.), *Vanbrugh and Landscape Architecture*, chapter 9. For quotations from Switzer's *Ichnographia Rustica* see John Dixon Hunt & Peter Willis (eds.), *The Genius of the Place: The English Landscape Garden 1620-1820* (Cambridge, Massachusetts, 1988), pp.151-63.

27   The wings were demolished after 1870 by Alfred Waterhouse.

28   From the title page.

29   Stephen Switzer, *Ichnographia Rustica: or, The Nobleman, Gentleman, and Gardener's Recreation*, 3 vols., 1718, 3, p.88.

30   Ibid., 1, p.198.

31   Ibid., 1, p.317.

32   Ibid., 1, p.198.

33   Ibid.

34   This was prepared for the Garden History Society in 1978 and is reproduced here with the Society's permission.

35   At first glance this looks to be late-eighteenth-century or Regency in date, but on closer inspection it shares a certain angular blockish profile with the Bath House.

36   Switzer, *Ichnographia Rustica*, 2, p.198.

37   An early eighteenth-century map at Castle Howard would suggest that Wray Wood was far more formally laid out with straight axes and circular clearings, much in the manner of early Bridgeman designs. I am indebted to Caroline Dalton for bringing this map to my attention and for her views on the supposed informal character of the Wood. The Temple of Venus was not built until 1731-5, long after Vanbrugh's death.

38   Quoted in Charles Saumarez Smith, *The Building of Castle Howard*, 1990, p.124.

39   The best account of the Wood was written in 1732 by John Tracy Atkyns and it is quoted liberally by Saumarez Smith, *Castle Howard*, pp.126-7.

40   Switzer, *Ichnographia Rustica*, 1, p.87.

41   Ibid., 2, pp.223-4.

42   Ibid., 3, p.89.

43   Ibid., 3, p.88.

44   Ibid.

45   Ibid., 1, p.197.

46   Ibid., 3, p.89.

47   All these features post-date the Classical Grove.

4

OXFORDSHIRE AS THE BIRTHPLACE OF THE ENGLISH ARCADIA

Stephen Switzer's *Ichnographia Rustica* was a quite unusually persuasive and culturally impressive work, with all its literary references and psychological awareness of the range of human mood involved in responses to Nature. Among the writers on aesthetics of the period he could be described as Prince Hamlet, revelling in self-indulgent poetic melancholy, a mood that would prevail in the later, full-blown Romantic Movement of Wordsworth, Beckford, Byron and Keats. If so much influence is to be attributed to three notably heavy-handed, yet modest garden buildings of about 1708 in the Classical Grove at Heythrop, then it is worth looking at other isolated garden buildings of the county to see them in the context of their times. Were there in Oxfordshire any general leanings towards an Arcadian mood?

While minor players in the Oxfordshire garden league like Souldern House, near Banbury, and Hordley, outside Wootton near Blenheim, were building their desperately plain garden pavilions on formal axes[1], major landscapes of this period like Ditchley and Shotover were being laid out on heavy, unimaginative geometric lines, remote from any Arcadian grouping. The entrance front to Ditchley was the octagonal focus to a goose-foot of avenues, but for the garden front James Gibbs, the architect of the house, settled for a massive gravelled terrace overlooking a valley which, by 1750, would be considered the perfect site for a large natural-looking lake. On Edward Grantham's survey map of 1726[2], however, there is no lake and the drive coming in from Kiddington and the north-west leads more to the farm buildings than to Gibbs' stately semi-Palladian house. Even as late as 1745 Sermingham's survey[3] only shows that great terrace overlooking a medium-sized rectangular pond or canal down in the valley; so formalism retained its hold. Trees were being clumped in the park and the little octagonal Menagerie (*colour plate 5*) is in place. It would end up as a 'Gas Works' in 1881[4], and some kind of generator today, but it is completely hidden from the house by a dense yew thicket, and never, even when first built, was in any way Arcadian.

Shotover Park's garden history is more rewarding, though it is perhaps the most frustrating garden in the county. When the names of the men associated with it are totalled up, it should have been an innovative layout of Arcadian delights, but in reality it is axially fixated and interesting largely for what it might have been. The two James Tyrells, father and son, who owned and gardened it, had a talent for friendship rather than for garden design. There had been Tyrells holding the rangership of the royal forest of Shotover since 1613; then, when it was de-forested in 1666, they bought it. James, the father of James the Colonel, having inherited the property in 1701, built a new, notionally Palladian house on the site in 1714-18, keeping the old house as stables and laying out an axial garden to the east (*colour plate 6*). He was friendly with the great scientist, Robert Boyle, and with the philosopher, John Locke, but that closeness did not necessarily influence his garden planning. The casual reach of the gardens to the west of the house was, presumably, also the elder James' creation, though no authority actually confirms this, and it was Colonel James who brought William Kent in to work, with rather less of his usual lively competence, on that western half of the axial line.

The name of Charles Bridgeman has been mentioned in association with this ruthless axial planning, but there is no evidence that he ever came near Shotover[5]; and there is nothing in the way that the crude axial line slices across the house, making little geometric response to the rise and fall of the land, to suggest the subtle way in which Bridgeman's geometrical layouts usually respond to topography, setting amphitheatres into curves of hillsides and intersecting avenues to link points of visual focus. What the elder James Tyrell did introduce into his garden complex was that essential element of the ideal Arcadian gardens: an eclectic as opposed to a classical pavilion. That was a real step towards an Oxfordshire Arcadia and we probably owe it to the influence of Locke upon Tyrell. As Mavis Batey has pointed out in her excellent, though curiously titled *Country Life* articles: 'An Early Naturalistic Garden'[6], Locke, Tyrell and the Whigs believed most earnestly that the basic principles of English parliamentary authority and liberty could be traced back historically to the Middle Ages and beyond, to precedents like the Saxon Witan and Magna Carta. That faith in a Gothic period explains why, at roughly 1720, though the precise date has never been established, the elder Tyrell had an architect design the large, awkwardly proportioned Gothick Temple (*26*) that stands, not tucked away in the woods like some hermit's residence, but brazenly facing the new house at the far end of the second of two canals which Tyrell had constructed in the place of some fishponds. It symbolises a declaration of principles rather than functions simply as a garden ornament.

A plaque in the Gothick Temple claims unhelpfully that William Kent designed it. Kent was to digest the medieval originals and whip them into light-hearted Rococo-Gothic curvaceousness, but only after his work at Richmond and Esher of the early 1730s.[7] The Shotover Gothick Temple is Oxford Collegiate Survival in style and probably designed by William Townesend working with his eye fixed slavishly upon Nicholas Hawksmoor's contemporary work at All Souls. But, whoever designed it, the Temple sets a most important precedent in garden architecture. In the future, various styles, not just Gothick, but Chinese, Turkish and Moorish, would be introduced to vary the charm and historic reference of Arcadian gardens, all sited illogically, but entertainingly, alongside classical temples. Shotover's Gothick Temple is a perfect example of the University driving the design of the county's gardens in new directions.

The other, western, half of this obsessive axial garden is the half where the younger Tyrell, Colonel James, was in control, working, as his epitaph in Oakley church,

26 William Townesend's 1720s Gothick Temple at Shotover Park is consciously modelled on Nicholas Hawksmoor's contemporary work at All Souls College

Buckinghamshire proves, in a spirit of filial piety to complete his father's severe garden design. Its Latin is roughly translated as: 'lest after the hardships of war his leisure should be mispent, this remarkable lover and cultivator of all elegant things pressed on with the completion of his house and gardens at Shotover'.[8] Colonel James was a close friend of Colonel Robert Dormer of Rousham, and it has been suggested that Colonel Robert brought Bridgeman in to lay out Rousham's grounds in 1725 in a geometry of straight lines in imitation of the axial geometry of Shotover.[9]

The great interest in these two Oxfordshire gardens lies in their contrasting response to the harrowing experiences of war. The younger Tyrell and both the Dormers had served under Marlborough. But whereas Tyrell seems to have conceived that western half of Shotover in terms of lines of fire from raised control points, like Kent's Rotunda on its hill, General James Dormer would express death and the horror of war in statuary, but then concentrate upon his garden as a memorial to famous historical figures and to his own sexual tastes. Rousham is a far more satisfying and subtle garden than Shotover, and whereas Shotover is inward-looking, tied down visually by its presiding trees to that one long axial line, Rousham has its seats and vantage points so arranged as to oblige visitors to look outwards at the landscape beyond. It was the county's good fortune to contain two such gardens of contrast. With that in mind, a walk from Shotover's north-west facing entrance front along Colonel James' half of the axial line makes a gloomy kind of sense. Working on it in Shotover's second, 1733, burst of garden activity, 13 years after the elder Tyrell's Gothick exercise, must have taught Kent some hard lessons, preparing him for Rousham in 1738.

An engraving of the grounds (27), a bird's eye view of 1750 by George Bickham[10], explains how this western arm was meant to work and why it does not work today. Kent's Obelisk, rather than the house, was the centre of a composition. The axis ran on to an octagonal pool, but out to the left of the Obelisk a widening, fan-shaped clearing climaxed in the octagonal Temple (28) on its steep, artificial mound. From one octagonal pool to one octagonal temple ran a long straight ride. The triangle of trees between these rides was threaded by a maze of winding paths leading casually to a centre point. That high raised Temple sat at the top of another broad ride leading down to a rectangular, tree-lined clearing and bastion where a drive came in towards the house. Quite strikingly there was a second straight ride running parallel to the western ride and passing through geometric clearings to end at the Octagon Pool. That has completely disappeared and so has the maze of winding paths, though a recent attempt to restore them as a 'Millennium Garden', beset with fat white cherubs and statues of shepherds and shepherdesses, indicates where the maze of paths once ran.

The problem that Kent failed to solve was Shotover's initial conception as an English version of a French-style forest garden. Trees work well in clumps or sited individually, en masse they take over in a wall of undifferentiated greenery. For all its siting on a mound, Kent's Temple is only occasionally visible in the grounds, and that Octagon Pool cannot be seen until the last minute of an approach. But is this criticism fair to Kent? Remembering the complexity of that 1750 aerial view, was there once a proto-Arcadia here that has not survived because there were no stone pavilions to punctuate it, and which has been overwhelmed by trees? It is possible; but Arcadias do not flourish in forest gardens; the present overgrown condition of Heythrop's little Classical Grove is proof of that.

When he came to Rousham, Kent would have found no such problems with suffocating tree growth. Charles Bridgeman had been working there before him as early as 1721.[11] All Kent had to do, though he took his time in doing it, was to lighten and curve some of Bridgeman's geometry, paint a mildly erotic ceiling for his patron and advise, in person when he could be persuaded to attend, upon the plantings of trees and shrubs. He had been involved with the Dormers of Rousham for some years. Sketches which he made for the Temple of the Mill, Townesend's Temple and Venus' Vale were executed between 1735 and 1738. Kent and Alexander Pope were quite close friends and Pope was a frequent visitor to Rousham.

The chronology of work at Rousham can become confusing with so many childless brothers succeeding each other. In 1719 John Dormer died, to be succeeded at Rousham by his brother, Colonel Robert Dormer, the friend of the younger James Tyrell, also

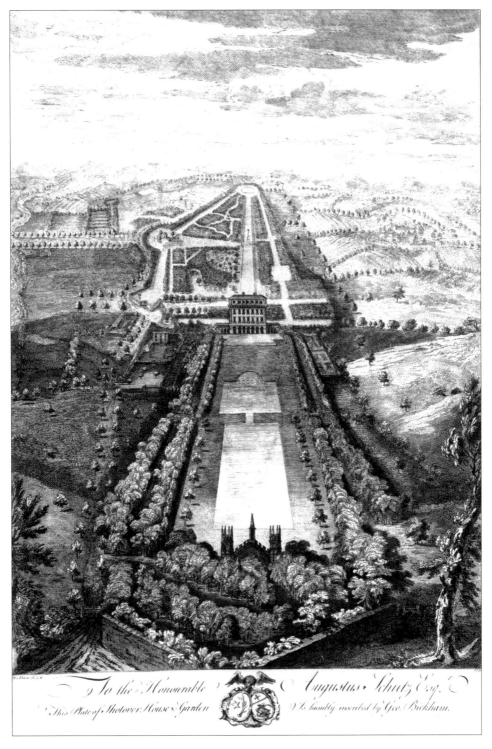

27 George Bickham's 1750 engraving of the grounds at Shotover shows the axial garden to the east and the William Kent–designed, informal Wilderness to the west. *Bodleian Library, MS. Gough Maps 26. F.71*

28 Kent's 1730s octagonal Temple at Shotover, originally encircled by four trees, commands three avenues in the Wilderness and a fourth in the wider parkland

a colonel, at Shotover. In 1721 Robert employed Charles Bridgeman to plan out his garden in Bridgeman's usual hard geometry imposed upon an existing topography. In 1725 another brother, James Dormer, was sent to Lisbon as British Minister as a reward for his successful campaigning in Spain. As a Minister he was less than successful, proving himself a roistering bully. James was recalled in 1730, yet rose to the rank of Lt General in 1735, so he must have had influential friends. In 1737 Colonel Robert Dormer died and James succeeded to Rousham. None of the three brothers ever married and it is evident, from the paintings which, miraculously, survive at Rousham, and from the statuary in the gardens, that General James Dormer was a confident bisexual. In addition, he was highly educated, Cicero and Chaucer being his favourite authors; the one notably severe, the other cheerfully bawdy. What matters at Rousham is that General James Dormer did exactly what Stephen Switzer had urged garden owners to do back in 1718: express uninhibitedly the 'sorrowful Reflexions' he had drawn from his warrior career, but also the 'Joy, Love, Fear, Contrition, and Repentence' which had sustained him. The fact that his favourite non-commissioned officer, William White, who was a leading bruiser in that Lisbon street fracas, followed his master-superior to Rousham, becoming his Steward, indicates that 'Contritions and Repentence' played little part in the General's scheme of things.

Rousham is a unique time capsule. The Cottrell-Dormers still own the house, and its contents, those of the Saloon in particular, are amazingly intact. It is as if that naughty, ruthless, honest, sophisticated old gentleman, General James, had just left the room to take a bracing cold bath in that wood of self-revelation which William Kent, a fellow bachelor and sympathiser, had helped him to create. Up on the ceiling of the Saloon is Kent's grotesque-style painting to illustrate the Merton educated General's chosen line from Terence: 'Sine Cerere Et Baccho Frigit Venus' (Without Food And Wine Love Grows Cold). How many lecherous suppers concluded in that low-ceilinged room where Venus and Cupid are uncomfortably supported by Ceres and Bacchus with a generous display of flesh? As if that ceiling were not enough to rouse his appetite, the General had hung his walls with fair copies of erotic originals. One painting of Cupid's big, bare backside is dominant; Kent's own Medusa head glares from the chimneypiece.

Nowhere else in England is there such a revealing introduction to the spirit of a garden as here at Rousham. After absorbing the art of the Saloon the exterior of the house and the statues of the garden will make sense. But together with all that sexual revelation and self-indulgence there is always the General, and Kent's delight in the beauties of the landscape. Among the satyrs and naked nymphs there are seats precisely sited so that a garden visitor must look in the correct direction for the ideal composition of a hillside, a dark wood overhanging a river, a triumphal arch, a bridge or a Gothick mill. The sensual aspects of Rousham should never hide its ingenious brilliance as a training course in landscape awareness. The reverse is true: the inspired sequence of views, enclosures and sudden realisations which make the garden so popular with genteel visitors should not distract from the fact that the garden at Rousham is one randy, rumbustious old soldier and art fancier's exploration of his own character. If the eighteenth century in England produced little in the way of analytical theatre, it did produce, as Switzer had hoped at its beginning, great gardens of self-expression, with Rousham foremost among them, a garden every bit as important nationally as Blenheim, though mercifully less tourist ridden.

Before walking its magical glades and erotic avenues one other point should be made. Its iconography is never remotely Christian. To an extent which is difficult to appreciate today, classical myths and classical gods and goddesses became mainstream in the Augustan eighteenth century; not because people believed in them as a faith is believed, but because their symbols and their aesthetic had become, via public school education, modern. Alexander Pope was the laureate of the Augustan Age not because he was creatively original, but because he introduced Virgil and Homer into the English poetic canon; and Pope, it should be remembered, was a close friend and admirer of a sensual man like General James Dormer. 'I lay one night at Rousham', Pope wrote on 4 September 1728 to Martha Blount, 'which is the prettiest place for water-falls, jetts, ponds inclosed with beautiful scenes of green and hanging wood, that I ever saw'[12], and that was 10 years before Kent was brought in. He was enjoying Charles Bridgeman's Rousham, the first edition as it were. What we find intellectually difficult to appreciate is that men like the Dormers, Pope, William Shenstone, Lord Burlington, Thomas Whately and William Mason, all the eighteenth-century garden arbiters, really cared about statues.[13] The Revd Joseph Spence, Professor of Classics at Oxford and Pope's most enthusiastic admirer, built his reputation on *Polymetis*, a mythological treatise which gave readers, who wished to place statues in their gardens, the correct order, selection and pose for those statues. It is worth making an effort to recreate their weird mindset: a Christian nation's aristocracy had virtually apostatised at one level of consciousness to the gods of Olympus, and Rousham was a sacred grove to apostates.

In a letter of 28 November 1738 to Lord Burlington, Kent related that 'the Genll is still bronzo mad, & they have bought him the Quattro Shiavi of Gio: di Bologna at Leghorn'.[14] Those bronzes were almost all studies of naked males, the General's polite pornography, and they still litter the shelves and alcoves of Rousham's Saloon. At the very least the Cottrell-Dormer family deserve a baronetcy for their fidelity over the years in preserving this strange national treasure. Their garden too is open under the most civilised and reasonable system of entrance anywhere in the country. We owe them a debt as true guardians of one of the great sites of our national heritage.

A walk around Rousham is further enriched by the accident of the MacClary letter.[15] John MacClary was the Head Gardener who outlived the General. When the Cottrells, to whom the General had bequeathed the estate, proved reluctant to stay in a house which had acquired such a louche reputation from the General's activities, MacClary wrote a racy and tempting account of the garden and its delights in an effort to persuade them to come up from London and revive the estate. So we have an invaluable contemporary account of how Rousham was meant to be experienced; and again by good Oxfordshire fortune, virtually everything, except the droves of cows passing over Heyford Bridge, can still be enjoyed.

Reeling morally from the artistic impact of the Saloon, visitors pass out and skirt the ha-ha to reach the garden front of the house. A naked Venus and a nude Antinous (or Apollo according to interpretation) are set in Kent's Gothick niches on the west wing, but a singing Faun and a Bacchante give the east wing a lively counterpoint. The Bowling Green and the scoop of green hillside from the Green to the river are Bridgemanic geometry. The disturbing statue (*29*) of a horse being savaged by a lion[16] must be the General's sensitive protest against the horrors of war as he had experienced them in Spain. MacClary turns away, 'your eye drops upon a very fine Concave Slope, at the bottom of which runs the Beautiful River Charvel, and at the top stands two pretty Garden Seats ... here you sit down first in the one, and then in the other' to appreciate 'the prettiest view in the whole World'. At the centre of this view (*30*) is the 'Temple of the Mill', a cottage enhanced by Kent's Gothick buttressing and pinnacles.[17] The inauthentic Triumphal Arch on the horizon is also by Kent, intended to focus the eye. Kent relaxed and naturalised the course of the Cherwell; Bridgeman had canalised it to prove man's authority over Nature, but Nature had now become fashionable. So had Death.[18] The General was well aware of death, hence the statue of the Dying Gladiator (*colour plate 8*). But those two herms of Duty – Hercules, and self-indulgence – Pan, that flank the soldier were meant to urge moral choices and they stand above the General's most original concept, the Praeneste: a loggia-terrace, delicately limewashed, for leisurely enjoyment of conversation and the view.

29 Scheemakers' horrific sculpture of a horse being savaged by a lion on the top terrace at Rousham – the first suggestion of the intensely psychological nature of General Dormer's layout

30 Kent's drawing of the 'Temple of the Mill and Eye Catcher' at Rousham, which extends the visual bounds of the garden out into the wider landscape. *Country Life Picture Library. By kind permission of Mr & Mrs Cottrell-Dormer*

31 The naked Antinous at the head of the former Elm Walk at Rousham – General Dormer's homage to Hadrian's boy lover who drowned in the Nile

We need to bypass Venus' Vale for the moment and follow the Serpentine Rill (*colour plate 9*) to the General's Cold Bath with a grotto-like changing room for indulgences in stoic nudity. In its first state the Rill was wider, rougher and had trout in it. The next statue was the General's pride, a 'Colossus', naked of course, of the Emperor Hadrian's boy-lover, Antinous (*31*), drowned mysteriously in the Nile, hence the reeds at his feet. He could be enjoyed, first from the long avenue walk, originally lined with elms, leading up to him, then from the Tuscan, Kent-designed, Townesend's Temple, which, when the Antinous paled, offered gazebo-type views of traffic on Heyford bridge and the causeway. So unlike inward-looking Shotover, Rousham looks affectionately out at the real world one way, at Antinous' nudity on the other. All this time visitors have been encouraged to interact with the garden rather than to enjoy it passively.

On the way back Venus' Vale emphasises the General's broadminded sexual outlook. This is one of Kent's best compositions (*32*) of water bubbling from grotto arches, fountains spouting, so MacClary claimed, one 50ft high, one 30ft, an erotically modest Venus being eyed up by a lecherous Pan and an evil, predatory Satyr, both by John Van Nost.[19] This is the conclusion of the artistic journey from that gloomy set of buildings at Heythrop: the English Garden now has its perfect model thanks to two artists and one wilful old soldier. At this half-way point in the circuit Kent placed his most original and topographically satisfying garden building, the Praeneste (*colour plate 7*), an arcade of seven arches fitting neatly into the curve of the hillside to provide a viewing place with painted wooden settees for private meetings.[20] The nature of these meetings is indicated by the busts that MacClary listed in his account: 'a young Cleopatra, Shakspeer, a Bacchanal, Alexander, the Roman Sistenor [Senator], and Niaba'[21]; a range from lovers to celebrities with the Bacchanal to hint at passion.

In exciting contrast in that dark wooded corner of the grounds, beyond Bridgeman's concave theatre, the yews close in and the General became mindful of the classical establishment. Here stands the Pyramid, sacred to the noble dead. MacClary lists the busts and bas reliefs it once contained: 'on one side is the Head of Julius Caesar, on the other is Calpurnia, in Bass Relief, on each side is a nich, in which stands Busts of Marcus Aurelius, and Socratus'[22], very much an Oxford man's choice. MacClary praises the views again at this point: 'the pretty naturial turnings and windings of the River and the delightful naturial Cascade'.[23] Originally a wooden bridge here allowed visitors to cross to the Mill and the Arch.

32 Venus' Vale, as sketched by Kent, is essentially a theatrical promenading area for Georgian couples, but one with an underlying sexual tension. *Country Life Picture Library. By kind permission of Mr & Mrs Cottrell-Dormer*

After Rousham there could hardly be a turning back from such a seductive triumph of image and arrangement. Its prevailing stylistic reference was, it is true, classical, but the Castellated Barn in the Paddock and the Pyramid were markers of the eclecticism which, for the Continental copiers, was a particular charm of this English Garden experiment. So what, precisely, were the sources of that intrusive fashion for things foreign? Not all garden quests end satisfactorily, but the follow-up to the garden of Francis Wise, an Oxford antiquary who, despite a dubious reputation for bad judgements, eventually became the first Librarian of the new Radcliffe Library, does throw a certain slanting light on that garden eclecticism in the middle years of the eighteenth century. The quest begins with an attractive print (33), 'A View from Elsfield near Oxford'[24], which illustrates an open columned and tent-roofed Chinese temple on a small round island, accessed by a bridge across an oval pond. Woodland around the pond has been cut down on one side to give a striking view of the spires and the Radcliffe dome of Oxford about a mile distant. What inspired an Oxford scholar to go Chinese in a garden building?

Wise was one of a group of Oxford men working to revive, not the study of Chinese, but of Anglo-Saxon.[25] As a Whig he believed that the primitive Saxon love of liberty within a jury-bound legal system was the underpinning of parliamentary democracy. He knew more about numismatics than Anglo-Saxon, but none of his Oxford colleagues knew much more and his scholarly 1722 edition of Aser's *Life of King Alfred* was a useful contribution.[26] Rather less valuable was his fieldwork on the Uffington White Horse, which he claimed was cut to celebrate one of King Alfred's victories. If he had looked at one of the Iron Age coins in his own collection he would have seen that the horse was much earlier and his claim, published in *A Letter to Dr Mead* (1738), was soon contradicted and ridiculed in *The Impertinence and Impatience of Modern Antiquaries display'd*, a pamphlet by Philalethes Rusticus (George North), published in 1739. After fighting back for a time, Wise came to admit his own error.

By his friendship with the Earl of Guilford, Wise had obtained the living of Elsfield, a small village on the ridge of high land immediately north-east of Oxford, and been given a lease of land, 'a little piece of ground, which had formerly been a garden, with two ponds in it' and 'a marshy bit of ground heretofore a pond, now a spinney, lying at the bottom of Homestead Close'.[27] He owed the Earl's favour to the warm relationship he had developed with his son when tutoring him at Trinity College. The 1772 *Life of Hearne*, a biography of another Oxford antiquary, records that Wise spent his time 'in forming an elegant Garden, which, though a small piece of Ground, was diversified with every object in Miniature that can be found in a larger Scale in the most admired Places of this Kingdom'.[28] Dr Huddesford particularised these, writing that in 'a few acres you was surprized with ponds, cascades, seats, a triumphal arch, the tower of Babel, a Druid temple, and an Aegyptian pyramid', but no mention of a Chinese temple, the engraving of which Wise included in his *Catalogus* together with another illustrating a cataract falling through a ruined arch. There was also a Hermitage where Wise entertained Samuel Johnson in 1754, just before the publication of his *Dictionary*.

Such a garden of compressed eclectic ornaments was clearly important. However, the present Manor at Elsfield is not the neat Georgian vicarage that might be expected but a gaunt, grey, mainly Victorian building, like a hotel, built immediately on the roadside;

33 The Anglo-Saxon antiquary Francis Wise's Rococo-style garden at Elsfield Manor with its Chinese Temple in the foreground and the spires of Oxford in the distance. *Bodleian Library, MS. Gough Maps 26. F.65B*

behind it the garden falls steeply down a lawn to rough woodland. Far from being ecclesiastical in associations, the house was the last English home of the novelist John Buchan. Site investigation is not easy as the wood is dense with nettles and bog myrtle, but a pond survives, with neither an island nor a Chinese temple, though a little classical stone temple seat lacking its columns overlooks the water. Trees have grown up and Oxford's spires are completely hidden. Up on the edge of the wood in a grove of yews is a sturdy dog's gravestone with a Latin inscription. Nothing else remains except some possible Druids' stones. So why, with all that Anglo-Saxon background, a barn disguised as a Norman keep and a stable designed to look like a Saxon convent, did Wise go Chinese and cram his little garden with Rococo eclecticism? The answer is obvious. His friend and patron was Francis North, Earl of Guilford, whose seat at Wroxton Abbey in the same county had one of the most complete collections of eclectic garden buildings in the country: classical, Gothick and, most prominently, Chinese. What Francis Wise built at Elsfield was the grounds of Wroxton in miniature and the garden structure he most valued and had illustrated was a Chinese temple, not a Saxon relic.

Elsfield was an antiquary's indulgence, but perhaps the most poetic influence for really eclectic indulgence in the county was Wroxton.[29] A first impression on approaching the Abbey will be one of surprise that any garden in this immaculately tended area of shaven lawns and rose beds could ever be described as lost. This, however, is the western, upper park; the Willow Pattern garden lies in the lower park and that is satisfyingly forlorn, bedraggled and imperfect. Up on the hillside to the right of the entrance drive is an octagonal dovecote of 1746, designed to look like one of the towers of Warwick Castle with arrow slits and battlements. This was the work of Sanderson Miller. He was a local squire and antiquary who, by making rough drawings for his friends, achieved quite a reputation in the Midlands as a gentleman architect with a flair for the Gothick. At this period Miller was designing very similar buildings, with an unfortunate tendency to fall down, at Ambrosden, 10 miles north of Oxford, for another friend, Sir Edward Turner, an Oxford association with political undertones.[30] In 1747 he designed a Gothick Barn with a pediment and pinnacles, something of a hybrid structure, and in 1748 a Ruin and a Lodge with rusticated entrance gates; Miller copied the rustication from that of Oxford's Physic Garden. But in March 1750 the Ruin collapsed only two years after it had been built. 'Down is fallen, fallen, fallen the Gothick! … Come and deplore the ruin of my Ruins', Sir Edward wrote philosophically.[31] Miller is supposed to have supplied him with a Castle Ruin and advised on some pools; but everything was demolished in 1779. Miller was a little luckier with his Wroxton designs. The dovecote deserves close inspection as it explains some of the changes that occurred in the Willow Pattern garden during the 1740s.

On the other side of the Abbey, past the 1st Baron Guildford's handsome late seventeenth-century stable block, is a vast expanse of manicured but oddly ridged and terraced lawn and it is there, standing next to the Doric Temple, that the North family's unusual relationship to Wroxton Abbey and the motivation behind their activities in the gardens needs to be explained.[32] The Norths did not build Wroxton, Sir William Pope did that, and though the Norths lived in the house for 250 years, the extraordinary truth is that they never owned it; they rented it, or more precisely they leased it, year by year, from Trinity College, Oxford, the real owners. The 2nd Baron Guilford of the North dynasty employed Tilleman Bobart, a gardener in the old, Franco-Dutch formal manner, who had learned his trade under William III's Royal Gardener, George London. Bobart worked fast and in the two years before the 2nd Baron's death in 1729 the entire green sweep of lawn below the house had been formalised with bedding and 'greens' (shrubs) in the Dutch manner.[33] Bobart had obviously converted the 2nd Baron to Dutch garden design. He regularised two monastic fishponds in a little side valley over to the right and hidden today behind a grove of trees. But then, before the geometry had had time to mature and soften, the 2nd Baron died and his son, yet another Francis, aged 25, succeeded to the lease. It was this Francis North who, in his long leasehold from 1729-90 as 3rd Baron and, after 1752, 1st Earl of Guilford, made the grounds of Wroxton into a miniature rural version of the Vauxhall pleasure gardens in London. Under his direction Wroxton gained, if not the first Chinese garden building in England – Stowe has that honour – then the country's first full-scale Chinese fantasy garden of winding rivers and Willow Pattern plate topography.

In 1729 ambitious young men like the 3rd Baron were gathering themselves naturally around the King's elder son, Frederick Louis, Prince of Wales, in the confident expectation that George II would not live too long and that soon there would be a King Frederick on the throne. He was a cheerful, probably a shallow man, but a devoted husband and father, devoted also to sports and entertainment. The obvious way to Frederick's friendship without too much expense was by providing, in a private park like Wroxton, a venue for night time pleasures and day time picnic expeditions with boats for music on calm waters, fireworks to make the dark sky light and fanciful eclectic structures – Chinese, Gothick, Turkish, it did not matter greatly, provided they offered exotic settings for alfresco eating and drinking. Chinese would be the cheapest as Chinese buildings were made of wood and canvas, brightly painted. Willow Pattern china had, however, set up a popular expectation that Chinese buildings were closely linked to bridges and wandering streams. Tilleman Bobart still had three years to serve at Wroxton, but when the old Baron died there were no more rectangular ponds dug or straight avenues planted. 'Sharawadgi' was the new craze, the Chinese art of asymmetrical grace notes: winding streamlets, lakes with wooded islands and natural shore lines, surprise compositions of rocks, falling waters, quaint bridges and pagoda roofs.[34]

Francis North was a young man in a hurry. In 1730 he was appointed one of the Prince's Lords of the Bedchamber, who were actually congenial friends and political advisors. Fixing his mind upon a provisional royal visit to Wroxton to attend Banbury races, he put Bobart to extending the existing earth dam at the foot of the last fishpond to create the Great Pond, seven acres of natural-looking water with winding inlets, peninsulas and an island. The earth dam created an impressive 20ft cascade and below that Bobart's team were busy digging a serpentine course for the little river, damming it up to widen its meagre flow and enlivening it with stepped waterfalls. Lastly, to achieve a bewildering riverine maze of waterways, an alternative double course was dug for the Sor brook, one of which was just wide enough for rowing boats to make oriental voyages from the Chinese Lodge, past the Chinese House to the last Chinese Bridge by the Chinese Seat. All this was achieved before Bobart's dismissal in 1732 and remains to be explored today with, admittedly, the help of a good spell of wet weather to fill the channels and boost the Cascade. What was required next were eclectic pleasure buildings. Here the Wroxton account books are not very helpful, but for the year 1739-40, when the Prince was finally persuaded to make his visit, there is a mention of payments for lead to cover the roof of the Chinese House.[35] By that time, on the evidence of an undated map, full of enchanting details and bordered with illustrations of the garden buildings, all drawn by Francis Booth, there was a Chinese House, a Chinese Lodge, a Chinese Seat and three Chinese bridges. Wroxton had its Willow Pattern world.

A copy of Francis Booth's plan (34) is an essential if an exploration of the Chinese lower park is to make sense. Using the plan, the carefully prepared carriage way that still circles the pleasure grounds can be followed, and when the Chinese area is reached, it helps to enrich visually the bramble bushes with the appropriate numbered item from Booth's delightful vignettes. The carriage way, many of its original kerb stones still visible in the earth, leads along the winding shores of the Great Pond and soon the

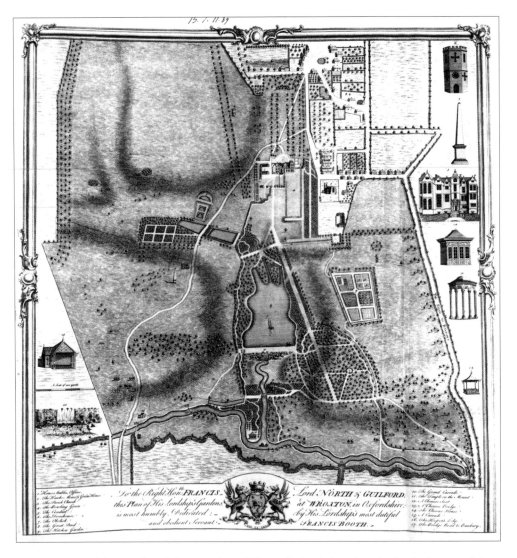

34 Francis Booth's 1750 plan of Wroxton shows Tilleman Bobart's formal garden by the house and the Chinoiserie-Gothick, Willow Pattern garden below the lake. *Bodleian Library, MS. Gough Maps 26, f.68*

splash, if not the roar, of the Great Cascade (35) can be heard. Not every visitor was impressed, however, by Wroxton's head of water. Philip Yorke reported in 1746, 'it only plays occasionally'[36], and Walpole had to wait for a signal to be given raising a sluice, which then provided a brief but tolerable flow. My luck was to be there in sunshine after appallingly wet weather when not only was the Cascade an impressive fall of white water with the lower, stepped fall well covered, but all Lord North's water courses, which are usually dried up, were full and flowing.

To revive the eighteenth-century visual experience the miniature Willow Pattern valley has to be viewed from two vantage points: from the dam first and then from the top of the mount. Looking down from the dam a serpentine stream, a mere eight feet across, wriggles in correct Rococo curves for 100 yards down to a steep mount clothed in dark yew trees. When the garden fancier, Mrs Delany, sketched this mount in 1747 a Gothick tower with two pointed windows, a most un-Chinese object, crowned it. Philip Yorke of Wrest Park had heard that such a building was planned and it is most likely to have been the design of Miller, like the church tower at Wroxton, and like that church tower it must have fallen down. Soon after, in 1750, Lord North and Miller were debating the model of a new temple to be built on the same strategic visual site: a domed octagon on arches half Gothic, half classical. The Temple had 'curtains, that by turning screws let down so as to afford shelter which ever way you please'.[37] This was a favourite picnic venue from the Abbey. But, for all the curtains, it would still have been a breezy spot and Lord North, who would live to be 86, was already a hopeless hypochondriac, nervous of draughts and damps.

For the next viewpoint the visitor must cross the stream by a three-arched bridge, Chinese in name though now stripped of its distinctive parapet, and climb the mount which impends quite impressively and Willow Pattern-wise above it. Now the view is, despite its diminutive scale, striking. Not only does the Great Cascade tumble noisily down over the arched recess in Bobart's dam, but the serpentine stream is broken by two stepped waterfalls. The scene would be improved if the two mounds that flank the Great Cascade were stripped of their vegetation and exposed as Lord North intended: two massy heaps of

35 The Great Cascade at Wroxton has a seat set behind the waterfall for views through the spray down the serpentine to the Gothick Temple on its Mount, now lost

36 Mrs Delany's 1754 sketch of the Chinese House at Wroxton where the Norths enjoyed cold meats and ice cream. *By courtesy of the National Gallery of Ireland (2722 (55))*

broken rock, the *rocaille* that was an essential feature of Rococo scenery.[38] It is worth following the course of the stream for its last 50 yards to the watersmeet. The Chinese House (*36*) stood here overlooking a world of toy waters.[39] 'I hope we shall have the pleasure of your company to cold meat and Iced cream', Lord North wrote to Miller in July 1749, 'at the Chinese House … . Our compliments wait on the good woman &c &c. My Chinese House is so warm she will not get cold'.[40] A short walk downstream leads to the site of a second Chinese bridge and the Chinese or Keeper's Lodge. This was the liveliest of Wroxton's three Chinese houses with a neat, geometrically ornamented loggia. Rather further upstream the twin rivers reach the Banbury road and there the Chinese Seat (*37*), which must have doubled as a gazebo, stood on a second mount, clothed like the other in dark evergreens. From the Seat a drive led back through the woods to the Great Pond and a completed circuit of pleasures.

As a sad footnote it has to be recorded that in 1751 all Lord North's political hopes crashed down when Prince Frederick died nine years before his father, George II. Always allergic to Oxfordshire weather, Lord North retired to his third wife's home, Waldershare in the warmer, drier airs of Kent, visiting Wroxton only occasionally to attend to elections. It may have been no coincidence that the year that ended his hopes of high office under a Rococo monarch also dampened permanently his interest in the Chinese.

William Kent, who had enlivened, and indeed transformed, Rousham from a collection of geometrical pools and straight avenues beside a disciplined river, never returned to work again in Oxfordshire gardens. But his influence is present in the gardens of another house where one of his close friends was brought in, as he had been brought in at Rousham, to rescue a rather lifeless late seventeenth-century layout. The Manor House at Milton has such attractive Carolean façades of about 1667 that visitors tend not to notice the charmingly run-down, Kentian-style water garden of its park. This was designed with help from the owner, Bryant Barrett, by one of William Kent's closest friends, Stephen Wright. It was Wright who added the wings to the Manor in 1776, and by a fortunate freak of patronage was able to create in the new Library a more splendidly imaginative and playful domestic Rococo-Gothick interior than Kent was ever allowed to design. For the single-storey offices on the east side of the house Wright devised a canted Rococo viewing bay looking out onto the park. It is, therefore, no surprise to find the relics of a Rococo-style water garden on both sides of the house, a layout that was planned and completed by Bryant Barrett and Wright before they began the remodelling of the house. It is recorded in a 'Plan of the Parish of Milton', made by James Glaspole in 1771 and preserved at the house.[41]

37 The Chinese Seat at Wroxton, shown in another Delany sketch, was the climax of a boat trip that began at the Chinese Bridge, passed the Chinese House and ended at the south-eastern corner of the estate by a cascade. *By courtesy of the National Gallery of Ireland (2772 (83))*

Initially the impact of the wandering Serpentine that threads the grounds is more whimsically comical than Rococo, as the present owners have set up a 'ferry' on which, for payment of a modest fee and at their own risk, visitors can propel themselves the 20 yards across the water. The source of this Serpentine lies on the other side of the house, the water being conducted by a hidden system of pipes running from the perimeter stream across the north grounds and under the service range. The charm of Milton is its unkempt, casual air: the brick-walled Conservatory in the Walled Garden has little glass left yet a peach tree manages to struggle on. The hot houses at the entrance to the enclosure are roofless and forlorn; only their water ducts survive. In contrast to the attractive confinement of the Walled Garden the pleasure grounds on the north side of the Manor are green, open and superbly tree planted and they boast a large pool, once circular, but now naturalised. Beech, willow and redwood grow around its banks and it has a metal heron standing in its shining waters; many of the trees in this area are likely to be early nineteenth-century introductions. This whole area was originally precisely circular like its pool and a Loggia with two Ionic columns commands it, not a very sophisticated design. On the entrance front to the Manor the Serpentine takes off confidently by the ferry and winds its way, pleasantly overshadowed by trees, one of them a wonderfully distorted plane, until it fades waterless away into the back gardens of the village. Just one classical rotunda, raised on its banks and visible from the Manor, would have made this a well-known, if minor, Rococo layout. As it is we have only the wet bones of a garden that Kent would have been happy to acknowledge: a clear pointer to the link in this insular county between the Gothick and the half-grasped Rococo.

An even more satisfying linking between two styles, the full-blooded Rococo and the natural elegance of Brownian landscaping, survives intact at Buckland House, near Faringdon, a seat of the Throckmortons in what was once Berkshire. Buckland is a confusion of the Mr Woods. John Wood the younger of Bath, who wrapped a confident Gothick façade around the decayed sixteenth-century manor house to provide stables, also designed, possibly with help from his father, Wood the elder, the ill-proportioned but memorable main block of Buckland House[42], while William Wood, possibly an uncle, acted as agent on the site. The park was also laid out by a 'Mr Wood', but one unrelated to the architects. This was the Catholic Richard Woods, an inspired follower of the Brownian-style of park composition. He was working at Buckland from 1758 for a fellow Catholic, Sir Robert Throckmorton and, although his layout is not shown on Roque's 1761 map of Berkshire, it was described in a poem of 1774 by Henry Pye who relates how Throckmorton has 'Clothed the declining slopes with pendant wood/ And o'er the sedge grown meadows poured the flood'.[43] Whereas Brown would have circled the valley and lakes with a carriage drive hemmed in by a shelter-belt of trees and contrived green vacancies with occasional tree clumps in the valley floor, Woods produced a circuit for strolling aesthetes with lively architectural incidents along the route, one that miraculously, with a little help from Lady Fitzgerald in the Edwardian period, survives today.

Just below W.H. Romaine's 1910 Dairy by the stables a wicket gate leads down to evergreen woods of yew, box and ilex, and the start of Woods' circuit or alternatively

38 Richard Woods' 1760s Ice House on the walking circuit at Buckland House has his trademark vermiculated rustication

its conclusion. Deep in this gloomy woodland belt is Woods' Ice House (*38*). It has a thatched conical roof and a wide loggia with Woods' trademark of alternate stone blocks and vermiculated rustication. It was probably intended for rustic picnics as it has a fine view of the upper lake. Below it the path crosses a rocky cascade by an elegant ironwork bridge, then turns left to begin a magical course along the bank of the lower lake. What makes this section of the circuit so attractive is the architecturally solid wall of close-clipped box that defines a series of little lakeside glades, concealing the rough woodland behind it almost completely and thus extending the garden out into the wild.

At the arm of land between the lower and upper lake there is a rustic boathouse and a round rustic hut, both probably Regency in date, but the box-hedged way continues winding its course and offering spectacular views across the lake to where the seemingly over-scaled house is in fact perfectly scaled to make a handsome garden ornament from this distance. The lakes are a conscious attempt on Woods' part to simulate a river, the Thames-Isis at Buckland, a landscape design motif that would remain a constant throughout his 30 year career. This upper lake has a small Grotto on the opposite shore and ends with a much larger rusticated Grotto Arch, darkly mysterious but only reached by a boat. High up on the wooded hillside, framed by evergreens and a towering row

39 The Duck House is another destination point on the perambulation at Buckland, giving wide views across the lake – a conscious imitation by Woods of the river Thames

of sweet chestnuts, the Rotunda of post-1767[44] offers the necessary architectural lure to persuade the walker uphill, past the rusticated Duck House (*39*) by the lakeside and on to the high ground leading back to the house. If visitors were taken round in the reverse direction they would have been able to end their tour at the Dairy with a sampling of the estate's milk and cheese or, if it were Sunday, with a short extra walk on to the Catholic chapel to attend Mass. In all they would have enjoyed eight garden structures and a series of perfect landscape compositions of wood and water: a more humanly-scaled Brownian-style park enlivened with diverting Rococo enrichment.

NOTES

1 Souldern's is dated 1706; Hordley's 1750.
2 Illustrated in Geoffrey Jellicoe, 'Ronald Tree and the Gardens of Ditchley Park: The Human Face of History', *Garden History*, vol.10, no.1 (Spring, 1982), figure 2, p.82.
3 Oxfordshire Record Office (hereafter ORO), Survey of Ditchley Park, DIL I/i/4.
4 ORO, DIL I/i/12.
5 Willis, *Bridgeman*, mentions Shotover in passing when discussing Bridgeman's contribution to Rousham but does not suggest an attribution.

6   *Country Life*, 22 & 29 December 1977.

7   See Timothy Mowl, *William Kent: Architect, Designer, Opportunist*, 2006.

8   Sherwood & Pevsner, *Oxfordshire*, p.764.

9   EH Register entry.

10 Bodleian Library, MS. Gough Maps 26, f.71.

11 Willis, *Bridgeman*, suggests that Bridgeman's plan for Rousham (Bodleian Library, MSGD a4, f.63) was based on a survey of 1721, preserved at the house. See his discussion on pp.66-8, and plate 61 for the plan.

12 George Sherburn (ed.), *The Correspondence of Alexander Pope*, 5 vols (Oxford, 1956), 2, p.513.

13 For a comprehensive survey of this phenomenon see Susan Gordon, 'The Iconography and Mythology of the Eighteenth-Century English Landscape Garden', University of Bristol, PhD, 1999.

14 Sherburn, *Correspondence*, 4, p.150.

15 Mavis Batey, 'The Way to View Rousham by Kent's Gardener', *Garden History*, vol.11, no.2 (Autumn, 1983), pp.125-32. See also Mavis Batey & David Lambert, *The English Garden Tour: A View into the Past*, 1990, pp.156-61, and Christopher Hussey, 'A Georgian Arcady – William Kent's gardens at Rousham, Oxfordshire', *Country Life*, 14 & 21 June 1946.

16 The General ordered from Scheemakers a copy of the work in the garden of the Villa d'Este at Tivoli.

17 Kent's drawing for this view with its Gothick enrichments is preserved at the house. It is illustrated in both John Dixon Hunt and Mavis Batey's articles cited above.

18 See David Coffin, *The English Garden: Meditation and Memorial* (Princeton, 1994).

19 Kent's drawing for Venus' Vale is preserved at the house and illustrated in Batey's MacClary article in *Garden History*.

20 These dove blue and white settees have now been taken inside the house for security.

21 Batey, *Garden History*, p.130.

22 Ibid.

23 Ibid., p.130.

24 Bodleian Library, MS. Gough Maps 26, f.65b.

25 See Rosemary Sweet, *Antiquaries: The Discovery of the Past in Eighteenth-Century Britain* (Hambledon & London, 2004).

26 This was based on a Bodleian manuscript: MS. Cotton Otho A XII, which was subsequently consumed by fire, leaving Wise's record a unique source. See Strickland Gibson, 'Francis Wise B D: Oxford Antiquary, Librarian, and Archivist', *Oxoniensia*, vol.1 (1936), pp.173-95.

27 Ibid., p.185.

28 Ibid.

29 In 1963 Fairleigh Dickinson College of New Jersey bought the Abbey and most of its parkland. The College allows interested visitors access to the grounds.

30 Jennifer Meir gives a brief account of Miller's Ambrosden ventures in her *Sanderson Miller and his Landscapes* (Chichester, 2006), pp.114-15, but reports that nothing survives of the Ruin except a small area of rushy ground. Miller also designed a Gothick Lodge for Middleton Park which survives to the south-east of the estate on the A43; it is illustrated in Meir, *Sanderson Miller*, colour plate XXVI.

31 Ibid., p.115.

32 John Cornforth, 'Wroxton Abbey, Oxfordshire I, II & III', *Country Life*, 3, 10 & 24 September 1981; Meir, *Sanderson Miller*, pp.93-105. This has excellent illustrations of Mrs Delany's sketches. See also Michael Cousins, 'Wroxton Abbey, Oxfordshire: An Eighteenth-Century Estate', *The Follies Journal*, no.5 (Winter, 2005), pp.39-72.

33 Bobart's plan is preserved at the Abbey and can be viewed, with permission, on the staircase wall.

34 Ciaran Murray, *Sharawadgi: The Romantic Return to Nature* (San Francisco, 1999).

35 Meir, *Sanderson Miller*, p.97.

36 Ibid., p.102.

37 Ibid., p.104: observed by Bishop Pococke, visiting in 1756.

38 Ibid., plate 65.

39 Illustrated by Cousins, *Follies Journal*, figures 8 & 9.

40 Meir, *Sanderson Miller,* pp.100-101.

41 The Plan is in the staircase hall of the Manor; I am grateful to Helen Hall for bringing it to my attention.

42 Its original attenuated proportions were made even worse by a general fattening out by Sir Maurice Fitzgerald to accommodate house parties in 1909.

43 Quoted in Timothy Mowl, 'Air of Irregularity', *Country Life*, 11 January 1990. Woods was paid for an initial consultation on 13 February 1758. For an account of Woods' career see Fiona Cowell's seminal articles in *Garden History*: 'Richard Woods (?1716-93): A Preliminary Account', vol.14, no.2 (Autumn, 1986), pp.85-119, 'Richard Woods (?1716-93): A Preliminary Account, Part II', vol.15, no.1 (Spring, 1987), pp.19-54, and 'Richard Woods (?1716-93): A Preliminary Account, Part II', vol.15, no.2 (Autumn, 1987), pp.115-35. Dr Cowell has recently completed a PhD thesis on Woods: 'Richard Woods (1715/6-1793): Surveyor, Improver and Master of the Pleasure Garden', University of East Anglia, 2005.

44 The urn under the dome contains the ashes of Sir Maurice Fitzgerald, 20th Knight of Kerry; Woods designed similar rotundas for Wardour Castle in 1764 and for Wormsley in 1779. The Rotunda was surrounded until recently by a circle of limes, but these were felled by Jill Wellesley to give the building more visual prominence in the landscape.

5

BROWN, MASON AND REPTON – MASCULINE VERSUS FEMININE

In the first half of the eighteenth century, as so often in the past, at places like Woodstock, Beckley, Heythrop and Rousham the county was at the cutting edge of garden innovation. In a new age of personality cults in garden design, Lancelot Brown, his very nickname, 'Capability', an obvious sales gimmick, and Humphry Repton, inventor of the ingenious 'before and after' watercolour slides of the Red Books, projected, not concurrently, but in succession, two basically different modes of landscape design. It may seem like a neat generalisation, but it will be helpful to think of Brown as producing garden-parks for men, and Repton as insinuating garden landscapes for women. In place of those enchanted Arcadias, Capability Brown offered, with his trained teams of skilled labourers, an elegant natural simplicity of landscape: an ideal England perfected, an Arcadia but with fewer temples, natural-seeming lakes and natural-seeming groves of trees.

Brown's parks satisfied the male ego. He provided evenly graded and surfaced drives for the new, well-sprung, almost streamlined carriages that industrial England could supply: speed together with a fast changing landscape appealed to the Toad in every man. Around these drives, one of which usually demonstrated by a circumnavigation the whole of a landowner's park, there were strategically placed coppices and belts of trees, sited not just for satisfying landscape compositions, but for the rearing and sheltering of game birds. With the invention and production of lighter, more efficient sporting guns, one of the chief attractions of a country weekend was the mass slaughter of game. Those were Brown's offerings: superficial beauty, ease of upkeep, exhilarating speed and sporting terrain. Delivered initially to patrons with a no-nonsense, masculine competence on personal visits, followed up by teams of ditchers, drainers, water manipulators and tree transplanters, it was irresistible. Kings and dukes persuaded him to visit, but before accepting the conventional image of Brown as a national treasure, two of Oxfordshire's gardens in which he had no hand should be considered.

One is Heythrop. Anyone who has squelched around Heythrop in Wellingtons or walking boots will appreciate what a service and a transformation Brown's teams effected in those parks which they drained, re-seeded and planted. The second non-Brownian landscape park is at Pusey House, once in Berkshire, now in Oxfordshire, and this is the reverse side of the Brownian coinage. Pusey is dramatic and even brilliant as a composition because it plays none of the Brownian tricks. There is no tasteful clumping of trees, no drive encircling the estate, in fact no drive at all on the south side of the house, and just one long, narrow bar of water. Instead, two woods face the house like two stage flats with a clear, open way between them leading to the horizon; there are no boundaries and it works. Pusey makes the point that avoiding Brown could be a stroke of luck. Heythrop, however, makes the opposite point; it desperately needed him and still does, two centuries later.

If in doubt about Brown's occasional predictability, it is useful to take a walk on one of the public rights-of-way across Kirtlington's park. Kirtlington lies on level country, unhelpful to a designer. Sir John Dashwood paid Brown £100, 'for work in hand', or possibly for a survey of the park, on 17 January 1752, early on in Brown's career.[1] Then, after a pause in 1754, his teams worked on from 1755-62 with very little dramatic effect on the landscape. A variant plan by Robert Greening had proposed cutting up the wood south-east of the house into a series of groves with classical temples: a typical mid-century Rococo-style layout. In two further plans Brown delivered instead loose groves south and east of the house with a belt of Scots pines and three tree clumps with one miniscule pond.[2] But then 1752 was quite early on in Brown's career, as he had only just left Stowe to set up on his own. Finmere's Rectory garden was an even earlier, perhaps 1740s, design when Brown was still working at Stowe. Lord Selborne described the Rector's demesne as: 'a slope of green turf … cedars, spruce firs, groups of other well chosen trees and shrubs and pretty flower beds; all disposed as to produce the effect of a long perspective and considerable space where there was really little'[3], which explains much about Brown's later work. He is also thought to have expanded the widenings on the Glyme into a lake below Kiddington Hall[4], but because he was so popular and so much copied he becomes a habit rather than a documented attribution. The perfect lake that now fills the valley below Ditchley and enlivens Gibbs' ley lines of trees looks to be a Brownian contrivance, but there is no record of him working to develop the water from an earlier pond or to enhance it with a Chinese bridge and a water grotto (40). Luke Sullivan's engraving of the landscape is dated 1759, so Stiff Leadbetter's 1760-3 oval Temple must have been a later enrichment of the scene.

Baldon House at Marsh Baldon, south-east of Oxford, preserves another instance of the Brownian style becoming a national vernacular with just a dash of Gothick eclecticism to liven up the composition. While Baldon House, for many generations a seat of the Willoughby family, has an early seventeenth-century gabled vernacular range to its entrance front, its rear façade is unassumingly Georgian in date and gives onto a perfect essay in amateur mid-eighteenth-century park design. A crude, quite uninhabitable, Gothick folly tower has been built, not out in the grounds as might be expected, but tacked onto the three-bay brick Orangery at the end of the bland, brick garden façade of the house. It seems likely that folly tower and Orangery were built when an eighteenth-century Willoughby was re-fronting that elevation with canted bays to take in the newly contrived views of the little park.

A deep ha-ha bounds the rear lawn, giving the back windows of the house a typical Brown-style view down a slope to a serpentine lake, green with duckweed and banked by huge sweet chestnuts. On the right of this lake a small peninsula juts out beyond a

40 An engraving of the Brownian landscape at Ditchley Park, designed in the 1760s by one of his followers with a water grotto in the foreground and a Chinese bridge across the lake. *Bodleian Library, MS. Gough Maps 26, f.57*

narrow inlet and this has a lidless, medieval stone coffin lying on the grass. Presumably there were originally a few other Gothic relics to accompany it and provide an interesting subject for a walk across the field. The farther arm of the sinisterly shaded serpentine is crossed by an approach drive, circuitous in the standard Brownian fashion, which bridges a tiny creek with a resounding classical causeway fronted by three limestone arches. Only a trickle of water passes through just one arch, and the bridge is placed out of sight from the house, though it must have been intended to enrich a view that also included the medieval coffin. Pevsner and Sherwood mention a second folly in the grounds, which incorporated a thirteenth-century window from the demolished church at nearby Nuneham Courtenay.[5] This has since disappeared, but is likely to have been sited on the peninsula.

In the same legendary spirit Adderbury House, up at the northern, ironstone end of the county, is supposed to have a Brownian landscape. The Duke of Buccleuch certainly bought a plan from Brown and sale particulars of that often-sold house, dated 1774, claim 'a fine serpentine stream of water … in full view of the house'.[6] Whatever the view from the house was in 1774, those serpentine streams are now hidden by trees but can be accessed as a village amenity.

After these minor layouts and uncertain attributions, Brown's overwhelmingly successful reshaping of Blenheim comes as a salutary reminder of his vision and of the authority he must have commanded. Northumbrian common sense and masculine charm achieved the intensive strategic planting: those tree clumps around the lake, that inspired afterthought of the Elizabeth Island on the foundations of a medieval causeway, a fringe of trees all around the vast park, rides that ignored any earlier formal planting and the Fourteen Acre Clump in the northern park. It is true that without a steep-sided valley, a towered palace of visionary oddity and an imperial viaduct to nowhere Brown would have been as dull as he was at Kirtlington; but at least he took his chances. If he had his romantic way, then Blenheim's park walls would have been castellated and a Gothick Bath House to match his Gothick High Lodge (*colour plate 10*) would have arisen on the site of Rosamond's Well.[7] Brown of the elegant natural simplicities had his eclectic leanings.

If it would not affect the tourist trade, vehicles would ideally be excluded from Brown's magical creation so that every able-bodied visitor would have to walk the approach and enjoy it as I did recently on a perfect April morning. After passing the theatrical curtain of Hawksmoor's Triumphal Arch, the composition of Palace, Park and Grand Bridge (*41*) is matchless: one of those man-made vistas that has Nature out-pointed. The Palace rides the skyline on the left, all its welcoming complexities focused by the big golden globes that catch the sunlight on its Indo-classical towers. Below it, down a steep, grassy slope, is Brown's lake, working almost like an inland sea, with the poplars and red dogwood of the Elizabeth Island drawing the eye, much as the golden spheres draw the eye to the Palace. And then, when nothing more than tree-planted slopes with a few superb cedars might be expected, there is the second palace of the Bridge itself, its proportions happily improved by Brown's flooding (*colour plate 11*). Nothing in Vanbrugh's architecture can be taken for granted; everything is novel. All that was needed was a frame to bring it together, and that Brown supplied.

Nuneham Courtenay, his next Oxfordshire exercise, was the garden where, though he and Repton did not actually come together physically to work, Brown designed the park and the poet William Mason designed the flower garden that Repton took as his model, thereby making future gardens essentially womens' worlds: neat, pretty and pint-sized, as they have remained ever since men took to their allotments. Nuneham Courtenay's 1st and 2nd Harcourt earls had two poet friends. The more important of the two was the Revd William Mason, also a friend of John Gay and Horace Walpole, and a writer who had the wit to notice that for some years flowers had been invading English 'hard' landscaping, in beds alongside the usual terraces, balustrades and flights of steps. The popular result was his 1777 poem, *The English Flower Garden* which, while not the sole fount and origin of the Gardenesque style of the next century, was a very important influence in popularising the whole picture-postcard vision of the garden with climbing plants upon arches and trellises, greenhouses and conservatories, arbours, hanging plant baskets, loggias, bird baths and general kitsch fripperies, as commerce and nurseries moved in on an increasingly affluent, industrialised country.

41 Capability Brown's masterly 1760s reshaping of the original raw, geometric forms of Blenheim's landscape into an ideal parkscape of lake, imperial Palace and Grand Bridge

The other poet was the under-talented William Whitehead, writer of the improving mottoes which featured among the daisy-rimmed flower beds, shrubberies, miniature Grotto Cave, Orangery and Temple of Flora at Nuneham, which the Harcourts raised up on the broad ledge below James (Athenian) Stuart's domed vision of the church as a garden building. In every way, Nuneham Flower Garden was a seminal site, a national archetype for the nineteenth century, and it would be an appropriate accolade for the family when, in the third generation, Archbishop Harcourt entertained Queen Victoria and her young husband, Prince Albert, for several days at the house and, of course, the garden. There is a running theme of royal connections in the county. York is too far from London to create a visiting axis, but Oxford, with its loyal and High Church University, is just the right distance. Charles I would never have retired with his Court to Cambridge, but Henry II, Edward II and Anne were all drawn in the Oxford way, and as George III admitted, royalty had no residence to match the Churchill Palace of Blenheim. It could well be that our monarchy's strength has been its bourgeois modesty; at Nuneham the superior British back garden, in all its modesty and bijoux charm, was invented. In 1772 Mason sent Lord Nuneham (the courtesy title of Earl Harcourt's eldest son and heir) a plan for the flower planting, and work began immediately with Lord Nuneham's gardener, Walter Clark, supervising the work.[8]

Before this, however, the 1st Earl Harcourt, like a cuckoo in the nest, had removed the village to a line of neat cottages on the high road, so that he could enjoy the glorious prospect of a great curve of the Thames with the spires of Oxford in the distance, undisturbed by lowly village activities. That was around 1760, and by 1764 he had had Athenian Stuart's new Church (42), built as far way from its congregation as possible. It stands, a true exotic, like an exile from the Roman Campagna, functioning on one side, together with what was originally a long, low Orangery, as parent figure to the colourful, dainty flowerbeds of Mason's garden. On its other, western side, it rises grandly from a steep slope above the Thames in what is essentially Brown's planting, the outer garden-park of the Nuneham hillside.

Mason's garden had been illustrated in Paul Sandby's *Collection of Landscapes*, published in 1777, though work was going on in 1778 to make the Grott-Cave; and in the same year, the year of the twin garden styles, Brown had begun to remodel and plant the outer slope of the park. The superb feathered beech immediately below the Church is one survivor of his planting and a long route of his trees runs south of the house to command the Thames views and reach the Carfax Conduit, a Jacobean structure from Oxford which the Harcourts rebuilt at Nuneham in 1787 as a substitute for a Gothick folly tower. For Picturesque as opposed to Gothick charm there was a riverside walk down to a thatched lock-keeper's cottage, which has, sadly, been burnt, as it would have lent a third element to these influential grounds.

Mason's Flower Garden (43) lies immediately north-east of the conventional Palladian house with a stepped rise in the ground cutting the garden off from the principal terraced grounds of the house.[9] A visitor is at once plunged into cosy paths running around flowering bushes with the little Temple of Flora seat and a decayed Grotto as a reminder of the recent fashion for Rococo eclecticism. Most of the busts that made the garden a semtimental memorial place to lost gurus and friends have been vandalised. Verses by Whitehead or Lord Harcourt's wife, Elizabeth, were hung about the necks of the busts and it must have come across as a superior version of William Shenstone's landscape garden at the Leasowes in Worcestershire, but with far more emphasis upon flowerbeds. These still stud the lawn, circular or crescent-shaped and never straight-edged. Each had a tight outer border and then rose to a central shrub or tall flower. As always, the art of flower planting had to be confused with an exotic science of colour arrangements: strong and soft colours as in women's dresses. Some original urns have survived, there is a later Venetian wellhead, and it is still easy to recreate Mason's intentions. The oddity is that it all looks rather like a modern garden, but then that is what it was and still is.

A very brief walk up past some sentimental tombs leads to the Church and the complete mood change of Brown's landscape. The poet Whitehead wrote a shrewd analytical poem, 'The Late Improvements'[10], in which Dame Nature and a Brown-type figure argue about their respective intentions and successes:

Dame Nature, the Goddess, one very bright day
In strolling thro' Nuneham, met *Brown* in her way;
And bless me, she said, with an insolent sneer,

42 A place of worship doubling as garden building – the first Earl Harcourt and Athenian Stuart's 1764 Greek Revival church at Nuneham Park

43 William Mason's 1770s Flower Garden at Nuneham ushered in the Gardenesque style and became the template for suburban gardens of the future

I wonder that fellow will dare to come here …
One question remains, Up the green of yon steep
Who threw the bold walk with that elegant sweep?

The answer, of course, being Brown, as his is the walk south to the Carfax Conduit. The
Dame continues her quizzing:

The ground of your moulding is certainly fine,
But the swell of that knoll, and those openings, are mine.

Brown replies:

The propsect, wherever beheld, must be good,
But has ten times its charms when you burst from this wood,
A wood of my planting. The Goddess cried, Hold!
Tis grown very hot, and tis grown very cold'.
She fann'd, and she shudder'd, she cough'd and she sneez'd,
Inclin'd to be angry, inclin'd to be pleas'd;
Half smil'd, and half pouted – then turn's from the view,
And dropp'd him a curtsie, and blushing withdrew.

She has given up, but comforts herself with a compliment, indirect, to Brown:

I may have my revenge on this fellow at last;
For a lucky conjecture comes into my head,
That, whate'er he has done, and whate'er he has said,
The world's little malice will balk his design:
Each fault they'll call his, and each excellence mine.

That, of course, is always the temptation when viewing a Brownian landscape. They are,
if anything, too natural.

In the next Harcourt generation the Archbishop Vernon Harcourt of York added
terraced gardens[11] to the west face of Leadbetter's house and, with the help of William
Sawrey Gilpin as landscape gardener, planted a Pinetum, accessed by an intensely refined
Greek Doric Lodge of 1838 by Sir Robert Smirke on the Oxford road.[12] Considering its
stylistic influence and stylistic constraints, it is surprising that the grounds at Nuneham are
not a more popular place of garden pilgrimage. Even the stables are exquisitely refined
and the 1st Lord Harcourt's new Nuneham village has a fair claim to be the mother of all
future housing estates: plain, functional semis, each with its own garden expressly enlarged
by the Archbishop, no squalor, but no real charm, and no new village green.

If Nuneham can be said to have delivered a prototype for the Gardenesque style
by 1783, then Oxfordshire had some time to wait for Humphry Repton's first essay
in garden shaping. It took place at Sarsden House, south-west of Chipping Norton,

1 Twentieth-century planting around medieval moats under the Tudor towers of Beckley Park

2 The Ladies' Garden at Broughton Castle was laid out in the 1880s and replanted after 1970 with advice from Lanning Roper

3 The forecourt to Chastleton House of 1603, a typical walled enclosure of the Tudor to Jacobean period

4 The 1723 Antique-style Triumphal Arch which Nicholas Hawksmoor designed as the curtain raiser to Blenheim's most dramatic vista

5 Originally built in the early eighteenth century as a Menagerie for Ditchley Park, this octagon later served as a 'gas works'

6 The 1714-18 Palladian-style Shotover Park commands a strictly axial Canal which leads to the Gothick Temple, the earliest revived medieval garden building in the country

7 A trysting place for lovers – William Kent's Praeneste Arcade at Rousham is sited at the top of a concave slope originally carved out by Charles Bridgeman

8 This copy of Scheemakers' Dying Gladiator at Rousham was General James Dormer's private memorial to the horrors of war

9 The sinuous, Rococo watery Rill at Rousham, which leads to the Cold Bath, was originally wide and deep enough to contain fish

10 Capability Brown's High Lodge of 1765 at Blenheim was all that was built of his scheme to Gothicise the estate walls and other park buildings

11 By raising the level of the lake and clumping the park with trees, Brown pulled together the whole composition of Palace and imperial Bridge at Blenheim

12 The lake at Sarsden with its bold planting is a rare realisation of a Humphry Repton design developed from existing fishponds

13 The essence of William Morris' Mulberry Garden at Kelmscott Manor is that it is practical and homely

14 Addison's Walk at Magdalen College is raised high above the fritillaries of its water meadow

15 New College has a legal duty to preserve the City Walls which give such drama to the undulating lawns and seventeenth-century viewing Mount

16 At St Catherine's College, Arne Jacobsen achieved his picturesque interplay of Podium and Canal while remaining chastely geometric

17 The walled enclosure of Oxford's Botanic Garden, begun in 1621 by the Earl of Danby, is overlooked by the tower of Magdalen College

18 A naked youth grapples improbably with a fat-nosed dolphin in the Water Garden, laid out between 1904 and 1913, at Buscot Park by Harold Peto for the first Lord Faringdon

Opposite: 19 Columnar Irish yews and a blaze of wonderfully kitsch colour in Lady Ottoline Morrell's Flower Garden at Garsington Manor

20 Lord Berners put a notice in his 1930s Gothic Folly Tower – 'Members of the public committing suicide from this tower do so at their own risk'. *By kind permission of Alan Powers*

Right: 21 Nicholas Dimbleby's statue of Dionysus was set up at Faringdon House by his grand-daughter, Sofia Zinovieff, as a memorial to Robert Heber Percy

Below: 22 A bronze of a very modern young woman by Judith Homes Drewry lolls casually by a lily pond in Raymond Blanc's postprandial garden at his Manoir aux Quat' Saisons

23 Emily Young's chalcedony quartz disk in Isabel and Julian Bannerman's terraced gardens behind Asthall Manor

24 The shard-like stone pavilions of New House and the pools of its Japanese Garden are exquisitely interlaced at Shipton-under-Wychwood

beginning in 1795, and owed more to Brown than Mason, so it is not a prime example of the Repton manner. What makes Sarsden's grounds so interesting and, to be honest, so much more impressive than the usual Repton treatment, is that his son, George Stanley, took over from Repton, working there between 1823 and 1825, moving on from his father's polite Picturesque to a more moody Savage Picturesque. It is possible to trace, by comparing Repton's proposals in 'before and after' watercolours from his Sarsden Red Book[13] with the present condition of the site he proposed to improve, what George Stanley actually altered.

Repton began his Sarsden Red Book in his usual devious manner by telling its new owner what a problem he faced: 'I must confess, that I was more alarmed at the unpromising appearance of Sarsden, than at any subject on which I had ever been consulted'.[14] He thought the park was an inauspicious plot without beauty, an area of naked hills, stone walls and ugly ploughed fields. Actually, Sarsden is one of Oxfordshire's major country houses, but grand in a rather subdued, retiring way. The house was, until George Stanley coaxed it into some ostentation, a modestly perfect, hip-roofed rebuilding of 1689 with all the good manners of the William and Mary period. It had all the elaborate formal compartmentalised gardens, which were then fashionable, enclosed by a wall surrounding the house to the east, west and south.[15] An estate map of 1788[16] shows three separate fishponds to the south of the house, and two of these would later be joined to create the lake which is pre-eminently the star of the present park. In 1792 a London merchant banker, James Haughton Langston, bought the house from the Rolle family and it was Langston's son, John, who brought Humphry Repton in to landscape the park.[17] Repton was so often a planner, not an achiever, but at Sarsden, as at Adlestrop a few miles away across the Gloucestershire border, his vision was achieved and, though several Reptonian Picturesque features have been demolished in the twentieth century[18], no one who has experienced his lake at Sarsden, with its wonderfully sited Temple-Boathouse and atmospheric, Cyclopean Bridge, will ever dismiss him as a mere verbal gardener or as just a clever book illustrator. That lake is one of the county's finest garden features, sensitively planted and imaginatively enriched with buildings.

As so often with Humphry Repton's schemes there was a concentration upon multiple park drives to command carriage views, and handsome gate piers, taken from that lost Rolle formal garden, are strewn around the park at drive entrances. The terrain is undulating and reasonably well wooded, and has extensive views to the west over Gloucestershire. George Stanley added a heavy Ionic colonnade, an angular Conservatory and a canted bay to command that west view from the 1689 house and a hedged and grassed formal garden dignifies George Stanley's façade, with box, holly and yew topiary. On the south side of the house there is a narrow paved garden with box edging and Portuguese laurels at the lower level and severely clipped and squared beeches on a higher terrace. Here there is a stone statue of a medieval figure standing on a globe. One splendidly shattered cedar and its less impressive, but intact, twin tend to distract the eye from the extensive, unremarkable reaches of the surrounding countryside.

Heading off south to relish Repton's lake the visitor's eye is taken by clumsy Gardenesque-style incidents on the way. There is a confused arc of topiary up one

44 George Stanley Repton's 1820s Temple-Boathouse at Sarsden was based on the theoretical origins of classical architecture as expounded by the Abbé Laugier

slope to the right and there is an absent-minded square of yew hedges with a parterre, flower planting and badly broken statuary up to the left of the path, related to nothing else in the grounds. But by that time the gleam of black water, backed with mature specimen trees, will have caught the attention (*colour plate 12*), so too will the Boathouse, a primitive templar seat, commandingly sited at the head of the lake. Until quite recently there was also a classical Rotunda up on the far shore. The rough carriage drive sweeps down towards the water, but then plunges into a small wood of dark yews and other evergreens. This works like a theatrical curtain because when the drive emerges on its far side the Temple-Boathouse (*44*) has become irresistibly complex in its textures, now that it is only a few yards away, and the stony cavern of the boathouse on which it is reared up is gaping like a black mouth.

The Reptons, father and son, who planned this temple-seat cum boathouse had taken the Abbé Laugier's theory on the primitive origins of classical architecture most seriously.[19] The Abbé was normally content to urge that a classical column should be represented by a simple tree trunk, but the Reptons, or rather George Stanley, who dismissed his father's Red Book design with its conventional columns[20], went one subtle stage further and suggested that the fluting on a primitive Greek Doric column was a memory of the slim branches that were originally bound up lengthwise down the tree trunks. This is what survives here, with bands of metal securing the branches and producing an effect close to the Roman symbol of the fasces.[21] To make the primitive impact even stronger, big strips of rough bark have been nailed to any flat patches of render. A long seat in the broad temple recess invites a visitor to sit and enjoy the vista down the lake to the Cyclopean Bridge. Behind this Temple-Boathouse an exedra of yews supplies the necessary pleasing gloom. That George Stanley was the Laugier enthusiast is virtually clinched by the presence on the garden front of Sarsgrove, the Langstons' dower house in an adjoining wood, of a semi-circular bay window composed of stark tree trunks posing as primitive Doric columns. Sarsgrove House was entirely remodelled in 1825 by George Stanley. These columns, together with the grim Cyclopean Bridge, mark the son out as pressing the Savage Picturesque in contrast to his father's more genteel pastoral Picturesque.

A walk along the further shore of the lake will give an opportunity to enjoy the water lilies that enliven its surface and the small islet on the opposite shore. The Cyclopean Bridge (45), a single arch of distorted rocks, is as effective an evocation of the sinister and the primitive as the Temple-Boathouse. The dark evergreen specimen trees gathered along this shore work with it in melancholy accord: the father's vision carried through into realisation by his more practical son in the years when he was working on the two small, satellite, picturesque parks of Sarsden Glebe, the vicarage, and Sarsgrove, the

45 G.S. Repton's Cyclopean Bridge strikes a Savage Picturesque note of sinister primitivism in accord with the tree trunk Doric columns of his Temple-Boathouse

46 Humphry Repton's 'before' view of the fritillary meadow at Magdalen College with the New Buildings in the background. *By kind permission of the President and Fellows of Magdalen College, Oxford*

47 Repton's Magdalen with the slide pulled back to reveal a Gothick quadrangle reflected in the new lake – a view to rival the Backs at Cambridge. *By kind permission of the President and Fellows of Magdalen College, Oxford*

house in the wood, which he remodelled as a *cottage ornée* in 1825 for John Langston's unmarried daughters.[22] If Capability Brown had worked here he would have left the lake in a setting of clumped deciduous trees. The Reptonian creation is thoughtful, moody and memorable. If that Rotunda on the west slope had survived it would have been even more so.

To point to a Repton garden in the county, that owed a clear debt to those Gardenesque flowebeds of Mason's Nuneham, would have helped the argument of this chapter of which Nuneham is the pivot. Unfortunately, Sarsden's Gardenesque features, noted in the first stages of the walk from the house to the lake, are in decay. The rest of Sarsden, the proposals for Magdalen College, Oxford, and the lost works at Great Tew all seem to owe more to Brown than to Mason, though Sarsgrove House, hidden away in dark woodland, is close enough to cottages in the celebrated John Nash-designed Blaise Hamlet, near Bristol, to have a cosy Gardenesque feeling with Laugier overtones.[23] As might be expected, the elaborate and deferential Red Book which Repton prepared for Magdalen College during a 'Winter's Residence at Bath, 1800', a scheme already referred to in the chapter on Oxford gardens, is anything but Gardenesque or cosy.[24]

Repton treated the College exactly as he would a major country house. For him, Magdalen's key building was not its late fifteenth-century Cloister overlooked by the Chapel tower; it was that heavily classical New Buildings block designed by Dr Clarke, which had gone up in 1733. Not that the classical trim appealed to Repton as he hoped to persuade the fellows of Magdalen to convert it to Gothick and add a whole new three-sided Gothick quadrangle to the College, open to the Meadow and a new lake (*46 & 47*). Viewed dispassionately, the Repton scheme was brilliant. At a stroke he would have given Oxford some equivalent at last to the Backs that make Cambridge visually far more attractive than its rival university. He proposed a twin towered Gothick Lodge on Longwall Street and from that a truly Brownian system of carriage drives would expand. But first he intended to remove the existing ranges of high, raised walks running alongside melancholy ditches and the Cherwell. A large curved lake, hatchet-shaped, was to be dug out and the soil extracted was to raise the rest of Magdalen's grounds high above flood level. This would inevitably have destroyed the fritillary beds, but it would have been a master stroke with long elevations of Magdalen, Gothick of course, like St John's at Cambridge, rising above the lake waters, and all the towers, domes and belfries of the city clustered beyond them.

The drives were to function just as Brown's drives functioned: offering a Picturesque route to what would now become the new Porter's Lodge in the new quadrangle and also a carriage ride to circumnavigate the lake and the reduced Meadow over a system of three bridges. The first area of the grounds from that Longwall Lodge to the new quadrangle was to be planted with a cross of doubled tree avenues overlooking a new garden which might tempt the vote of the President of Magdalen. Perversely, all the drive around the lake and the surviving Meadow was to be lined on both sides with trees to conceal the views. At the far northern corner of the grounds Repton proposed an Addison memorial temple or rather an 'Addison Portico' to a Fellows' 'Summer Room', a feature that the dons of Merton already enjoyed. The

Portico sat snugly in the woods and confirmed the impression of a grand country house garden. It is even possible, though Repton blandly ignores them, that an area of snakeshead fritillaries might have survived the upheaval. It is easy to understand why Repton's proposals were rejected in the classically-inclined early Regency period. But if, instead of being put forward in 1801, they had been presented to the President and Fellows in 1850, in the High Victorian period, they might have stood a better chance. Repton was as much a voice for nineteenth-century gardens as Brown was for the eighteenth century, a man far ahead of his time, though not necessarily the wiser for that. But what a tourist attraction the fellows would have commanded, running visitors briskly around in pony traps, up the Grand Approach then round the lake and the Meadow over three bridges and two hairpin bends. For the Gardenesque successors to Mason's Flower Garden at Nuneham another chapter must serve.

NOTES

1   Dorothy Stroud, *Capability Brown*, 1950, p.49.

2   Ibid.

3   Ibid., p.34.

4   EH Register entry. Brown is likely to have worked for Lady Mostyn, who inherited in 1754.

5   Sherwood & Pevsner, *Oxfordshire*, p.699.

6   Dorothy Stroud, *Capability Brown*, p.213, Appendix II states that Brown was paid for his plan for alteration of the park and gardens at Adderbury, but gives no documnetary source. The sale particulars are quoted in *VCH*, 9, 1969, p.9.

7   See Green, *Blenheim*, plate 91 (castellated park walls), plate 92 (Brown's Gothick Park Farm Granary), plate 93 (plans and elevations of the Bath House).

8   Ibid.

9   For a full account of the garden see Mark Laird, *The Flowering of the English Landscape Garden: English Pleasure Grounds 1720-1800* (Pennsylvania, 1999), pp.350-60, which includes contemporary views of the garden and two plans.

10 Quoted by Dorothy Stroud, *Capability Brown*, pp.189-91; taken from the *Annual Review* of 1787.

11 The present Italian-style terraced garden to the west was added before 1913 by Lewis, Viscount Harcourt, and his American wife.

12 The Harcourt Arboretum is adminstered by the University of Oxford's Botanic Garden. The management of the arboretum has been aided by a recent Restoration and Management Plan by Kim Wilkie Associates, the research for which was carried out by David Lambert and Mavis Batey. A pdf file of this report can be accessed via: www.kimwilkie.com/images/projects/uk/harcourt_arb_report.pdf.

13 The Red Book is no longer kept at the house, but is well illustrated with copious quotation in Nigel Temple's article, 'Sarsden, Oxfordshire, "Qui fait aimer les champs, fait aimer la vertu"', in *Journal of Garden History*, vol.6, no.2 (1986), pp.89-111.

14 Ibid,. p.89.

15 White Kennett, *Parochial Antiquities in the Counties of Oxford and Bucks*, 1695, plates 8 & 9 show it.

16 ORO, 'A Map of the Several Farms and Grounds of Denys and John Rolle', 1788, illustrated as figure 2 in Temple's article on Sarsden.

17 Until recently the Red Book was kept at the house, but was taken away by the last owners when they sold up recently.

18 Including G.S. Repton's Green Lodge, Keeper's Lodge, the Kennels and New Farm. There was also a Rotunda above the lake.

19 The Abbé published his *Essai sur l'Architecture* in 1753 and Sir William Chambers recommended his views in the first part of his 1759 *Treatise on Civil Architecture*.

20 See figure 13 in Temple's article in *Journal of Garden History*. Figure 14 illustrates a George Stanley drawing in the RIBA Drawings Collection showing 'Boat House, Sarsden' as a predictable Doric temple front. So when did George Stanley decide to imitate Laugier?

21 For another example of Laugier's theory applied to a garden building see Timothy Mowl, *Historic Gardens of Dorset* (Stroud, 2004), pp.76-7.

22 John died in 1812, to be succeeded by his son, James, who employed G.S. Repton from 1817 to continue improvements to the estate; hence the building of Sarsden Glebe and Sarsgrove.

23 G.S. Repton worked in Nash's office for some years and would have been familiar with the Blaise estate.

24 Frontispiece to the Red Book, which is preserved at Magdalen; I am most grateful to the Magdalen Archivist, Robin Darwall-Smith for allowing me access to the book. Several of the Repton views from the Red Book are illustrated in Roger White & Robin Darwall-Smith, *The Architectural Drawings of Magdalen College, Oxford: A Catalogue* (Oxford, 2001), pp.38-42. See also John Steane's series of short articles on the College grounds in the *Magdalen College Record*, between 1997 and 2000: 1997, pp.75-86; 1998, pp.97-102; 1999, pp.92-9; 2000, pp.97-100.

6

THE GARDENESQUE CENTURY –
A NAME IN SEARCH OF A STYLE

Victorian gardens are as difficult to define, as is Victorian architecture and for the same reasons: increasing wealth and widening cultural awareness. There is no such thing as a typical Victorian garden, yet from a certain brash confidence and technical display it is usually easy to recognise one. In a vain effort to compartmentalise them, though hardly to define anything, the term 'Gardenesque' has been invented and books written to support it. In reality, if these gardens had been called 'Gardenish' it would have been equally unhelpful, though less academic in resonance. In the latter years of the preceeding century, the poetry of the Revd William Mason and the persuasive salesmanship of Humphry Repton resulted in a colourful, disciplined melange of flowerbeds, garden furniture and technology with an eager indulgence in any foreign exotics that could be coaxed to grow, and preferably to flower, in our climate. Both Mason and Repton were responding naturally to industrial advances and social change. If neither man had lived or written, someone else would have taken over their function, as indeed John Claudius Loudon did with his confident practice and his publications: the *Encyclopaedia of Gardening* (1822) and *The Suburban Gardener and Villa Companion* (1838).

Loudon is an intriguing figure. A calculating, combative Scot, he knew that Repton was the rival he needed to knock down and replace as the nation's garden guide. At Great Tew, where Repton had, as usual, concentrated on persuading the owners to rebuild the house to either Grecian or Jacobethan designs by his son[1], Loudon was brought in by the owner, George Frederick Stratton, who had read his *An immediate and effectual mode of raising the rental of landed property* of 1808.[2] In an effort to demonstrate the superiority of Scottish farming methods Loudon replaced six English tenants with one Scot, spent a fortune of Stratton's money on a model farmhouse, which would be demolished in the 1830s, created the Lodge Ponds to power a threshing mill, laid out farm roads with easy gradients and put his own theories of the Picturesque into practice by a liberal, all-over scatter of trees across the landscape. Loudon's tenure only lasted from 1808-11 and was not a financial success, but Great Tew's present picturesque cottages owe something in the way of porches and thatched roofs to Loudon's Picturesque aesthetic.

His *Treatise on Farming, Improving and Managing Country Residences* of 1806 has illustrations demonstrating with brilliant clarity the difference in estate design between traditional, Brownian, Reptonian and his own style. He favoured scattered tree planting and opposed

Brownian clumps. In a cruel, but convincing, plate: 'Strictures on Mr Repton's mode of using Slides', he produced a 'before' slide which was exactly the same as the after illustration beneath it.[3] This proves, at least to Loudon's own satisfaction, that the 'after' always looks superior to the 'before' because it lacks the distracting, wobbly lines of the before slide. In that way he presented himself as the technical expert for a new scientific age of gardening. It was, quite simply, becoming easier and cheaper in nineteenth-century Britain to make a lively, individually themed garden, so the Gardenesque was not so much a garden style as a capitalist phenomenon. Any middle class household could indulge in a greenhouse or a conservatory and bed out regiments of red, white and blue flowers. A trellis or a bird-bath was in the reach of all but the truly poor. This chapter will, consequently, prove a bumpy ride for anyone who enjoys clear definitions.

As usual with every county, Oxfordshire went its own way. The typical county garden pattern was to settle down, as an Edwardian era succeeded the Victorian, at least a decade before the old Queen Empress died, into an aristocratic historicist patriotism, with Elizabethan-Jacobean-style garden forms sleekly adapted to modern lawn mowers. Oxfordshire did produce a few such gardens in this later, specialised and distinctive branch of eclectic historicism. Yarnton Manor, Shipton Court and High Wall in the Headington suburb of Oxford are modest examples, but idiosyncratically, towards the end of the period, when everywhere else a suave Jacobethan of balustraded terraces, long lawns and clipped yew hedges was becoming a near-national garden idiom, the county produced in Friar Park, the creation of Sir Frank Crisp on the suburban outskirts of Henley-on Thames, the ultimate exotic, eclectic and technically assured Gardenesque layout. Nowhere else in Britain is there a garden that so richly deserves that vague, all-inclusive stylistic title. It is so outrageously impressive and yet so late, post-1890, when the garden Edwardian manner should have taken over, that it must have a chapter to itself. No other garden in the county seems to be leading up to it; yet like Woodstock, Blenheim and Rousham, the county seems able, perhaps by that London–Oxford axis, a fashionable tension, to produce the best gardens, nationally, of several ages. Henley could be described as a fashionable outer suburb of London and Friar Park is definitely a suburban rather than a country garden. High Wall is similarly urban in feeling. With the Gardenesque, were the suburbs taking over the centuries-long lead from country houses in garden advances?

To turn from Friar Park to Kiddington Hall is a dramatic switch in scale. The Hall stands high up above a reach of Oxfordshire's own version of the Veneto's Brenta, the slow-winding Glyme. Its garden, though small and compact, is a very fair introduction to the Victorian Gardenesque because it was shaped by the architect, Sir Charles Barry, in his favourite Italianate mood, and if the Gardenesque has any kind of typical profile it is the Italianate echoes of the Queen's Osborne House on the Isle of Wight. Barry's ten-bay Orangery, with four of its windows opened up to make a loggia, is one of the prettiest garden buildings in the county, almost as large as the Barry-remodelled classical house next to it.[4] Mortimer Ricardo, a son of the political economist, employed Barry for the Orangery around 1850.[5] A lawn fronts it, but the house alongside has a terrace dropping down to an eight-part formal garden (48) with roses in rectangular beds, some box-edged, and miniature topiary pyramids, surrounding octagonal punctuations with shallow bowled urns. The real Italian touch comes next. Beyond a balustrade the land falls steeply to the Glyme with a flight of steps that divides half way down then unites to meet the south drive. Urns flank the paths, there is an angular *scola* seat[6], and an impressive rockery careers down by the steps, radiant with flowers, all delightfully fussy and intimate. There was a large Rose Garden to the east in a pleasure Wilderness of dark yews shown on an 1881 Ordnance Survey map, but a dower house has replaced it. North of the garden a seventeenth-century dovecote with a conical roof gives the complex a French tilt. On one of the lakes, recorded in the last chapter as possibly one of Brown's very earliest works, is an octagonal Boathouse for very modest boat trips. North, upriver, is a new twentieth-century lake. The whole garden is active and eventful and, in that sense, the epitome of a Gardenesque layout.

After leaving Kiddington I discovered in subsequent researches that I had missed the garden's oddest feature. That was a stone font brought in 1660 by Sir Henry Browne from a ruined chapel of King Edward the Confessor at Islip. According to tradition, St Edward was supposed to have been baptised in it. In a more disgraceful distinction the future King Ethelred the Unready, who sold England out to the Danes, was not only baptised in it, but relieved himself incontinently in the holy water to the disgust of Archbishop Dunstan, who was performing the ritual and cried out: 'Per Deum Et Matreum Eius, Ignacius Homo Est' (This will prove to be a shameful man), a prophecy that was fulfilled.[7]

48 Charles Barry's 1850s balustraded formal garden and Orangery at Kiddington Hall – the Italian mood of the Gardenesque

A more orderly yet essentially Gardenesque archaeological spirit prevailed a few years earlier in Cuddesdon parish. But Denton House is the perfect proof of how unpredictable a Victorian garden, in this case one of 1844-5, can be. Denton's Gothic furnishings are neither Early English pointed and pure, nor yet eighteenth-century Gothick and Rococo frivolous. They are of that rarest of all the English Gothic styles: seventeenth-century Gothic Survival, but set up at Denton in the 1840s. The explanation for this garden phenomenon lies in Oxford. Brasenose College's Chapel and Library quadrangle was built in the Commonwealth, going up between 1656 and 1666. Its architect was John Jackson, who had recently supervised the construction of the Gothic-Baroque Canterbury Quadrangle at St John's College, and had designed a similar, mixed style porch for St Mary's Church in 1637.[8] Consequently Jackson's Gothic is, to put it mildly, idiosyncratic, and when James Wyatt came to remodel the Library in 1779-80, the stylistic tangle got worse with new two-light Gothick windows with classical aprons below them that were more severe than Jackson's stunningly wild, five-light Chapel east window looking out onto Radcliffe Square.

Then came the Victorians with their earnest drive to trim and repair stonework with any sign of mellow decay. In 1844 they replaced the tracery of both the Chapel and the Library at Brasenose, at which Denton's owner, the Revd Snyde[9], thought that he saw a Gothic bargain going with rich Oxford associations. He snapped up the stonework and re-erected the tracery of the Brasenose windows in the walls of his garden at Denton. The first sign of Brasenose survival comes at the roadside front of Denton. The main house is a severe classical block, remodelled in 1757, but to the left of the façade, shaded a little by a titanic wisteria which seems to be intent on covering the whole building, is a strange garden doorway with a leathery, almost Art Nouveau cartouche set within a broken pediment. It is clearly another exile from Brasenose.[10] It leads on to a large Croquet Lawn with a wide, well-stocked herbaceous border. This is all to the south of the house; the Gothic garden lies to the west. Inwardly, viewed from the house, there is nothing remarkable: a big lawn with average fine trees bordering it firmly on three sides, with bushes below them. But if we enter this dark border a path leads into the leafy gloom, creating a rustic cloister of shade, and on the outer garden wall, seen at intervals, are the Brasenose windows, still surviving the elements after 160 years' exposure. That great Chapel east window (49) is particularly impressive with its cusped mandorla tracery radiating from a central oval above five slender lights. The heavy leaf cover and lowering bushes create just the right darkness for the exiled lights to continue their task of illumination. It is a rare, indeed a unique, experience: a Gothic Survival garden cloister walk.

Denton was a one-off garden experiment, using second-hand artefacts in a scheme that had no natural stylistic relationship with the parent house. At Yarnton Manor the garden work was quite different. There an informed and scholarly mind made a considered assessment of the style of the house and the relics of its original garden, then carried out a thoughtful restoration as close to the original as possible. It would have been a task made easier by the mood prevailing in garden circles in the 1890s, which favoured the hybrid Jacobethan style as patriotic and appropriate.[11]

49 The great east window on the cloister walk at Denton House is a seventeenth-century refugee from Oxford's Brasenose College

Neither the Manor House at Yarnton nor its gardens are quite what they seem. During the nineteenth century the impressive post-1610 Jacobean house of the Spencers had fallen on bad times, becoming nothing more than an inconvenient farmhouse.[12] It had lost the two, largely service, wings that had created an entrance courtyard, an entire bay of the main house, and the arch leading into the courtyard had been pulled down. So when, in 1895, the Dashwoods sold the farm to Henry Robert Franklin, the head of a building firm with a good reputation for restorations, there is not likely to have been an orginal Jacobean garden for him to restore. He was, however, wealthy and had a feeling for the early seventeenth century. In 1897 he commissioned Thomas Garner not only to rebuild the lost south bay, but also to add the three curly gables that do so much to enliven the entrance front.[13] Whether the gardens now lying around the restored house should be termed as 'Edwardian' is doubtful. Edwardian-Jacobethan layouts tend towards long yew hedges and ambitious vistas, but the principal garden at Yarnton feels compact and authentic in its planning, though stylistically uncertain in its detail.

The lawn in itself is a problem as it has a clearly depressed area running around its four sides and no terrace walk where one would be expected next to the house. High around it on three sides runs a viewing terrace with a central ogee-gabled and pinnacled archway. Its sundial reads: 'Amidst the flowers I count the hours', which is typical of this period. But the archway leads to a pleached lime alley set on the cross axis and, via a wrought iron gate dated 1907, to a long poplar avenue across the field towards Yarnton's lost railway station. This west range of the viewing terrace has a recessed stone seat at its north end, but a stone Garden Pavilion at its south end. That Pavilion, however, cannot be accessed directly from the high terrace; it is approached from the lower orchard to the side. Inside on its plasterwork walls there is a delightfully effete, and typically Aesthetic Movement inscription, supposedly composed by the architect, George Bodley, with whom Garner and Franklin often worked:

> Here shall green summer golden autumn bring,
> And winter wrap the silver heart of spring.

But why make the access to the Pavilion from the orchard? And why focus an axial line of trees on the local railway station? It is not as lordly and aristocratic or as pavilion-twinned and generally symmetrical as the best Jacobethan layouts of the Edwardian period. But then Franklin was only a wealthy builder, not an aesthetic aristocrat. Another oddity is the absence of parterres or topiary work to be enjoyed from that lofty viewing terrace. This suggests that Franklin bought the wreck of an original seventeenth-century viewing garden, but then contented himself with laying the enclosed rectangle out to lawn and grassing over the path from which the farm's vegetable patch had been gardened.[14] Only a very small door leads from the house on this side into its garden. Were there lost doors that once accessed directly onto those high terraces?

Easily Yarnton's best surprise is the little Sundial Garden (50), enclosed by yew hedges and sunk quite deeply at the south end of the house. This once had the topiary shapes that the main back garden lacks; it was originally the kitchen herb garden for the Manor. It was probably the creation of that dangerously decadent don from Oxford, 'Colonel' George Kolkhorst, University Reader in Spanish. He presided as Lord of the Manor here from 1936-58. John Betjeman was quite a close friend of the Colonel and stayed at the Manor for much of the summer of 1945 when he was working at Oxford for the British Council. Unfortunately a plan to have John Piper do a painting of the house came to nothing; he could have made it look very haunted and the room over its porch is supposed to have a ghost. Around the back of the house is a rare survival: a polygonal stone Game Larder with a pyramidal roof and Stonesfield slates set as louvres in the window openings.

There is a paradox and a problem over this pending revival of Elizabethan-Jacobean-style historicist gardens. Most of them surround large aristocratic country houses; they have a reassuring elegance, are spacious and costly of upkeep. So to what extent was this historicism influenced by William Morris' single-handed revival of historic forms, not in gardens only, but also in wallpaper, furnishings and poetry? Morris, for all his loving traditionalisms, was a man of the left in politics and society. Yet his firm supplied the wealthy with expensive crafts in the way of furniture, fabrics and artefacts. Did the gardens of the Edwardian upper classes owe much to Morris' own carefully revived rural simplicities at Kelmscott Manor on the Gloucestershire border, or is its undoubted current popularity a recent phenomenon? It is not easy to answer this because the dates of Kelmscott's Morris occupation – 1871-96 – place it exactly where it could have nudged the historicist layouts of places like Yarnton over into the rising Edwardian. Morris' inspiration was unquestionably historicist; he was a Romantic Socialist.

50 The Sundial Garden at Yarnton Manor – one of several Edwardian enclosures around the Jacobean house of the Spencers

A visit today on one of the Society of Antiquaries open dates for the house and its small gardens may suggest some answers.[15] But do not expect to be alone. That front garden, praised and illustrated in Morris' 1892 *News from Nowhere*, is crowded enough to make photography difficult. The farm buildings are bigger than the house, vernacular jewels set casually around a yard, and every one of the barns and shippons has a tourist function. Morris' fabrics are omnipresent and the winning thing is that the flowers and leaves on which he modelled those patterns are still blooming and blowing around the mellow walls. His wild strawberries fruit from cracks in the paving stones[16], his thrushes sing among his leaves. To see the source and the success side by side is a rare artistic pleasure.

Where gardens and their relationship with a house were concerned Morris was very wise and hugely influential. He saw that a garden could be an extension to the house, a number of outdoor rooms, their stone walls a part of the house walls. That way a three-seater lavatory could be as attractive as a garden pavilion and where a stone wall was usually inadequate a clipped yew hedge could take over effortlessly. At this period Morris and Sir Reginald Blomfield were in accord.[17] They believed in hard landscaping, but what Blomfield would delineate with a stone balustrade, Morris would mark out by fences and arches of branches tied roughly together; he devised a new snobbery of rustic vernacular and it worked brilliantly because its inherent lower class, socialist cachet must have been irresistible to left-wing middle class folk.

51 An idyllic enclosure for a Romantic Socialist and medieval obsessive – Kelmscott Manor's front garden, which featured as the frontispiece to William Morris' 1892 *News from Nowhere*

The gardens of Kelmscott, long and narrow in front, modest in size and private at the back, are the ideal models for today's middle class terrace or semi-detached suburban houses: simple, green and, above all, wholesome. The entrance front of the Manor overlooks an enclosed garden (*51*) with a stone-flagged path lined with rose bushes, a little garden hut for assignations or elevenses, and the dragon Fafnir of Icelandic legends clipped out of the yew hedge. Tolkien's *Lord of the Rings* saga is a continuation of Morris' *Sigurd the Volsung*. Both men wrote in a slightly embarrassing Brewer's English prose, where stone tiles are 'besprent' with lichen, rustic voices are 'merry' and the 'herdsmen of the manor slept … a-nights' in 'quaint garrets amongst the great timbers of the roof'.[18] As the twentieth century bore down with frightening innovations, Morris offered an easy retreat to a sanitised past. Even his love life, the menage of Morris, his wife Janey and her lover, Dante Gabriel Rossetti, was correct for Edwardians bored by insistent Victorian morality. Their gardens needed those private nooks for secret meetings conveniently close to front parlours. Bearded gentlemen like Morris looked the other way and went swimming, or headed off to Iceland.

Craft and homely produce are concentrated in the Mulberry Garden behind and at the side of the old house (*colour plate 13*). This and the Front Garden were sensitively restored in 1993 by Hal Moggridge and Janet Carter of Colvin and Moggridge. The old mulberry drips Elizabethan fruit and is underplanted with wild tulips, but there are also a quince and a medlar, equally sixteenth-century in fashion, for the making of Tudor preserves. There are red apples and black grapes dangling from a vine arbour of rough branches; nothing is machine made. The little lawn is only for drying clothes, which can also be hung out on yew and box bushes, and in the beds, besides a few native flowers, are planted utilitarian herbs, bays, pineapple mint and southernwood. There is a yew hedge for some enclosure, then an orchard, then the flat fields, which have lost the elms that once supplied verticality, and lastly the Thames for those essential cold dips. One feels guilty at not driving away in a horse and cart.

Bewitchingly full of simple charm, Kelmscott is, with its hard landscaping and particularly with its tendency to create small garden rooms for privacy, the lordly Edwardian garden in miniature, and there is this strong suspicion that Morris and Blomfield were both working on the same aim: to restore the garden to its proper function as an extension of the house. Whether that makes Kelmscott one aspect of the Gardenesque movement depends upon whether its garden is seen as an authentic historicist revival, in which case it was, or as a revolutionary social statement, in which case it was not. But it did unbdoubtedly offer a template of the fashionable aristocratic Edwardian garden for the middle classes of the polite suburbs.

Shipton Court, an authentic Jacobean property of 1603, was taken in hand for a garden restoration around 1903 at exactly the right time for its revived historicism to be influenced by Kelmscott. Built for the Lacey family, it is a rambling yet impressive and outrageously picturesque complex pent in by village houses, roads and the Trot's Brook.[19] Its gardens are an interesting instance of the usual Edwardian styling having to work on a very irregular, limited site. The Pulham firm of London and Broxbourne did its best in 1903-6 for the owner, W.F. Pepper, but Pepper's alterations, a billiard room and a Winter Garden by the architects Perkins and Bulmer made the spaces available for garden layouts even more confined. What has happened after a destructive military occupation during the 1939-45 War years has led to further complications. The property was sold in 1977 to create apartments, the same fate that overtook Hanwell Castle, and each of the apartments has its own private garden carved out of areas littered with listed structures.[20]

There was, and remains though it is little used, a short, formal main approach to the Court from the A361. This has ironwork gates and low clipped topiary leading into what was the entrance court. The usual way now leads in alongside the Trot's Brook on the left, which runs exactly straight and canalised through a pleasant, lawned and walled garden. Another equally enclosed garden with a pool and willow trees lies up on the right, but hidden behind a high stone wall. In front of the house the most successful Edwardian garden takes over, with the east front of the house up on a high narrow Long Walk overlooking the long Main Lawn. This is confined on the house side by a yew hedge and the terrace wall with the Trot's Brook on the far side, now widened out into a rectangular swimming pool that falls into a Canal. As the Pulham firm left it, the Canal ended with a single Garden Pavilion (52); this has now been enlarged with some sympathy into a detached house, which has inevitably urbanised the garden's formal airs. The richly balustraded bridge over the Canal used to lead into another garden cutting out at at right-angles, but this area has been sold off.

Eynsham Hall is a more elusive case: a landscape and garden with a long past and a rich Gardenesque present, behind which that interesting past can easily be forgotten.

52 The 1903-6 Canal with its terminal summerhouse, now enlarged into a house – part of the Pulham firm's Edwardian enrichments to Shipton Court

The grounds have never quite recovered from being initially too extensive for their owner's income to support, and the place has passed so often to different owners with different ideas on how to shape both house and grounds that Eynsham belongs in no particular chapter. Essentially the park is the estate to a lost classical house of the Lacy family, built by them around 1760-70, but altered for the next owner, Robert Langford about 1780. However, the gardens around the house are actively Gardenesque, the setting for a house that had suffered another alteration by Sir Charles Barry for the 5th Earl of Macclesfield in 1843, but was then completely rebuilt in 1904-8 for Lady Evelyn Mason by Sir Ernest George in Jacobethan style, with a heavy reference to Montacute. With so many alterations the Hall needed a helping hand from its topography but got none; the park is flat as a board, apart from the odd relic of an Iron Age hill fort.

Across its level expanses a system of drives, one from the north, one from the south and another from the east, attempts to assert some order. It is as if a Rococo garden of the immediately pre-Brown period, one designed to be experienced on foot with incidents close together, had been widely expanded and made to be hurried past in fast carriages. The south drive skirts the wooded hill fort, then leads picturesquely past a small pool, which once had a Hermitage beside it, and finally curls up to the house from the west. Two-thirds of the park have a tree-belted, circumnavigatory drive and there are clumps past counting. That east drive swings alongside a small lake but this was not created until 1866 when the Mason family had bought the house from Lord Macclesfield. The area around the lake with its typical Victorian exotic trees was landscaped by Robert Marnock, and the Swiss Cottage in the west half of the park, near the Monument, dates from the same period.[21]

All those features initially supported that classical house of the Lacey occupation, so they seem unrelated to the Ernest George house that replaced it and which sits more comfortably within its Gardenesque grounds. As the main north drive leaves a tract of splendid mature oaks it phases near the house into pollarded limes around a forecourt with balustraded walls. One ilex here has an umbrella-like growth enclosing a sheltered arbour and is a probable Marnock survivor. Nearby, in typically Gardenesque inconsequence, are two charmingly rustic, branch-walled structures of 1883 by C.H. Howell: a hexagonal Game Larder and a Dairy. The Home Farm lies on this east side of the house, and one of the disturbing features of the whole, ambitious layout is that it is not, in the usual sense of the word, a park, but normal agricultural land with field divisions.

On the south side of the house there is a conventional terraced garden, originally laid out by Owen Jones in 1872[22], but, in this ever-altered demesne, with additions by Sir Ernest George and, around 1910, by Thomas Garner.[23] The terrace walls have a number of playful stone cherubs prancing, others of lead balance on ball finials, a fountain plays in a rectangular central pool, and in another round pool down steps to the west, two cherubs squeeze water out from bunches of grapes (53) below a dramatically blasted, slanting cypress. This eye-catching tree is unlikely to be the result of an accident. John Claudius Loudon gave exact illustrated instructions, with five figures, to demonstrate the stages, showing 'How to bend Conifers'.[24] The topiary work in this garden is laid out in a dense, symmetrical maze formation, severely cropped to enclose beds of mixed hebes. In Spring this produces an unusual Scottish tweed effect, not at all traditional. Below the Jacobean-style balustrades is a series of semi abstract, half bird- or animal-shaped topiary bushes, growing dark behind the obelisk finials and those inescapable cherubs. But there, and this is typical of Eynsham, a grand flight of steps leads anti-climactically down into an ordinary agricultural field, as if money, or inspiration, had run out.

The same could not be said about the garden campaigns which 'Sunny', the remarkable Charles, 9th Duke of Marlborough, was waging at the same time in Blenheim park. At first sight the 9th Duke, pressuring his distinguished French landscape architect, Achille Duchêne, to create Italian gardens on a Lancelot Brown landscape, appears an exotic oddity in the Edwardian period.[25] Certainly he had a mind of his own and a finely-honed visual judgement. He was sufficiently involved in the perspectives of garden design to have travelled to Versailles with Duchêne and to agree with him that Le Nôtre had made the canal there too narrow. But there were echoes of both J.C. Loudon and the mystical in his make-up. By laying out hundreds of his pasture land acres to grow corn he made a handsome profit, and he was so other-worldly that he accepted the magical qualities of the waters flowing from Rosamond's Well, valuing them so highly that he had them piped under the lake at considerable expense to run in his garden fountains.

53 Cherubs grapple with grapes in a pool of the formal Edwardian garden at Eynsham Hall, while the parterres of mixed hebes produce a Scottish tweed effect

Coming to the title in 1892 and marrying the very wealthy Consuelo Vanderbilt in 1895, he determined to restore the run-down grounds of the Palace and to undo any harm that Brown's simplifying processes might have caused. The lake was dredged and by 1896 the Great Avenue had been replanted. In 10 years he is said to have had 465,000 trees planted in the park. The Avenue was in place by 1902 and then, between 1900 and 1910, he carried through a programme of restoration on the north forecourt. Brown's soil and turfs were removed, urns and some statues were restored and Vanbrugh's vision of granite sets was back in place. In 1910, shirking any recovery of the State Garden to the south, he brought in Duchêne for his first work: the laying out of a flower and topiary parterre with flowery, almost Paisley-patterned, beds to refront the east side of the Palace.[26] Sumptuously rich, the beds were centred by a fountain of Venus holding aloft the ducal coronet.

Joy was a ducal obsession. He wrote Duchêne a philosophical lecture on the theme: 'Whether you modify your Plans and your decoration or whether you do not, try and inspire in them a feeling of joyousness, for joy means the birth of everything; of spirit, hope and aspiration'.[27] He had detected a gloomy streak in the Frenchman: 'With that tinge of melancholy in your temperament you are inclined to be sombre and therefore severe'.[28] That was not what 'Sunny' Marlborough wanted. Rather than trust that fountain statue of Venus to a Frenchman he gave the American, Waldo Story, whom he and Consuelo had met in Venice, the job and Venus is certainly cheerful.

But then the Great War of 1914-18 intervened, when the Duke was busy setting a national example in thrift and industry. Consuelo divorced him, though he married again in 1921 and, after 1925, set about his two Italian water garden terraces to the west, between the Palace and the lake. He had originally intended several more terraces, leading right down to the water, but the topography was against him. Duchêne's first scheme, with cypresses, was scorned. The Duke insisted upon obelisks for vertical emphasis; Duchêne wanted several fountains. 'Bear in mind', the Duke lectured him,

> that the situation is grandiose. Limpidity of water is pleasing and possesses a romance … Be careful not to destroy this major emotion which Nature has granted to you for the sake of what may possibly be a vulgar display of waterworks which can be seen at any exhibition or public park.[29]

So there were only two fountains on the lower of Duchêne's terraces below the west front. One, however, was a repaired modello for the river gods fountain in the Piazza Navona that the Papal Envoy had presented to the 1st Duke, a Bernini original which had been lying around in pieces for two centuries, the other is a copy (54). Duchêne was allowed to bring water effects with shells and caryatids up to the foot of the first terrace in a grotto-like wall and the Duke congratulated him generously on his vision. Limpidity was not, apparently, all. This was the Bernini spirit that the Duke had asked for.

54 Achille Duchêne's 1920s Italian water terrace at Blenheim — one of the obelisks is a modello by Bernini for his Fontana dei Quattro Fiumi in Rome's Piazza Navona

NOTES

1   For Repton's proposals see Stephen Daniels, *Humphry Repton: Landscape Gardening and the Geography of Georgian England*, 1999, p.145; also Christopher Hussey, 'Great Tew, Oxfordshire – I', *Country Life*, 22 July 1949.

2   EH Register entry. See also Mavis Batey, 'Pioneer in Preservation: Great Tew, Oxfordshire', *Country Life*, 8 March 1979.

3   Plate opposite p.642 in vol.2.

4   Its cast iron and glass roof has been replaced by a solid covering.

5   EH Register entry.

6   A Pompeii-inspired semicircular seat much in vogue at this period; see Robin Whalley, 'Harold Peto: Shadows from Pompeii and the Work of Sir Lawrence Alma-Tadema', *Garden History*, vol.33, no.2 (Winter, 2005), pp.256-73.

7   Thomas Warton, *The History and Antiquities of Kiddington* (first published as a *Specimen of a History of Oxfordshire*), 3rd ed., 1815. Warton was Rector of Kiddington (1771-90) and also Poet Laureate from 1785-91. John Buckler did the illustrations and from those it is unlikely that the font was Saxon.

8   See Timothy Mowl & Brian Earnshaw, *Architecture Without Kings: The rise of puritan classicism under Cromwell* (Manchester, 1995), pp.197-9.

9   Information on their re-siting from the present owner, John Luke.

10 For other refugees from Oxford see Timothy Mowl & Brian Earnshaw, 'Exiles From Oxford', *Country Life*, 21 January 1982.

11 For this patriotic tendency see Anne Helmreich, *The English Garden & National Identity: The Competing Styles of Garden Design, 1870-1914* (Cambridge, 2002).

12 The *VCH*, 12, 1990, p.476, gives the date as 'c.1611', and records that by 1718 it was in 'ruinated condition' and the park had 'lately been destroyed'.

13 See Gordon Nares, Yarnton Manor, Oxfordshire I & II', *Country Life*, 21 & 28 December 1951; also Jeremy Schonfield, *A Short History of Yarnton Manor* (Oxford Centre for Jewish Studies, 2004).

14 The EH Register entry agrees with this interpretation.

15 The Society has published an excellent guide: *Kelmscott Manor*, 2004, which has a chapter devoted to the garden. For the best modern biography see Fiona MacCarthy, *William Morris: A Life for Our Time*, 1994.

16 His 'Strawberry Thief' design is of 1883.

17 Reginald Blomfield, *The Formal Garden in England*, 1892.

18 Morris, *News from Nowhere*, Chapter XXXI: 'An Old House Amongst New Folk'.

19 See 'Shipton Court, Oxfordshire', *Country Life*, 3 February 1900, which records the house before its alterations, but shows some of the landscape features in place. Evidently there were two successive phases of intervention.

20 I was given a most helpful tour of the grounds by David Yates. It is thanks to his wife Trudy's researches, and her collection of old photographs of Shipton, that I was made aware of the Pulham firm's work on the grounds.

21 EH Register entry.

22 Sherwood & Pevsner, *Oxfordshire*, p.602.

23 EH Register entry.

24 Loudon, *A Treatise in Forming, Improving and Managing Country Residences*, 2 vols., 1806, 2, p.477.

25 For this campaign see Green, *Blenheim*, pp.203-18.

26 Ibid., plate 100.

27 Ibid., pp.205-6.

28 Ibid., p.206.

29 Ibid., p.217.

7

UNDERGROUND LAKES, ICE CAVES AND A MATTERHORN – SIR FRANK CRISP AND FRIAR PARK

Friar Park lies on the same gentle slope of the Chilterns as Greys Court, but about a mile to the east of Greys and overlooking Henley and the Thames. Whether to describe it as a garden, a park or a pleasure ground is a problem, but whichever category is chosen it is one of the most important and memorable in the county.[1] Far smaller than Blenheim's grounds, a mere 40 well-wooded acres gathered about its high towered, multi-turreted, red brick and white stone, Franco-Flemish parent house of the 1890s, the Friar Park grounds contrive to include at least as many intriguing garden incidents as Blenheim encloses in its 400 acres.

It was the creation, like the house itself, of Sir Frank Crisp, a wealthy lawyer and microscopist, and a member of the Linnean Society. He received the Society's Victoria medal of honour, its highest award, and was an expert on mediaeval gardens.[2] Its restoration, one of the most inspired and sensitive of the twentieth century, was carried out by the current owners. When they bought Friar Park in 1969 the grounds were on the edge of ruin, but after the most generous expenditure, they have brought them back to a radiant new life. Back in 1969 the scene was one of 'a great neglected but not ruined Gothic pile', lived in by 'a handful of nuns and a segregated priest with a rude twinkle in his eye and a broken arm'.[3] Soon there were seven gardeners working on a great restoration. They cut the grass, dug out the three lakes and bored down 350ft to get the cascades running again. So the park which desperately needed an inspired and caring owner found owners who were perfectly in tune with the character of the original creator.

Sir Frank Crisp had a lively and irreverent sense of humour, a questing, detached interest in religion, a love of plants and a quirky feeling for fair-ground rides, ghost-trains, garden gnomes and philosophical paradox. For this is a philosophical garden. It was designed in 1890[4] deliberately to explore what a garden or a park, or a pleasure ground, is meant to offer to those who enter it: the 'I.V.'s' as Crisp mockingly described us – which could stand for either 'Ignorant Visitors' or 'Intelligent Visitors'.[5] Crisp carried to its ultimate that William Kentian vision of the garden as a place where visitors have to perform like actors, by being plunged into a succession of areas or stages that enforce a response. I freely admit to having emerged from my private tour of the grounds overwhelmed by the experience. They are not simply beautiful, a triumph of decorative plant shading, by both Crisp and the current owners, they carry the visitor through a dream-like sequence of improbable visual collisions. The comparison with a compression of exhilarating fairground rides is inescapable, but fairground rides set in an idyllic English Eden. It is an astonishing creation.

Ignorant or Intelligent, Crisp wanted visitors to pour through his gates: 'a great part of the enjoyment of a garden lying in the power to give pleasure to others and to share the pleasure of one's friends'.[6] Today the grounds are a private place, but Friar Park is one of the county's greatest garden achievements. We are up in the Blenheim, Buscot, Rousham league, but with a garden so intensely individual and disarmingly perverse that it has multi-tiered lakes where, by concealed stepping-stones, Crisp's guests or members of the paying public would appear to be walking on water. Crisp had impressed his personality and his beliefs lavishly upon Friar Park in a host of painted or incised inscriptions and quirky, ingenious carved figures (55). The grounds had a notice at the entrance reading: 'Don't keep off the Grass'[7], a double negative designed to leave visitors in a healthy linguistic and moral uncertainty: do two negatives make a positive? Should they or shouldn't they? He was challenging both Victorian assumptions and the docile legality of the English. Crisp had thought long and hard about the function of a garden: 'Let a garden possess some special feature and then conceal it', was one of his favourite aphorisms. 'One of the principal things to aim at in laying out a garden is mystery', was another. 'Even a garden may become monotonous, and lose something of its enticement if the whole is seen at one glance', should be balanced against 'the making of surprises … must always be considered as evidences of debased taste; the prostituting of a beautiful art, for the sake of securing a momentary exclamation of astonishment'.[8] Crisp was as illusive as his garden is various, and if my account of a visit leaves the reader confused, then my account is an accurate one. The only way to grasp Friar Park's topography is to walk it with a very good plan (56), and fortunately Crisp had one made to guide his many visitors around the grounds.[9]

On the entrance lodge, which is guarded by an outlying bastion turret with portholes, the delicately carved ornaments of 'grave' and 'gay' friars, 'Noah in the Ark', a 'Woolly Hen', 'Flying Horse', 'Angel', 'Devil', 'Harpy' and 'Dragons' give a Chaucerian touch to the Loire château-style building and set the tone of earthy, idiosyncratic diversity for what comes next. First come beautifully manicured lawns, Crisp's 'Alpine Meadow' on the plan of the gardens, and specimen trees – blue Californian pines for spring foliage and, on the right, scarlet oak and beech for an intense crimson in the autumn – with the addition of a colour toning of acers. The serpentine path through the tree belt on the right leads past a cascade, the first of several in the grounds, and is bordered by more acers and grasses. There are glimpses, through the belt, down to the roofs of Henley and the valley of the Thames. This is Crisp's 'gloomie Glenne' where the path is laid with bark and leads to the one serious loss in the grounds. Half of Crisp's 'Herbaceous Garden', together with his 'Valley of dancing Downdaffodillies', his 'songster's Bower' and a Kitchen Garden 'for ye Friar's eatinge', the latter bordered by 'ye duskie lovers' walke', had been sold off to build a primary school before the current owners came to the rescue. Towering leylandiae hide the wound, but there are still the brick bones of two quadrants of the Herbaceous Garden with its central 'pathe of Bliss' in the clearing.

Right: 55 The gnomes that dotted the grounds and underground caves at Sir Frank Crisp's Friar Park are some of the earliest Swiss imports in this country. *English Heritage: National Monuments Record*

Below: 56 Crisp's own medieval-style plan of the grounds at Friar Park shows its extreme complexity of themed enclosures. *By kind permission of Mrs Olivia Harrison*

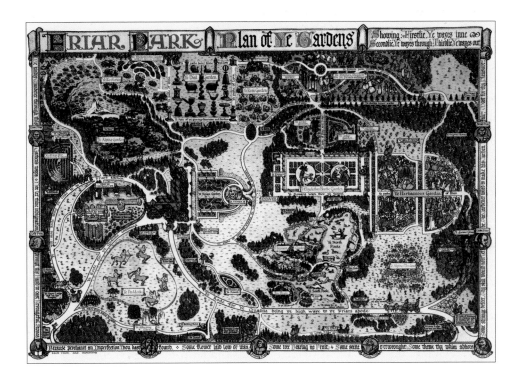

This is the first relic of Crisp's eight medieval gardens in the original grounds.[10] His *Guide* is richly illustrated with plates taken from paintings and illuminated manuscripts and one from the garden in the *Roman de la Rose* provided the design for the Palisade Garden (*57*).

Other losses in this area are the 'Gray Garden' and the 'Blue Garden' that flanked Crisp's 'Elizabethan Hearbe Garden', the enclosure of which survives. Somewhere in this area was the Garden of Sweet Smells and Savours, with its brick-faced terraces in the form of concentric horseshoes, centred by a globe sundial surmounted by a winged cupid (*58*). There was a collection of over 200 plants in this enclosure, all chosen for their scents: lavenders, rosemary, bergamots, mints and thymes, scented pelargoniums, verbenas, piperella, patchouli and crosswort. Given Crisp's almost obsessive interest in the medieval period the loss of these gardens is particularly to be regretted.

57 The Palisade Garden at Friar Park – a scholarly adaptation of a medieval garden illustrated in the Roman de la Rose. *English Heritage: National Monuments Record*

58 Crisp's didactic programme at Friar Park extended to horticulture with the Garden of Sweet Smells and Savours where there were over 200 different plants. *English Heritage: National Monuments Record*

Then the path leads up through the remains of a rockery, under a cast iron pergola, on through a Pulhamite[11] tunnel into the Sun Garden, created by the current owners from Crisp's Elizabethan Garden. It has yellow and orange planting with superb variegated mollinia grasses and neat balls of box. A walk through a Bamboo Gate leads out into the lawns again and down to the three lakes that make the garden's central feature.

The first lake is more precisely two, with an upper and lower section divided by a cascade. Flanking the second section, at a much lower level, is the third lake, fed by a seven-tiered stepped cascade. Crisp calls these Upper, Middle and Lower[12], though his Plan marks them 'North Poole and South Poole'. There are no natural springs on this hilltop and the water is all ingeniously recycled from the waterfalls and basins of the Alpine Garden in the north, and then fed through underground pipes, to feed the lakes in the south. The lower of these lakes was where Crisp's guests and visitors appeared to walk on water. As the lawns end, visitors advance on huge, irregular stepping-stones along the shore. Carved into these stones is the entirely spurious record of a prehistoric drama: the imprint of the naked feet of a man, a woman and six children. The man's feet are carved to face the sinister clawed impressions of a four-footed monster; the woman's and the childrens' footprints face away from the monster, as if in flight. This is a revelation of Sir Frank Crisp as the showman, not the scientist or the moralist. At one point in his *Guide* to the grounds Crisp admits that such false attractions have been forced out of him:

> For his own pleasure he would have been content with much less variety – say the Alpine Garden, the Herbaceous Garden, and the Pools – but such a limitation would have largely diminished the pleasure of several thousands of people who are found to take their special delight in the variety presented to them.[13]

From the very beginning Crisp always intended Friar Park to be a public attraction. That his personal interest was 'centred in what, for want of a better word, may be termed their 'scientific' (including 'horticultural') aspect; in the wonderful complexity and diversity of the ways of 'Nature'', was apprently secondary: 'The convalescent poor of Henley and the widows and orphans of the Gardener's Societies might look in vain for their sea-side trips or their pensions if nothing more was to be seen'.[14] All the entrance fees paid by the public went to those two charities: Henley's poor and the Gardener's Society. 'Hence the Admission Fee of sixpence has to be extracted by the ordinary old-world processes … and so Caves are provided with uncanny, even ghostly, subjects … and Chamois that seem to gambol on the rocks'.[15] There was actually a big telescope set up from which the public could spy the tin chamoix perched on the fake Matterhorn. That explains the caves full of garden gnomes and the pottery cranes that ceaselessly dipped their beaks into pools of water. The garden was contrived as a popular venue, though never a tea garden. The nearest surviving example of another Edwardian pleasure ground is the Larmer Tree Gardens on the Dorset-Wiltshire border, set up by General Pitt Rivers in the early 1880s entirely as a philanthropic project to educate and amuse the new affluent and bicycling working classes.[16] To understand Friar Park's conception it is helpful to read H.G. Wells' *Kipps*. The English upper classes had realised, as they had done in the eighteenth century, that if they wanted to maintain their political hold then they had to be populist.

Those faked prehistoric footprints were one part of the education; the various eclectic gardens – Japanese, Elizabethan and Mediaeval – were another part. If the working classes could not afford the Ruskinian pleasures of travel in the Alps then Crisp would bring Switzerland and the Alps down to Oxfordshire for their pleasure. It was an essentially pre-1914-18 World War moment, when the old class structures of politics were still holding fast by their elasticity and charm, as witness Friar Park, but before the awful realities of the Somme and trench warfare had undermined trust in the gentry's judgement and shifted voters to the left. As a Liberal of Asquith's rather than Lloyd George's persuasion, Crisp was a shrewd visionary. Just two pages of his revealing *Guide* prove that he had foreseen the inevitable breakaway of an Irish republic, on the carvings of the house: 'The Rose and the Thistle are shown separated from the Shamrock – carved as long ago as 1891 by way of prophetic anticipation!'[17] Yet in a positive spirit he intended to transform a dull stretch of ground: 'An attempt is being made to grow in it the flowers found in the lower Alpine meadows, but the result can at present only be hoped for, but not seen'.[18] And, of course, his vision has been rewarded.

There was, however, a dark side to Sir Frank Crisp, an agnostic cynicism, as he describes a 'Friar watching the Owner's Hearse [his own, apparently] passing and chuckling in the mood of the lower inscription: – *Vestigia nulla retrorsum*. – 'No footsteps backwards – for you'.[19] The Friar in question is carved gloating over the inevitability of death.[20] But, like his 'Blondin' Friar[21], Crisp could walk a balancing tightrope between agnosticism and faith. On his Summer-House Lawn the Summer-House displayed 'a catalogue of flowers for every day in the year, compiled by monks or other steadfast observers of the Roman Catholic Ritual, the Saints' Days, festivals and feasts being symbolised in Catholic countries by their appropriate flowers'.[22] Today, Friar Park, with all its carefully composed beauties set next to dark caves with skeletons and naughty gnomes, preserves that intriguing contrast between light and dark, science, horticulture and just sheer fun. In the Gnome Cave 'a special mirror at the E. end of the cave turns the visitor himself into a Gnome'[23], and according to Crisp's iconography gnomes are heartless, drunken, irresponsible snuff takers who torment flies, steal small birds and laugh at a fellow gnome in pain, so the message is clear enough.

After the melodrama of the prehistoric footprints on the stepping-stones comes aesthetic, eclectic relief: an island with Japanese lanterns set among acers and rodgersias. Crisp based his Japanese Garden (59) on an illustration in J. Conder's *Landscape Gardening in Japan*.[24] He was well aware of the Japanese avoidance of flowers. One of his horticulturalist friends, having laboriously constructed what he supposed was an authentic Japanese garden, invited a Japanese gentleman to inspect it. At the end of his tour the Japanese remarked politely: 'It is very beautfiul; we have nothing like it in Japan'.[25] Point taken. Pulhamite rocks shape the banks and there are two Pulhamite cave openings, one on each side of the lake, which lead to underground caverns. A cascade pours down the rock face above the lower, third lake and a Japanese Tea House tops that cliff with a sign beside it which reads: 'Ye House for ye Goodlie View'.

In the Japanese Garden, set alongside the Upper and Middle lakes of the North Poole, visitors truly have to perform themselves. Steps lead down into one cave, an evocation, by its blue tinted skylights, of the Blue Grotto on the Island of Capri. Iridescent chips glitter in stalactites of soft cement and a gnarled handrail protects visitors as they walk along a channel, down which, in Crisp's time, they would have passed magically by boat. That needs to be restored in places, now that the core is largely intact and clear of all the debris and rubbish. The impact of dark water, shadows and the faint sparkling roof is awesome after the brightness of the rest of the grounds. The walkway leads to an even bigger cavern of columnar stalactites and stalagmites, a cross between a medieval chapter house and the caves at Wookey Hole, or perhaps the Grotto at Painshill Park in Surrey. To manipulate our mood even further, at the head of the exit steps is a statue of a laughing figure with both hands thrown joyfully up into the air. And that is the essence of these pleasure grounds and also their parent house: one of exhilarating jollity. The visitor is now back at another point of the rocky Japanese Garden with lanterns and a kiosk set among English ferns, moss and shallow pools, all of which are shown in early photographs of the grounds.

To cross the lower lake the visitor must follow the 'Mystery' path on those stepping-stones concealed from anyone sitting up by the house. This path runs at the foot of the seven-tiered cascade mounting up to the romantic turrets of the house. The drive can be accessed here and I was taken back a little way along it to read the very Crispian

59 The Japanese Garden at Friar Park with its acers and rodgersias is planted around the lakes above the underground caves. *English Heritage: National Monuments Record*

injunctions on two 'Stones of Precation'.[26] These urge visitors not to throw stones 'because perchance an imperfection thou has found', for 'the gardener toiled to make his garden fair, most for thy pleasure'.[27] The other stone curses any 'wayward swain, who dares these hallow'd haunts profane'.[28] From the drive the house in all its elaborations of red and white colour contrasts is seen mirrored in the upper section of the Lower Lake. Fronting the house there is now a simplified parterre; in Crisps's time the swirls of the hedges were infilled with gravel and punctutated by ornamental peacocks. At the head of this 'Terrace Garden' is Crisp's 'Fountain of perpetual mirth'. For a time now Crisp's creativity dominates the route with the Topiary Garden, leading to the Alpine Garden, which climaxes with the most surpring illusion of all, Crisp's Matterhorn, towering up ahead in a shimmer of snow and ice, all ten feet of it!

But first comes the Topiary or Dial Garden (*60*), laid out on the plan of the Labyrinth at Versailles with almost 200 clipped bushes and enclosed by walks such as the 'pathe twixt Time and Love'. The bushes originally had animal heads but now most of

60 Crisp's Dial Garden is laid out on the plan of the Labyrinth at Versailles and was punctuated with sundials on which were improving mottoes. *English Heritage: National Monuments Record*

them have grown out of shape and G.J. Gibbs' Helio-Chronometer, which corrected sun shadow time, has gone too.[29] The yew and box bushes spiralling round their own stems remain. There were 39 sundials in the garden with mottoes like: 'It is always morning somewhere in the world'. My favourite Crispism here was: 'Time wastes our bodies and our wits/But we waste time and so we're quits'.[30] At the west end of the garden there were three stands: 'one with a skull eating a bone, one with a heart pierced by an arrow, and the third a comic-faced sun'; there was also a stone that bore the mischevious inscription: 'Turn me up and I'll tell you more'.[31] Crisp's *Guide* reads: 'Male I.V.'s desiring to interest their lady friends should turn the stone over and show *what* more the stone has to tell'.[32]

The scale and artistry of Crisp's rockworks, devised in consultation with his Head Gardener, Frank Knowles, are the greatest wonder in a garden of many prodigies. There are no precise dates for the construction of the Alpine Garden (*61*), but it was in place by 1905.[33] Just one of the 7,000 tons of millstone grit boulders, brought down from

61 Oxfordshire's greatest rockwork – the Alpine Garden at Friar Park constructed with boulders of Yorkshire millstone grit and topped by a replica of the Matterhorn. *English Heritage: National Monuments Record*

Yorkshire to construct its maze of paths and Alpine plant pockets, weighs more than 12.5 tons, and the composition of the rocks is masterly. Dwarf conifers, dwarf mallows and tiny geraniums flatter the scale of the enormous sandy-coloured rocks. Hailing Crisp's achievement in 1913, Henry Correvon, an expert on Alpine flora, wrote:

> So harmonious is the picture, so charming are the proportions, that one feels suddenly transported to the secret heart of Alpine nature. Old climber as I am, whose whole life has been spent among the mountains, I felt myself one fair morning, as I sat alone beside a brook that murmurs at the foot of this rocky flower-gemmed mountain-side, carried in spirit to my native Alps; I caught myself whistling an Alpine song.[34]

This is not over-praise. April, May and June are the best months in which to enjoy what remains of Crisp's ambitious flowering sequences of pinks, heaths, sun roses, primulas, orchids (Lady's Slipper and *orchis maculata alba* particularly), gentians, anemones and harebells. Rareties like the Chilean *tropaeolum*, Daphne *Blagayana* from Bosnia and *Schizocodon soldanelloides* were coaxed into responsive growth. Edelweiss was commonplace. Crisp made his intention clear in his *Guide*:

The fact, however, is that the personal interest of the owner himself in the grounds is centred in what, for want of a better word, may be termed their 'scientific' (including 'horticultural') aspect; in the wonderful complexity and diversity of the ways of 'Nature' and the marvellous adaptation of means to an end which a special collection of plants is capable of demonstrating in so high a degree.[35]

Frank Knowles' Matterhorn is admittedly an ingenious toy. It only works at certain distances and from flattering angles, but what panache it represents! The tin chamoix which used to stand in profile on a ridge have gone; but as Correvon laughingly pointed out: 'a bird, perchance a simple sparrow; he perches on the Matterhorn, and with the ruin of the scale every illusion tumbles down, for the charm is broken'.[36] But if Worlitz, an eighteenth-century German garden, could sport an occasionally erupting fake volcano, then surely Henley can be proud of its Swiss Alps. Crisp was ready to debate the propriety of his mock mountain and its metal chamoix. He even quoted in his 1910 *Guide* that one lady's judgement of the chamoix was: 'How silly'.[37] On the far north side of the Matterhorn Crisp was constructing in 1913 a scree, a Moraine Garden, and his Plan also shows 'Ye Rooteries' planted with roses and 'Ye Rhododendron Garden with ye spiral walkes'. His Ice Grotto leading to an Ice Cave, dug into the base of the mountain, was 'but one of the countless surprises which the genial host of Friar Park keeps for his visitors'.[38] Today, sadly, it is inaccessible to the public; as are the whole network of caves under the foothills of the Matterhorn: the Vine Cave, the Wishing Well Cave, the Skeleton Cave, The Illusion Cave with its 'optical illusion showing the upper part of a Friar who instantaneously passes from life to death, after the manner of American 'electrocution', a ferocious tiger, and, finally, the Gnome Cave.[39] All these, as well as the caverns by the lakes, were lit by electric lamps.

After the rocks and the screes with their Nepalese plants, giant lilies and *meconopsis* (blue poppies), like some lost world up on Roraima or the setting for an exotic Rider Haggard novel, there is a Holy Well and then the walled Kitchen Garden at the rear of the house. The Holy Well had above it, rather unfortunately, a carved Swastika whose arms, when bent to the left, signify cursing, and when bent to the right, as in Hitler's version and Crisp's choice, symbolise blessing. This has since been re-carved as a cross by a subsequent owner.

In the Kitchen Garden the glasshouses, 'where are many plants quaint and rare'[40], have now gone, but on the upper wall is a large Conservatory with Pulhamite pools of faintly Art Nouveau feeling and cast iron heating ducts. Impressive cast iron spandrels support the roof. Beside it and originally roofed is the Fernery, now an area of writhing cement and clinker boughs smothered in mostly common ferns. At the heart of the Kitchen Garden is a fountain in a circular enclosure bordered by tall sunflowers and pear trees. In the potager are beet, chard and ornamental grasses. Here true pear trees are shaded by Weeping Pears.

On the clock in the Garden Offices was inscribed a typical Crispian linguistic knot: 'Yesterday to-day was to-morrow/To-morrow to-day will be yesterday.'[41] And, predictably, the Stables had a Latin version of 'Don't shut the stable door after the steer is stolen'.[42]

A Jewish Weeping Corner with weeping trees stood next to the Dogs' Cemetery where Crisp had inscribed Alexander Pope's lines on 'the poor Indian' who:

asks no angel's wings, no seraph's fire
But thinks, admitted to that equal sky,
His faithful dog shall bear him company.[43]

Of all the many pets' cemeteries in country house gardens only the cemetery at Longleat gives its dogs equal literary graces.

The rear of the house dominates this area of the grounds, its hyperactive elevations alive with comical friar carvings: friars washing up, the four ages of friars and friars of the four winds. Was Friar Park, house and garden, Sir Frank Crisp's contribution to the Darwin versus Bishop Wilberforce debate? His illusion of walking on water was a typically specious piece of legal point scoring, as if there had been several different levels of the Sea of Galilee to produce that visual trick of Christ walking on the water. Friar Park is a fascinating encapsulation of its age and its survival through the current owners is a near miraculous blessing. When the restoration is complete and the grounds are perhaps occasionally accessible to true garden enthusiasts, it is likely to become one of England's and certainly one of Oxfordshire's most celebrated gardens: a fitting memorial to Crisp and the current owners.

The Park has already welcomed one remarkable and significant visitor. In May 1912, 120 continental visitors, brought to London for the International Exhibition of that year, were invited to pass a Sunday in the grounds of Friar Park. Among them, and loudest in his admiration, was His Imperial Highness, the Archduke Francis Ferdinand, who had become heir to the throne of the Austrian Empire after Rudolph, the Emperor's son, had committed suicide. The Archduke was, Correvon maintains, scarcely able to trust his eyes when he found the slopes with a complete collection of the flora of the high Tyrolean Alps of his own country, and wondered, such was the air of Crispian trickery, if he 'were the victim of an optical illusion'.[44] Two years later the Archduke's assassination at Sarajevo set off the 1914-18 War and the destruction of old Europe's aristocratic and royal order. It is the presence of that man at Henley, delighted by Crisp's gardening and probably amused by Crisp's mischevious humour, which makes one appreciate how tight was the upper class world of country houses and aristocratic house parties, and what a jolt to that world the brutal shooting of the Archduke and his wife must have been. All Europe, its upper class at least, was inter-related and friendly in the golden afternoon of Edwardian-Georgian England, and Oxfordshire was the perfect aristocrat's county. It was easily accessed by rail from London, attractively hilly, threaded by the Thames, centred by the University with a Physic Garden familiar to generations of wealthy, elite youths, and unusually rich in great houses. And there, in the midst of them, impudently cocking a snook at religion, but filling his garden with wit and invention and perfectly acceptable to all, from the heir to an imperial throne downwards, was Sir Frank Crisp and Friar Park. It was the symbol of a stable, gracious world of humour as well as beauty, but it only took the murder of one man, one among 120 in that garden party, when the

Alpine flowers of the rockworks were at their May-time perfection, to end forever that era of civilised charm and creativity which Friar Park exemplified: Europe as it might and should have been.

NOTES

1   I am most grateful to the current owners for allowing access to these private grounds, and to the estate manager for his expert tour of the site. As will become apparent in the main text, that morning in August was, without doubt, the most enjoyable and visually stimulating that I have spent visiting a garden for this series.

2   DNB. Crisp's daughter saw his monograph on mediaeval gardens through the press after her father's death in 1919: Sir Frank Crisp (ed. Catherine Paterson), *Mediaeval Gardens*, 2 vols., 1924.

3   George Harrison, *I Me Mine*, 1980 (2002 edition, with an introduction by Olivia Harrison, consulted here), p.67.

4   Friar Park was the subject of an article in *Country Life*, 5 August 1905, where the author was specifically concerned with the Alpine Garden. However, he made a general comment about the site as whole: 'It is a garden of hill and dell, of grassy ways and sunny slopes, and has been a source of delight and recreation to its owner from its formation some fifteen years ago, when this was an untouched hill-top rising from the wooded valley of the Thames'. That would put the start date for construction at 1890, once the house had been completed.

5   I consulted two guides in Henley-on-Thames public library, both written by Sir Frank Crisp: *Guide for the Use of Visitors to Friar Park, Henley-on-Thames,* 3rd edition (corrected issue), 1910, and a later, expanded version of this dated 1914.

6   1914 *Guide*, p.5. The 1910 *Guide* records that 'The Grounds are open to Visitors on WEDNESDAYS, in the months of MAY to SEPTEMBER inclusive from 2pm until 6pm'.

7   Ibid., pp.9-10. The first version, which read: 'The grass may be walked upon', was considered to be too simple and direct.

8   Ibid., p.5.

9   The current owner has kindly supplied me with an illustration of Crisp's original, beautifully illuminated, as in a mediaeval manuscript, 'Plan of Ye Gardens' on fake parchment, which records all the many garden areas, some now completely lost.

10 See Crisp's 1910 *Guide*, p.37.

11 Most of the rockworks here and around the lakes are made from Pulhamite. Crisp mentions the material when describing the Bridge connecting two sides of the Middle Lake in his 1910 *Guide*, p.34.

12 1914 *Guide*, p.12.

13 Ibid., p.6.

14 Ibid., p.7.

15 Ibid.

16 See Timothy Mowl, *Historic Gardens of Wiltshire* (Stroud, 2005), pp.135-8.

17 1914 *Guide*, p.11.

18 Ibid.

19 Ibid., p.10.

20 See fig.5 on p.23 of the 1914 *Guide*.

21 See fig.35 on p.34 of the 1914 *Guide*. The Friar, walking a tightrope, was carved on the Middle Lodge.

22 Ibid., p.22.

23 Ibid., p.20.

24   Ibid., p.12.
25   Ibid.
26   Originally there were 10 of these inscribed Japanese stones set around the grounds.
27   1914 *Guide*, p.11.
28   Ibid.
29   1910 *Guide*, p.71.
30   1914 *Guide*, 16.
31   Ibid., p.17.
32   1910 *Guide*, p.72.
33   'The Alpine Garden, Friar Park, Henley', *Country Life*, 5 August 1905.
34   Henry Correvon, 'The Rock Garden at Friar Park', *Country Life*, 3 May 1913. Correvon
     wrote another short, valedictory, article on the garden in *Country Life*, 9 August 1919, just
     after Sir Frank's death, where he cites his own book, *Flore Alpine*. Both articles give a fully
     illustrated account of the rockworks in their prime.
35   1914 *Guide*, p.7.
36   *Country Life*, 3 May 1913.
37   1914 *Guide*, p.7.
38   *Country Life*, 3 May 1913.
39   1914 *Guide*, p.19.
40   On Crisp's Plan.
41   1914 *Guide,* p.20.
42   Ibid.
43   Ibid., p.22.
44   *Country Life*, 3 May 1913.

8

THE COLLEGE GARDENS OF OXFORD

Rather more sentimental aesthetic prose has been lavished upon the gardens of Oxford's colleges than they actually deserve. Henry James set the fashion of praise: 'We repaired in turn to a series of gardens and spent long hours sitting in their greenest places ... Locked in their antique verdure ... filled with nightingales and memories, a sort of chorus of tradition'.[1] In 1912, R.T. Günther, a fellow of Magdalen College, wrote a laboured hagiography of the gardens, recording the height and the girth at various points in their multi-centuried life, of several 'legendary' wych elms, walnut trees, oaks and acacias.[2] Few writers can resist Lady Isabella Thynne who, during the Civil War, would make her entry into the gardens of Trinity 'with a theorbo or lute played before her' and who was told by the President, Dr Kettell, 'I know you to be a gentlewoman, I will not say you are a whore; but get you gone for a very woman'.[3] Another well-worn anecdote relates that one day, when the elder Jacob Bobart, the second Keeper of the Physic Garden, was walking in the street with his pet goat, another and rival eccentric seized hold of his immense beard and cried out: 'Help! Help! Bobart hath eaten his horse and his tayle hung out of his mouth'.[4]

If we cross these comical historic whimsicalities with hierarchy, with a large number of cheerful, intelligent young people and with a few, extra clever, older ones we have some highly unusual gardens. But the hierarchical aspect should be emphasised. Every college has a special, usually walled, garden for its leader, whether he or she is called the Master, the Warden, the Provost or the President. Then there is a second garden, also walled though rather larger, for the fellows. This is supposed to be private, but is generally accessible. Lastly there are the gardens for the undergraduates, open or closed to the general public by a notice at the porter's lodge. This uncertain accessibility actually adds to the charm; where else does one find such a complex garden apartheid, or so many intelligent people?

The college gardens are essentially peopled places, not solitary retreats; they function daily. One late October afternoon, for instance, I had talked my way into Worcester College's water gardens, which are ambitious enough for a major country house. They were initiated by Whittington Landon, Provost of Worcester from 1795-1839, so are essentially a scheme of the Regency Picturesque. The 1788 extension of the Oxford Canal made the creation of the lake simple. But what held my attention on the heavy Hawksmoor-influenced terrace of Main Quad, against a backdrop of jazzy canna lilies and what looked like medium-sized banana plants, was a group of girl students laughing together. In contrast with the wild tropical planting, the Virginia Creeper above them had been shaved back severely to the platband of the first floor. To reach the Sainsbury Building of 1981, poised in airy geometry over an arm of the lake, it was necessary to make a long deviation, wonderfully melancholy, with trees trained to droop over a weir and a canal; all this had to be done to avoid the Provost's private garden that bulges in front of Henry Keene's hammy façade of 1773-6.[5] A mellow golden sunlight was slanting across the chestnut trees. Then, out of the light, quitting Worcester's vast playing field, came a rugby 15 of young men making for the showers, stripping off their shirts to exhibit elegantly muscled torsoes in that flattering, theatrical garden glow. The garden's people are as vital to it as its plants, a horticultural category of their own. Oxford is a legend and its college gardens have intellectual intensity added on to sport, grass, trees, water and flowers.

A cool truth which must, however, be added, is that most of the 22 older college gardens depend for their seductive charm on the buildings that they front and the students who inhabit them. A few gardens – Magdalen, Worcester and New College – merit serious attention. The addition to that list of Merton, St John's and Trinity is arguable. St Catherine's is the honourable exception, a modern twentieth-century college with a designed garden that will, if it is allowed to survive a growth of cloaking trees, become historic in time. The rest have gardens thought up in episodes of senior common room chat after dinner. In any one common room at a given time there will be one don ready to make his mark, not by research, publication or able lecturing, but by pottering around to create a suburban rockery in the wrong place, to plant a winter garden of hellebores in some sheltered nook or to sink water lilies in an isolated pond.

There is a description in one English Heritage Register entry that could be applied to virtually every medium-sized Oxford college garden. It runs: 'The Fellows' Public Garden is laid largely to lawn and planted with scattered, mature ornamental trees, with a perimeter path giving access to a doorway into the Fellows' Private Garden set at the east end of the north wall and border'.[6] That was Wadham, though it could just as easily be Trinity or St John's. Yet Wadham's garden was, during the Commonwealth, truly historic, probably the most influential garden in the country and the nursery of what would become, in the next reign, The Royal Society. Scientific discoveries need impressive toys to catch the public's imagination and Wadham, under the enlightened, and clearly lively, rule of its Warden, Dr John Wilkins, had a garden of remarkable toys.[7]

It appears, from John Evelyn's account of the visit which he made to Oxford with his wife in July 1654, that the University was in a mood for curiosities and odd experiments, even though the sermon which he sat through at St Mary's advised students to 'Search after true Wisdome, not to be had in the books of *Philosophers*, but *Scriptures*'.[8] It was probably no coincidence that this surge of scientific experiment took place at a time when the established Church was discredited and students were in an environment of free thinking and questioning. According to Evelyn, Dr Wilkins was a most obliging Puritan, but had married the Lord Protector Oliver Cromwell's sister Robina 'to preserve the *Universities* from the ignorant Sacrilegious Commander & Souldiers, who would faine have been at demolishing all both places & persons that pretended to Learning'.[9] Cromwell was indeed the Chancellor of Oxford and Dr Wilkins had married Robina in 1656.

The eccentric spirit of Oxford research at this time is indicated by the 'treasures' which Evelyn was allowed to examine in the Bodleian after meeting 'that miracle of a Youth, Mr. *Christopher Wren*', a fellow of All Souls.[10] He was shown '*Josephs* parti colour'd Coate', miraculously preserved, 'A Muscovian Ladys Whip, some Indian Waepons, *Urnes, Lamps*', but the rarest was 'the Whole *Alcoran* written in one large sheet of *Calico*, which is made up in a Priests Vesture or Cape after the *Turkish*, & the *Arabic* Character so exquisitely written, as no printed letter comes neere it'.[11] All of which naïve oddities from the Tradescant collection give a perspective on the contents of Dr Wilkins' Wadham garden:

> *Transparent Apiaries* ... adorn'd with a variety of *Dials, little Statues, Vanes,* &c: very ornamental ... He had also contriv'd an hollow Statue which gave a Voice, & utter'd words, by a long & conceal'd pipe which went to its mouth, whilst one spake thro it, at a good distance, & which at first was very Surprizing'.[12]

Loggan's view of Wadham illustrates the Atlas statue set on a mount in the centre of the garden and surrounded by a balustrade, the viewing platform reached by a flight of steps, but the 1733 print of the garden made by Williams (62) shows far more detail of the planting in the squares of lawn around it, with obelisks in circular enclosures. It also suggests how Atlas was made to speak. Set into his mount on the other side from the steps is a small hut. Concealed in that, and speaking down the pipe, which was connected with the giant, Dr Wilkins could have surprised his guests either with compliments to the ladies or witty insults to the gentlemen. The Williams print also shows one of Wren's glass-windowed apiaries.

In his Gallery, Dr Wilkins had a 'Way-Wiser [an instrument for measuring and indicating a distance travelled by road], a *Thermometer*, a monstrous *Magnes, Conic* & other *Sections*, a Balance on a demie Circle, most of them his owne', together with the notes for a new language composed not of words but of notions.[13] Twelve years later in Surrey, Evelyn would find Dr Wilkins, Sir William Pettit and Robert Hooke 'contriving Charriots, new rigges for *ships*, a Wheele for one to run races in, & other mechanical inventions'.[14] These 'Charriots' may well have been the first prototypes for the new, well-sprung, light carriages that created the need for the network of drives that threaded the Brownian landscape park in the next century. Evelyn seems to have been shown one Wadham rarity whereby a rainbow was produced by passing sunlight through misting water vapour and reflecting it through mirrors, much in the same way that rainbows were a scientific curiosity of the Enstone Marvels and in the Grotto at Wilton House, Wiltshire.[15] Such was the experimental ground from which Newton's conclusions would eventually rise: Wadham was the ultimate Garden of Curiosities, more a laboratory than a grove. But none of these extraordinary features survive; only the standard, easy upkeep lawn with a few trees, the perimeter path and disconnected flower beds, the whole flattered and made to seem historic by the façades of Wadham's Jacobean ranges.

62 Williams' 1733 view of the scientifically inspired Commonwealth gardens of Wadham College with their Atlas Mount and transparent beehive. *Bristol University, Special Collections*

The tantalising fact is that virtually every college once had an historic garden. Celia Fiennes gives a clear description of their charm and their detail with her 1694 account of New College:

> the Garden was new-makeing, there is large bason of water in the middle, there is little walkes and mazes and round mounts for the schollars to divert themselves in ... and here they may live very neately and well if sober, and have all their curiosityes; they take much delight in greens of all sorts Myrtle Orinje and Lemons and Lorrestine [Laurustinus] growing in potts of earth, and so moved from place to place and into the aire sometymes.[16]

There are three important illustrated sources for Oxford's gardens: the 1578 Agas map, David Loggan's 1675 *Oxonia Illustrata* and W. Williams' 1733 *Oxonia Depicta*. Loggan's richly detailed bird's eye views show a number of intricate knots and later *parterres de broderie*, fashionable once Queen Henrietta Maria had brought their sinuous patterns over from France. His engraving of Brasenose Old Quad (*63*) shows the space quartered with elaborate double-noosed knots of the Staffords[17], the destruction of which Thomas Hearne, a local eighteenth-century antiquary, described:

> Last week they cut down the fine pleasant garden in Brasenose College Quadrangle, which was not only a great Ornament to it, and was agreeable to the quadrangles of our old monasteries, but was a delightful pleasant Shade in Summer Time, and made the rooms, in hot seasons, much cooler than otherwise they would have been. This is done, by the direction of the Principal and some others purely to turn it into a grass Plot and erect some silly statue there.[18]

Loggan's view of Jesus College shows three enclosed gardens set within its northern retaining wall, one with two grass squares bordered by topiary and two others with ornate box parterres[19], and the 1598 Hovenden map of All Souls records four geometric knot gardens in the college precincts.[20] Earlier, in 1575 at Lincoln College, a payment of 6d is recorded 'for herbs to sett our knotts'.[21] Yet every one of these gardens has now fallen victim either to new building or to the economy of the plain lawn.

Mavis Batey's *Historic Gardens of Oxford and Cambridge* is a delightfully readable and scholarly survey, but when she claims of these colleges that they 'are now the only places where the true atmosphere of the middle ages still exists',[22] she is ignoring the destructive intrusion of the machine-mown lawn. Every quadrangle would have originally been densely patterned with herbs and vegetables, a potager with untidy but attractive turf seats set under shades. Simplicity is a modern heresy in gardens. Loggan shows that in the 1670s there were some 15 or more small walled or hedged gardens in the grounds of Christ Church alone.[23] Each canon had his garden variously hedged or squared, there was a long bowling alley and a three-arched pavilion at the end of a formal allée. In another was a low mount with a catslide-roofed structure. The only major avenue was out on Christ Church Meadows. Lawns are simply cheap solutions

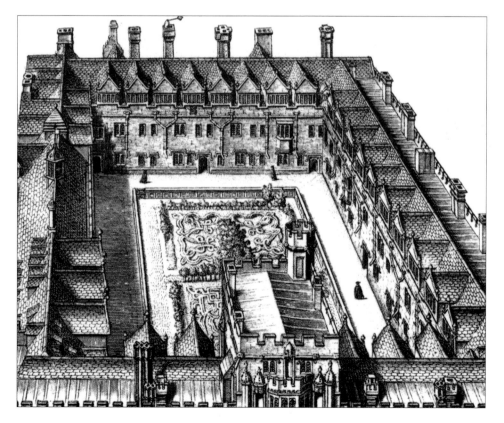

63 Many Oxford college gardens once had elaborate sixteenth-century knot gardens as here at Brasenose, illustrated in Loggan's 1675 *Oxonia Illustrata*. *Bristol University, Special Collections*

in a time when labour costs are high. A sunken knot garden may be a pleasure to view from a raised path, but it is labour intensive.

The real villain in Oxford's formal garden history was Joseph Addison, a Magdalen man, though he matriculated at Queen's in 1687, and Magdalen's grounds today are an interesting testimony to his malign influence. He wrote, in clear populist prose, that Nature was superior to formal gardening:

> In the wide Fields of Nature, the Sight wanders up and down without Confinement, and is fed with an infinite variety of Images, without any stint or Number. For this reason we always find the Poet in love with a Country Life, where Nature appears in the greatest Perfection, and furnishes out all the Scenes that are most apt to delight the Imagination.[24]

This doctrine led inexorably to the elegantly sterile, perfected Nature that Capability Brown was to devise, where woods and lakes and slopes of land would all be manicured into acceptable versions of real, wild Nature; but initially, long before the Brown revolution of the mid-century, the result could be seen at Magdalen's grounds where Nature was left more or less as she was.

Here it is essential to tread carefully. At certain times of the year Magdalen's grounds are a rather dull fen, set with lines of trees and bisected by straight canal-like reaches of the Cherwell river, its prospects raised to some beauty by the background of towers and attractive ranges of college buildings. Conscious of its limitations, in 1800 the dons called in Humphry Repton and he produced his scheme for a new quadrangle and its landscape setting, already discussed in an earlier chapter.[25] Though it would have been Addison's and Brown's vision of Nature realised, it is impossible not to rejoice that the proposal fell through because it would have drowned Magdalen's fritillary meadow. For about two weeks every year when the fritillaries are in flower, Magdalen has, not a dull fen, but one of the most overwhelmingly beautiful gardens in Oxfordshire. If that seems extravagant praise then a visit, in early April, though English seasons can vary wildly, will confirm the truth of it. The snakeshead fritillary (*fritillaria meleagris*) shares with the foxglove, and to a limited extent the bluebell, the quality of looking more like a cultivated garden flower than a wild flower. Its cap of purple chequers upon cream very nearly produces that rarest natural feature, a straight line, and with defiant panache it often produces white versions of itself. When hundreds of thousands of these normally rare wild flowers bloom on Magdalen's meadow it imitates shot silk with a subdued purple blush over sludge green grass. At the same breath-catching fortnight sufficient of the fritillaries have been persuaded to flower close to Addison's Walk (*colour plate 14*) so that their intricate perfections can be appreciated near at hand in the midst of a torrent of Spring primroses, anemones and the more banal daffodils and narcissi. It is as if Spring itself were sounding trumpet fanfares of fresh colour, 'a paradisiacal pointillism' or 'rare drifts of pixiliated purple' as Mark Griffiths has described them.[26]

Magdalen's Fellows' Garden is a notable planning failure. Addison's Walk runs high and gives a bird's eye angle on the fellows' grounds, but reveals no winding ways, no Gothick folly, shapely yew hedges or ballustraded terraces. With Addison's doctrine of leaving Nature to herself and considering a field to be a natural garden, the fellows have done very little. Neither Worcester College's deep-seeming woodland and intimate, winding serpentine, nor New College's bold use of battlemented walls has made any impact on Magdalen's unimaginative fen of straight lines. Oxford could easily have had its equivalent of the Cambridge Backs. Instead it had a William Morris, willow-banked river and Parson's Pleasure. Where Cambridge embraces and bolsters up its little Cam, Oxford merely disciplines its Cherwell and Isis then turns its back on them.

The city is, after all, one up on its rival. Cambridge has no formidably picturesque lengths of defensive walls to dramatise a garden. New College has a great garden as much by accident as by design. Everyone rhapsodises over the peaceful beauty of its cloister, which Charles I used as an arms dump while improvising a shot-tower in its 1396-1405 bell tower, but that solitary, solemn ilex, that shades about half of its otherwise empty lawn, is a parody of what a monastery-inspired cloister garden would historically have contained.[27]

At its other extremity, however, New College has been unusually enterprising and formal, though the fashion for a picturesque, cloaking, over-growth in trees has damaged a good concept. While the colleges must have spent more than half their lecturing and tutoring time in the eighteenth century delivering Greek and Latin learning, they were reluctant to indulge themselves often with classical garden structures. The Warden's very private and secluded garden behind the buildings at New College does have an early eighteenth-century classical Summerhouse by William Townesend, but no casual visitor is likely to set eyes on it.[28] Curiously, neither this, nor the handsome classical two-storey Pavilion, which the fellows of Merton built for themselves, feature in Loggan's views. But he does illustrate a domed, almost Baroque Pavilion on the garden wall of Pembroke College (64) and a more humble vernacular pavilion raised up on stilts to allow the President of St John's to look over his garden wall and observe the fellows in their garden.[29] The Williams engraving of Wadham gives an elevation of a classical temple, and there is an Ionic garden house in the garden of St Giles' House, now belonging to St John's College, which has a dome that is said to be a replica of the model by Gibbs for the stone dome he intended for his Radcliffe Camera.

What the colleges did set up, in the way of garden furnishings, were wrought iron screens, and New College has the best of these. Its central gates are of 1711 by Thomas Robinson, the wings being nineteenth-century replicas, and they are the focal point to one of the oddest garden style conjunctions in England.[30] Forming the open, fourth, side of William Byrd and William Townesend's 1682-1707 Garden Quadrangle, the screen allows that stately and entirely un-collegiate classical façade to confront, firstly, the Mount, a 10m high early sixteenth-century garden pleasance[31], and, secondly, the formidable, hollow interiors of the Oxford city wall towers which the College has been bound by statute to keep in good repair. The clash of buildings: urbane and jaggedly military, with undulant lawns and that screen between them, is almost as visually exciting as the Camera in Radcliffe Square. Add to these the raw, uncompromising tower of St Peter-in-the-East, looming up over the trees, and it is tempting to award New College the accolade of a great garden. What gives its vistas a particular vitality is the heave and swell of its long lawn, which has a Baroque movement of its own.

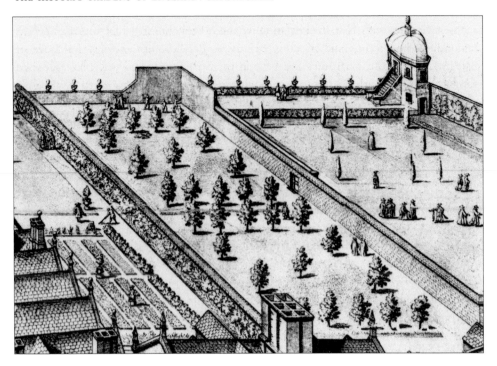

64 Loggan's view of Pembroke College shows a domed viewing pavilion on the garden wall. *Bristol University, Special Collections*

As originally planned and recorded in Loggan's 1675 view (*65*), this area was subdivided by walls; there were four elaborate ornamental gardens: one *parterre de broderie*, two armorial designs, and one a sun dial[32]; and the Mount, now conventionally smothered in trees, was bare grass, rising in three stepped levels to a viewing platform with a column. Celia Fiennes saw this elaborate formal garden in about 1694:

> there are severall New Lodgings added and beautifyed here, the Gardens also with gravell
> and grass walkes, some shady, and a great mount in the middle which is ascended by degrees
> in a round of green paths deffended by greens cutt low, and on the top is a Summer house.
> Beyond these gardens is a bowling-green, and round it a close shady walke, walled around
> and a cutt hedge to the bowling-green … in the plott there is the Colledge Arms cutt in box
> and the 24 letters round it; next plott a Sun-dial cutt in box and a true-lovers knotts.[33]

The building of the Garden Quadrangle changed all that, opened up a dramatic vista and, paradoxically, turned the classically formal Mount into a Romantic, natural visual conclusion (*colour plate 15*). If only Magdalen's garden had been so fortunate.

What was, in its prime, Oxford's most lordly and impressive formal garden was laid out before 1733 behind Trinity College (*66*). Blessed, like New College, with a three-sided court, Trinity planted a tremendous seven-lawn axial garden down to the palatial ironwork screen, which still fronts the road. It was not an imaginative garden, but rather an obsessive one, with two shallow mounts and a veritable forest of topiary obelisks surrounding the mounts and framing each lawn. Parallel with these was a grove of small trees set in four axial lines and beyond them the celebrated yew maze, scooped and curved into a swirl of paths which would not have disgraced a French royal palace garden. Vestiges of the yews survive in rugged old age.

While the circuit gardens of St John's and Trinity are beautiful enough, their actual gardens are incidental, mere foils to their backcloths of college ranges.[34] Merton's gardens are something else: a linear delight to explore, with enclosure opening up after enclosure, slung along a narrow belt between Merton Street and Christ Church Meadows. It is at Merton that just a ghost of what the college gardens and grounds must once have looked like and even smelt like still lingers on. So, perversely, the most interesting way to enter the linear complex is not from the Porter's Lodge on Merton Street. That leads into the pavements of Front Quad and the sterile, tasteful lawns of Fellows' and Mob Quads. In the past the Warden and fellows of Merton seem to have been more inclined to behave like country gentlemen in their gardening than the rulers of the other colleges. They set up a classical term, a handsome two-storey Summerhouse of 1706-7[35] for the fellows' alfresco fun and a Viewing Pavilion, on a bastion of the city wall, for the appreciation of a wide riverside vista. It would be gratifying if they were

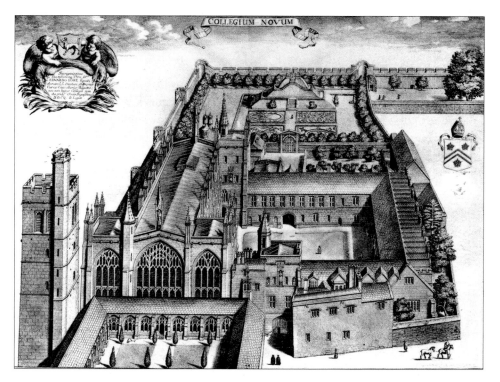

65 The great formal Mount Garden at New College, from Loggan's view – a vantage position from which to enjoy the elaborate parterre and College arms cut in box below. *Bristol University, Special Collections*

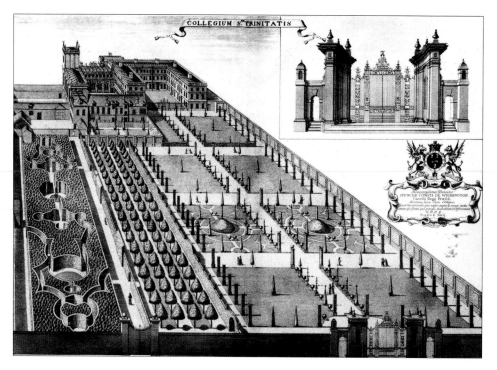

COLLEGIUM S.ᵗ TRINITATIS

66 Oxford's most impressive formal garden, at Trinity College, with its forest of topiary obelisks from a Williams view of 1733. *Bristol University, Special Collections*

to continue that tradition today and invest in two daringly imaginative modern gardens, all sculpture, water effects and exotic planting in the Fellows' and Mob Quads; the buildings deserve aesthetic responses, not cheap lawns. Mob Quad, the oldest in either of the two universities, has suffered an exceptionally dreary restoration and deserves a garden revival.

The way to experience a whiff of the past is to enter Merton through its most modern quarter off Rose Lane and by the North Lodge. Here there is that Oxford rarity, a real garden potager, sunk below the city wall. It has herbs mixed with dahlias, fennel, Indian corn, bright red chard, even a date palm. On the fruit trees behind it mistletoe hangs richly and a ripe smell of compost scents the air. The Loggan view of Christ Church illustrates an entire farmyard complex where the Meadow Buildings now stand[36], so that college must have once smelt even more homely than Merton does today. This random court area is much planted with rowans and there was, on my visit, a perfect vignette of a red admiral butterfly perched on a wall above a row of pink nerines and next to a Belle Helene rose in flower. Merton meticulously labels all its plants and seems to welcome visitors rather than to fleece them like Christ Church with its hefty entrance charges.

The Fellows' Garden at Merton has high terrace walks on three sides, one lined with lavender on one side, iris on the other, one lined with box and yew. The Fellows' Summerhouse looks enviably inhabitable, but is now the Music Room, and where the semi-classical viewing Pavilion once stood there is now a stone table and seating. St Alban's Quad, of 1904-10 by Basil Champneys, is in that irritatingly, almost Art Nouveau, free-style Tudor Gothic that England employed as a nervous salute to more committed Continental fashions. Its 1907 wrought iron screen is also by Champneys and leads down to an antique mulberry tree looking lost on a lawn, which seems to have been the Warden's garden before the Warden made the first of two moves to better housing, and the Fellows' and Warden's plots were merged into one ramblingly pleasant, rather than grand, whole.

To turn from the gardens of Merton, so various and so time-patterned, to those of St Catherine's College, which were planned and built between 1960 and 1964 by one man, the Danish architect Arne Jacobsen, is stimulating and a challenge to preconceptions. St Catherine's was coaxed into existence by Allan Bullock, its first Master, and began to function as a college in 1962 with Jacobsen designing everything from the cutlery to the squash courts and the disposition of the gardens.

What the St Catherine's gardens undoubtedly contrive to achieve is a close visual connection with the buildings of the college and the waterways near at hand: something that St John's, Cambridge also achieves, but that Magdalen, Oxford does not. From the start Jacobsen planned a campus rather than a garden. There is nothing else in Oxford remotely like it and it is to be hoped that it will be exactly preserved as an example of England's mid-twentieth-century reverence for all things Scandinavian and austerely elegant, rather as the Elizabethans revered Renaissance Italy despite its Catholicism.

Jacobsen gave firm orders that there should be no flowers in St Catherine's grounds so that his pale, buff brick ranges would be set against an entirely green background. What he may have forgotten, or overlooked as an unfortunate necessity, was the English autumn. Possibly it was cheating to make my third visit in November, a brilliantly cloudless day, cold after a long warm October that had left almost every tree on the campus in full yellow, siena or burnt umber leaf, but the place was a feast of subdued gold and the planting almost overwhelmed the long, low, rectangularities of the buildings. Was that why Jacobsen was against colour? His designs are so restrained, so desperate not to intrude, that the conifer in the quadrangle makes all his tasteful ranges look secondary. It is probably Oxford's greatest garden because the College itself offers no competition, only a dim steel-and-glass backdrop; also, the garden relates intimately to its river, the Mill Stream, which other Oxford colleges fail to do. From the octagonal Music Room in the south to the glum, leaden Punt House, two storeys high, in the north, it is a college by a stream, though punting it must be an exercise in avoidances.

As one enters the place, crossing the Mill Stream, the gardens take over. Unfocused by the retiring, rectangular blocks a visitor is given this amazing vista down a ruler-straight lily and reed-planted Canal (colour plate 16) that runs alongside the Podium which holds half the student rooms. This is not a vista to infinity, but it is still generously uncollegiate in scale, with dark woods gathering at the far end, dappped gold. After that it is not the usual movement from quad to quad; the design obliges a visitor to infiltrate. Only the Master's Lodgings, an unassuming grey box to the right, between the Mill Stream and the Canal, keeps itself apart. All else is open; even the Fellows' Garden is part of a united sympathy of spaces. It is in this, relatively un-private

67 The insistent geometries of Arne Jacobsen's 1960-4 St Catherine's College are continued in the gardens with the harsh angularities of his baffle walls and rectangular yew hedges

reserve off the fellows' private Dining Room, that Arne Jacobsen's fixation upon the rectangular segues in, outstandingly in isolated brick baffle walls often echoed by isolated rectangles of yew hedge (*67*). What do they demarcate? I never worked them out, nor did Sherwood and Pevsner. They call them screen walls set 'fin-wise'.[37] Some are harsh backs to slatted seats.

The hedges, some beech, but mostly yew, are as rectangular and exact as the baffle walls. Often they play wall-like tricks: recesses and protrusions, all clipped to six feet, one inch if they are yew, eight feet if they are of beech.[38] Among these straight lines that circular lawn in the only quadrangle comes like an alien intrusion. If a path turns a bend it does it in rectangular blocks laid sideways. At the Canal's south end there is one semi-circular arena, but it was an afterthought of the late 1960s, and Jacobsen gave it square flanking changing rooms of yew. What save the rectangles from being dispiriting are the trees. There is a walnut by the Music Room where the Mill Stream nudges in around the ditch of a Civil War defensive ravelin. Two mulberries have resulted in shameful bloody footprints on neutral Jacobsen carpets. A foxglove tree by the Fellows' Garden was still dutifully green on my visit. It only flowers profusely on alternate years. Two *Cecidia phyllums* smelt deliciously of burnt sugar in the November sun, an open air sweet-shop aura. There may not be any flowers, but there are some lively trees. In the strategic vista between the Podium, the Canal and the Mill Stream there is a contorted willow, considered something of a tree wonder. Near it a Barbara Hepworth bronze, 'Archaean', expresses itself with a ruggedness unusual in her work. To the north of it is an equally contorted bronze, like toppling stonework, by the Japanese, Ju Ming, of 1981. These sculptures, like the refined specimen trees – ginkgo, strawberry tree, liquid amber and robinnia – are as memorable as the Gothic shields on older colleges.

Perhaps in 100 years St Catherine's will be a college of grey and glass in a forest; just now it is an airy, idyllic grove. It wears its garden trees as a person wears a coat. Neither the Bell Tower nor the Dining Hall are memorable or even noticeable, merely self-effacing. I came away dazed and delighted, but wondered if Jacobsen had ever seen it in autumn and, if he had, might he have wished he had asserted his buildings just a shade more competitively. But this is Oxford's best garden, a 'garden-college', not a college garden.

That title of the best garden should belong to the garden which concludes this compressed survey of a massive topic; but the Oxford Physic Garden, or Botanic Garden as it now calls itself, should probably have been considered at the beginning of this study of the college gardens rather than at the end; or even found a place in the Introduction. Was it the inspiration, the source spring, that accounts for the quite unusual number of significant, nationally influential gardens clustered in this one average-sized county: Rousham, Wroxton, Buscot, Blenheim, Heythrop, or even Addison's much-written-about Walk, across the road in Magdalen? Reservations begin to set in because the Physic Garden did not have an auspicious beginning.

Henry, Lord Danvers, subsequently the Earl of Danby, who spent £5250 setting up the Garden between 1621 and 1633, suffered from ill-health and founded the place essentially as somewhere to grow medicinal herbs and to popularise them, 'to begin and finish a place whereby learning, especially the faculty of medicine, might be improved'.[39] It was a simple 'physic' garden long before it became a consciously 'botanic' garden in 1840.[40] The first Keeper, or 'Gardener' as he is referred to in Danby's correspondence, is now proven to have been the most distinguished contemporary plantsman, John Tradescant, but it took so long to secure his appointment that he had barely one growing season to plant the Garden at Oxford before he died in 1638.[41] Thereafter, when Danby met a German ex-soldier, the Brunswicker, Jacob Bobart, in the Greyhound Inn opposite Magdalen College in 1642, he identified him as a good practical gardener to take charge of the exotic plants that had been arriving, and offered him the post of *Horti Praefectus*. Bobart was succeeded, not by an enthusiastic academic, but by his son, another Jacob. The younger Jacob died in 1719, a year after enforced retirement; so the Bobart reign (Bobart was pronounced to rhyme with 'cupboard') lasted over 70 years.

Celia Fiennes writes that the Garden 'afforded great diversion and pleasure, the variety of flowers and plants would have entertained one week'. She saw 'the Aloes plant which is like a great flag in shape leaves and collour, and grows in the form of an open Hartichoake', the 'Sensible plant [Mimosa]', and the 'Humble plant that grows on a long slender stalke and do but strike it, it falls flatt on the ground stalke and all, and after some tyme revivces againe and stands up, but these are nice plants and are kept mostly under glass's, the aire being too rough for them'.[42] The walled enclosure with its three classical entrance gateways overlooked by Magdalen's tower (*colour plate 17*), was originally divided into four quarters by yew hedges, each quarter then subdivided into four. The taxonomy has often changed over the years; at present they follow the taxonomic system created by Bentham and Hooker. The public were only allowed into the two main cross alleys, perhaps because the Bobarts increased their salaries by growing fruit and vegetables in some of the subdivisions to sell in Oxford market.

68 Nicholas Stone's 1632-3 triumphal gateway to Lord Danby's Botanic Garden at Oxford, inspired by Serlio and carrying statues of Charles I and Charles II

A 1728 bequest made by Dr William Sherard was given under the condition that the celebrated Dr Dillenius should be chosen as the first Professor of Botany, but when Dillenius was appointed in 1734 he argued unproductively with the great Linnaeus when the Swede made a visit. Dr Humphrey Sibthorp[43] and Dr George Williams both allowed the garden to be run down during their professorial terms, but Dr Charles Daubeny succeeded in gathering funds to build new glasshouses in 1893, the first 'Conservatory for Evergreens' shown on Loggan's 1675 view of the '*Hortus Botanicus*' having been built in 1670.

Today the most impressive feature of the Garden is its 1632-3 entrance gate from the High (*68*) with a brilliant Nicholas Stone improvisation on Serlio's *Extraordinary Book* of archways to greet visitors.[44] Life-sized statues of Charles I and Charles II flank the arch and a bust of Danby himself is set in the niche above. The vast, almost square, garden within the walls is an open book for students, its bedding strips planted with the various plant families: *Ranunculaceae, Papaveraceae, Cruciferae, Caryophyllaceae* and the more exiciting *Cucurbitaceae*.[45] The sections with economic plants, like cereals, and medicinal plants are more accessible and memorable to amateurs, but attention can soon wander. The horrid insect-eating plants, succulents and water lilies in the greenhouses and palm house over on the left of the Danby Gate are easier viewing. Those hot houses offer, in a gentle halitosis of flowers, an attractive succession of exotics, though most such displays seem tame after the Eden Project in Cornwall. The multiple quartering of the square was, as Loggan's views of the colleges show, often copied in unenterprising gardens before the Addison revolution. Curiously Stone's three fine garden gates inspired no contemporary imitators.

The liveliest area of the Garden today lies just outside the walls on the south side where there are a Bog Garden in an exedral extension and some open prospects. In general, however, it has to be said that, while it may have inspired improvements in grafting techniques, the Physic Garden has had a limited impact on the college gardens and it is not apparent that it has had any inspirational force on the planting, the landscaping or the eclecticism of gardens in the county at large. The most charitable conclusion would be to quote John Ayliffe's 1714 *The Antient and Present State of the University of Oxford*. He believed that the Garden was:

> of great use ... as is easily found, among all persons willing to improve their Botanical inclinations and studies; and for the pleasant Contemplation and Experience of *Vegetative Philosophy*, for which is here supposed to be as good Convenience as in any Place of *Europe* (if not the best) and also for the service of all *Medicinal Practitioners*, supplying the Physicians, Apothecaries and who else shall have occasion for things of that nature with what is right and true, fresh and good for the Service of Health and Life.[46]

This was, after all, exactly what Lord Danby had intended. When Dr Robert Morison began lecturing in 1670 on herbs and plants three times a week, from a table set up in the walled enclosure, to a large crowd of students, he was perhaps setting up a dichotomy in the Garden between physic and botanic from which it has never quite settled down. If only Geoffrey Jellicoe had been let loose upon just one quarter.

NOTES

1 From *A Passionate Pilgrim*, 1875; quoted in Mavis Batey, *The Historic Gardens of Oxford and Cambridge*, 1989, p.7.
2 R.T. Günther, *Oxford Gardens based upon Daubeny's Popular Guide to the Physick Garden of Oxford: with Notes on the Gardens of the Colleges and on the University Park* (Oxford, 1912).
3 John Aubrey, who was Kettell's pupil, quoted in Christopher Hobhouse, *Oxford As it was And as it is to-day*, 1939, p.73.
4 Quoted in Mavis Batey, *Historic Gardens of Oxford and Cambridge*, 1989, p.63.
5 This private area was given a formal Arts and Crafts garden in its south-east corner in 1903 by Alfred Parsons. It contained 'a central sundial surrounded by beds of roses, pinks and snapdragons; delphiniums, tiger lilies, peonies, sweet peas and other herbaceous plants grew in the shelter of the stone wall dividing it from Main Quad (EH Register entry).
6 EH Register entry for Wadham College.
7 See Timothy Mowl, 'New Science, Old Order: The Gardens of the Great Rebellion', *Journal of Garden History*, vol.13, nos.1/2 (Spring/Summer, 1993), pp.16-35; also Timothy Mowl & Brian Earnshaw, *Architecture Without Kings: The rise of puritan classicism under Cromwell* (Manchester, 1995), chapter on 'Garden design', pp.205-24.
8 E.S. De Beer (ed.), *The Diary of John Evelyn*, 6 vols (Oxford, 1955), 3, pp.104-5.
9 Ibid., p.165.
10 Ibid., 4, p.106.
11 Ibid., pp.107-8.
12 Ibid., p.110.
13 Ibid., pp.110-11.

14 Ibid., p.416.

15 I am indebted to Paige Johnson's unpublished researches into these curiosities. For Enstone see Chapter Two.

16 Christopher Morris (ed.), *The Illustrated Journeys of Celia Fiennes c.1682-c.1712*, pp.57-9.

17 Illustrated in Batey, *Historic Gardens*, p.44.

18 Ibid., p.91. A lead statue of Samson slaying the Philistines was sold for scrap in 1881.

19 Aymer Vallance, *The Old Colleges of Oxford*, 1912, plate XLVI.

20 Ibid., p.44.

21 Batey, *Historic Gardens*, p.51.

22 Ibid., on the dust jacket blurb.

23 Vallence, *Old Colleges*, plate XXXIV.

24 Ibid., p.105; see also Mavis Batey, 'The Pleasures of the Imagination: Joseph Addison's Influence on Early Landscape Gardens', *Garden History*, vol.33: no.2 (Winter, 2005), pp.189-209.

25 See chapter 5. This proposal is discussed by Batey, *Historic Gardens*, p.138; see also Howard Colvin, *Unbuilt Oxford*, 1983, pp.92-3.

26 'Thank goodness for the fritillaries of Oxford', *Country Life*, 20 April 2006.

27 The space was once intended as the fellows' burial ground.

28 Attributed to Townesend by the EH Register entry.

29 See Vallance, *Old Colleges*, Plate XXXII.

30 Batey, *Historic Gardens*, p.85, records that Robinson had worked for Tijou, famous for his ironwork screens at Hampton Court.

31 The EH Register entry records that the Mount is not shown on the 1578 Agas map, but cites J. Buxton, *New College, Oxford, A Note on the Garden*, 1976, which reports that work started on it in 1529-30 when 500 waggon loads of rubbish were tipped in the garden for its foundation.

32 For this feature and other sundial gardens see Pete Smith, 'The Sundial Garden and House-Plan Mount: Two Gardens at Wollaton Hall, Nottinghamshire, by Robert (c.1535-1614) and John (-1634) Smythson', *Garden History*, vol.31, no.1 (Spring. 2003), pp.28. The sundial at New College is dated 1628 in its patterning and was laid out for Robert Pinke, Warden between 1616 and 1647.

33 Morris, *Celia Fiennes*, pp.59-60.

34 St John's does, however, have an ambitious Rock Garden, which was laid out by Henry Jardine Bidder (1847-1923), 'Keeper of the Groves'.

35 Jennifer Sherwood & Nikolaus Pevsner, *The Buildings of England: Oxfordshire*, 1974, p.164.

36 See Batey, *Historic Gardens*, pp.88-9.

37 Sherwood & Pevsner, *Oxfordshire*, p.242.

38 Simon Horwood, the Garden Manager who showed me around, was my informant.

39 J.K. Burras, 'Britain's Oldest Botanic Garden', *Country Life*, 15 July 1971. Physic gardens had been set up in Padua (1533), Pisa (1544), and at the Jardin des Plantes in Paris in 1597.

40 So named by Professor Daubeny in his *Guide*, upon which Günter's 1912 book is based.

41 See Jennifer Potter, *Strange Blooms: The Curious Lives and Adventures of the John Tradescants*, 2006, pp.248-51.

42 Morris, *Celia Fiennes*, p.57.

43 He should not be confused with his son, John Sibthorp of Lincoln College, who was made Professor of Botany in 1784 and 'will be ever memorable in the annals of botany for his zeal in the pursuit of science, no less than for his munificent designs to promote its advancement' (Günter, *Oxford Gardens*, p.20). His 1799 monument by Flaxman, showing him in profile in a short chlamys holding flowers in his hands, is in Bath Abbey.

44 Sherwood & Pevsner, *Oxfordshire*, p.267. Stone records the commission in his diary for 1631: 'to mak 3 gattes in to the phiseck garden'.

45 For a clear, full account see Ronald Gray & Ernest Frankl, *Oxford Gardens* (Cambridge, 1987).

46 Quoted in Günter, *Oxford Gardens*, pp.12-13.

9

LINGERING CONSERVATISM – EARLY TWENTIETH-CENTURY GARDENS

Once Edwardian historicism, an essentially conservative garden styling in thrall to the Jacobethan, had put an end to the chaotic, though often rewarding, Gardenesque, there would be no shortage of new twentieth-century gardens in the county. There are so many, in fact, that it is tempting to order them into two types, or themes: the conservative and the experimental, with a chapter for each. It is tempting to subdivide them that way, but not easy. There is no exact chronological division between the two; paradoxically the conservative gardens can appear late and the experimental surprisingly early. But two helpful reservations can be made about virtually all twentieth-century gardens. One is self-evident in an historic county: most apparently modern layouts have old structural bones. The second is that this was the century when flowers took over and hard landscaping, with solid features that will outlast the centuries, has tended to take a back seat.

As regards the reservation about old bones supporting new gardens, Stonor Park is a perfect example. A new generation of the Stonor family, a very distinguished race of aristocratic recusants, gave the twin gardens up the hill behind the house a complete makeover after 1978. What had been, in the bird's eye view painted in the late seventeenth century[1], a kitchen garden of 15 plots, became formally gracious with a herbaceous border backed by crab apple trees at the top and an axial path flanked by columnar yews leading down to white agapanthus and fuchsias at the bottom. Its twin, the Pleasure Garden alongside, got terracotta tiled paths and small lily ponds. The only radical changes at Stonor were to demolish the forecourt walls with their entry lodges, thereby opening up the house to the landscape, and to shift, in a move of decorous Catholic pietism, the genuine prehistoric stone circle, which had defied time in the forecourt of the house, out into the park to make an object of interest beside the drive. Curiously, the 1690s artist who recorded Stonor's grounds found it tactful, even then, to omit the stones. In the eighteenth century they were to have become mildly fashionable, like Druids, who were quite often represented in garden statues of the period.[2]

Buscot Park will make a broader and more flattering introduction to the twentieth century than Stonor; though again, when it was bought in 1885 by Alexander Henderson, the millionaire financier who was created Lord Faringdon in 1916, there were already the bones of his later cascade in place.[3] This was a shorter version that had been laid out in the 1860s as part of a scheme by Robert Campbell to create an industrial farm in the Loudon manner. Between 1904 and 1913, Henderson, living in an age when £1 million was real wealth, set Harold Peto to work on the steep hillside above Buscot's lake and below the lacklustre 1770s classical house. Sir Ernest George had given this building a few tweaks back in 1899, leaving it with a look of surprised confusion.

Buscot is one of the great gardens of the county, with three spectacular features, all formal and conservative. Peto's Water Garden down to the lake is a witty, poetic extension of a paltry existing nineteenth-century watercourse. On the other side of the hill, Tim Rees' and Peter Coats' late twentieth-century reshaping, for Charles Michael, 3rd Lord Faringdon, of the old Kitchen Garden into the amphitheatre of the Four Seasons Garden and the Melon Ground is a visual vortex; then, as if two totally successful gardens were not enough for one dim house, the house itself has Geddes Hyslop's 1936 twin garden pavilions, one of the rare occasions where England can look Florence in the face and not feel apologetic.[4] The western of Hyslop's pavilions is memorably pure, with Tuscan pedimented porticos and, a very British touch, nesting perches in their oculi; but the eastern pavilion is the national treasure. Not only does it overlook, as the house fails to do, Peto's Water Garden, but it encloses a swimming pool with socialist murals by John Hastings, a lively contemporary comment on upper and lower class life, painted in soft colours on chalky white plaster.[5] The frescoes depict Lord Faringdon addressing a political rally, Mr Bastion, his Head Gardener, and Lord Berners of neighbouring Faringdon House. Lord Faringdon was an inspired and daring patron of the arts, as was his grandson, Gavin Henderson, 2nd Lord Faringdon. If only Lord Burlington could have been as well served by his eighteenth-century painters our country houses might be the envy of Europe. Could it be just a coincidence that at Faringdon House, Robert Heber Percy commissioned, after Lord Berners' death in 1950, an equally poetic swimming pool, raised up to the face of heaven as if to out-point Buscot?

Down from this east pavilion Peto's Water Garden (*colour plate 18*) runs for 250m of wit, water and bronze nudity down to the lake, which on my last visit was as blue as the Mediterranean, with trees around it far more verdant than Italy can offer. On the far side of the lake a white Rotunda ties in the vista neatly. First come sphinxes with Greek inscriptions. Then the Water Garden runs down on the left in steps from one geometrically-shaped basin to another. Mature trees close in, low box hedges and spires of yew march down on either side of the stone watercourse, and statues of plump children posture in mimicry of the Roman gods. One laughing boy wears the helmet of Mars, one girl is tricked out as a silly Venus. Half-way down a Pompeian exedral *scola* has jambs of winged lions.[6] Evil satyr herms populate another clearing, while a third has herms of senatorial dignity. No one statue is conventional and the clear brown water is itself a garden, planted with reeds and water lilies, always noisy with its cascades. Most striking of all is a bronze fountain (*69*) where a naked youth grapples lewdly with a monstrous, fat-nosed dolphin, pressing jets of white water from the brute's nostrils, the water arcs focusing the eye all the way down the hill, as the bag jet does in the amphitheatre of the Four Seasons Garden.

69 The Boy and Dolphin fountain
is one of several sculptural incidents
which enliven Harold Peto's brilliant
Italian-syle Water Garden of 1904–13 at
Buscot Park

At each of those punctuating pools a cross-alley, more French forest garden than Italian, cuts away to a richness of *rond-point* gardens in the woods where a system of six avenues (one the Water Garden), in a goose-foot based upon the west front of the house, dives down through the trees. An afternoon is not long enough to explore all that Buscot has on offer. A statue of Antinous stands down one avenue of thin poplars, an icon for the sexually ambivalent. In one *rond-point* the Swinging Garden, a circle of silver-leafed weeping pears, surrounds big terracotta pots and swinging couches for siestas. Up a cross-alley to the next avenue is the Sunken Garden: an Orange Grove preceeded by two Eyptian statues of Coade stone. The Top Circle has a hedged circular lawn, a small pool and a tumulus with a whale's jawbone. It is a pleasure garden in the real sense of the term, eclecticism carried with light-hearted invention.

Visitors come to the Water Garden last as entrance to the grounds is from the stables in the north-west corner of the park, across an arm of the Little Lake. This service area is grand enough, with its 1781 stable block. The house itself is kept in reserve, externally the least of Buscot's attractions.[7] Instead, a way leads into the deep hollow of the Four Seasons Garden, a wonderful taster of things to come (*70*). Four axial paths swoop down vertiginously to a large bronze of a naked man squeezing a bag to produce another prodigious jet of water. He stands in a balustraded round pool and, such is the water

70 Naked statuary and water features prominently in the inventive Four Seasons Garden, laid out after 1977 by the third Lord Faringdon in the former Kitchen Garden at Buscot

pressure from a concealed reservoir up above[8], that the jet holds the eye exactly as those from the dolphin in the Water Garden. This is typical of Buscot's generous gusto. With so much rain England is curiously short of such grand water gardens. Hedges of pleached hop, hornbeam and Judas trees flank the cruciform paths. That to the west rises to a gazebo pavilion[9], from which it plunges down to the statue then up again, by five stages of clipped yew hedges, to the south lawns of the house and Hyslop's pavilions. Oddly the house commands long vistas north and south across the counties, but cannot see either its Water Garden or the Four Seasons amphitheatre.

At Peto's Water Garden, Oxfordshire was possibly moving ahead of the rest of the country in its eclecticism to a more controlled and sophisticated adaptation of foreign models. Meanwhile at High Wall, a country house in size and consequence, but entirely Oxford suburban in setting, Peto, together with the architect Walter Cave, appear to have been indulging in mystic symbolism. It was built in 1910 for Katharine Feilden, apparently on esoteric principles culled from W.R. Lethaby's *Architecture, Mysticism and Myth* of 1891. For Lethaby, and apparently for Walter Cave and Katharine Feilden, a house and its garden should be so constructed 'that beauty may flow into the soil like a breeze'.[10] He hated buildings of the past where 'each stone is cemented in the blood of a human creature'.[11] So what should the art of the future be?

> The message will still be of nature and man, of order and beauty, but all will be sweetness, simplicity, freedom, confidence and light; the other is past, and well is it, for its aim was to crush life: the new, the future, is to aid life and train it.[12]

So, after the random chaos and eclecticism of the Victorian period and the predictable historicism of the Edwardian, comes this first subtle hint of Modernism in the simplicities and hopeful morality of the Arts and Crafts movement. At High Wall the house, its interior, its terraces and its garden are a whole. The main structure of the gardens was to Cave's basic design worked out in harmonic Pythagorean and Masonic proportions to the house, with an agreed Pergola and planting overlay by Harold Peto.[13] As Lethaby wrote in his *Architecture, Nature and Magic*: 'all architecture – that is, all that is worth the name – is one vast symbolism, symbolism controlled by an experience of structure'.[14]

Just as William Morris had demonstrated at Kelmscott that a house and its garden could be an interlocking series of rooms, inner and outer, so the forecourt of High Wall seems itself to be a roofed room because it is so overshadowed by trees. This outer walled enclosure phases by shallow steps down to a sunless inner courtyard where the front door, with the mathematical sign of Pi contrived within Katharine Feilden's initials carved boldly over it[15], is hidden away to the left, at right-angles to its expected position, thus perversely unseen and shifting the axis. Where the door would normally be sited, in the centre of the multi-mullioned façade, there is a tall mullioned and transomed window, the lower lights having stained glass images of four women saints: St Margaret of Scotland, St Frideswide, St Werburga and St Bega. It is prudent in this strange period to meet scepticism head on and note that the long axis of the gardens on the other side of the house has been laid out so that the sun will rise along it on 19 October, which is St Frideswide's Feast Day; also to remember that the house is dated, below Katharine Feilden's initials, 1910. Other ley-line-type intersections between the alignment of the house and the places of birth or origination of the saints depicted in its windows, for instance at Dunfermline and St Bees Head in Cumbria, await publication by Arpad Turmezei.[16] Just as prehistoric man laid out Stonehenge, Maeshowe in the Orkneys and Newgrange in Co. Meath, Ireland so that the sun rose along their axes on a fixed equinoctial date, to represent rebirth and regeneration, so Cave, presumably in concert with Peto, laid out the gardens at High Wall to celebrate the saints venerated in the stained glass. It is fanciful, even improbable, but this was the Lethaby era of symbolism and patriotic magic.

To absorb the devious planning of the place it is necessary to walk through the house, from entrance front to south front, and then from garden to garden, from unexpected asymmetry to broken symmetry. After that left-handed entrance from the sunken courtyard a columned hall-dining room, dark with wood panelling but lit by the stained glass of those saints, swings the axial line to the right. It then wheels sharply back left again to exit into the rear garden terrace via an arched loggia room. The terrace then takes over the game of levels and directions, suggesting that Cave the architect rather than Peto the gardener was in charge.

This top terrace has four herringbone-laid brick squares, which were tiny lawns until Percy Cane's alterations of the 1920s.[17] A sinuous, almost Art Nouveau-style, fountain (71) overlooks these from a recessed niche, spraying its water out to overflow in a veil from its lip. Though the fountain is symmetrically central, the eye is directed sharply to the right and down a stepped level to where, at the end of the second terrace, an octagonal pool

Above: 71 Sprouting like an organic growth on the terrace at High Wall – Walter Cave's fountain is on an axis of the mystically orientated layout inspired by W. R. Lethaby

Left: 72 Harold Peto worked with Walter Cave at High Wall to link house and garden, in typical Arts and Crafts style, with the welcoming arms of his Doric columned Pergola and central Pavilion. *Countryfile Picture Library*

is so perfectly covered in duckweed as to pretend perilously to be a lawn. Paving leads out past the pool, far away from the main axis, out to the lawn, into a side terarce where a buttressed wall juts out over the leaf-shadowed public lane and the wooded gardens beyond it, to suggest another unity, this time with the woodlands. Immediately ahead across the wide lawn is an octagonal Pavilion (72) of Doric columns as the centre of a welcoming Doric Loggia enclosing a third of the lawn. Steps lead up out of it to the lane level, more steps lead on from it to another lawn and, when the Loggia arm reaches the rare formality around High Wall itelf, more steps lead down from a grand terrace to lawns and a lost Rose Garden on the Frideswide 19 October axis: level after level, directional change after directional change. Grape vines and, on my visit, autumn-turning creepers were hanging richly from the Loggia, but this is not a flowered garden.

Quoting César Daly's *Hautes Etudes*, Lethaby asked: 'Are there symbols which may be called constant: proper to all races, all societies, and all countries?'[18] To which the answer would be: sunrises, yes, but St Frideswide's Feast Day? High Wall toys with these unities. It was a signpost to the next age when gardens would not follow stylistic fashions but become personal statements by their owners, as Rousham had been: a modern garden two centuries before its time. High Wall spoke for sweetness and light. High Wall was a rare experiment in a county that held longer to traditional formal layouts and was more reluctant to break out and experiment.

If there was ever one garden of eminently successful floral traditionalism with an unparalleled guest list of well-known and influential people, it was Garsington Manor under the control of Lady Ottoline Morrell and her rather more retiring husband, Sir Philip. Set on its hillside at the edge of the little village, the compact, gabled Manor House, sixteenth-century in date with some seventeenth- and eighteenth-century additions, was ideally suited to offer weekend parties to Oxford dons and their visitors. Between 1915 and 1928, the wartime period and post-war Art Deco years of the 'Bright Young Things', Sir Philip and his angular, strikingly handsome wife entertained and probably impressed with their garden styling: Virginia Woolf, Duncan Grant, Clive Bell, D.H. Lawrence (who actually took his coat off and worked on the beds and the hedges), W.B. Yeats, Dora Carrington, Lytton Strachey, T.S. Eliot, E.M. Forster, Aldous Huxley, Katherine Mansfield, Vita Sackville-West, Bertrand Russell and Siegfried Sassoon. The wartime Prime Minister, Asquith, was another guest. If that is not awesome hospitality, what is? Garsington was as traditional in its design as Buscot, though with far more emphasis on flowers and rather less on water. The next owner, Dr Heaton, an Oxford don, was resident from 1928 to 46. Relatives of Mrs Heaton, the Wheeler-Bennetts, who were in residence from 1946 to 82, and after them the opera-promoting, but still keen-gardening, Leonard and Rosalind Ingrams, from 1982 to the present, have kept Garsington alive with social electricity at a time when it was sliding from Edwardian formalism into a flowery professionalism.

Garsington's back garden is a complex of separate garden rooms. The terrace lawn in front of the house was the worse for wear when I visited as it had just accommodated the marquees for the opera festivals.[19] Rosalind Ingrams has cut a gap through the lime grove that hid the view of half of Oxfordshire. A dominant ilex, that shed limbs in mourning when the Morrells left, comes next. Then, from right to left, which is from

73 Like many garden pools in Oxfordshire, that in the Italian Garden at Garsington Manor, designed by Lady Ottoline Morrell after 1915, was used for swimming

west to east, comes successively a wilder leafy area below a natural pond with the springs that feed the ambling water features. Its streamlet threads a tree-shadowed dell down to a pool with a white Chinese Bridge giving on to an island, before trickling down flowery terraces to the garden's finest note, the Italian Garden (*73*) with its large rectangular pool, classical pavilion-boathouse, originally called 'The Temple', yew hedges and weather-worn statues, some sourced locally, others brought from Italy. The pool pretends to be for swimming, but Dora Carrington described it uncharitably as 'a cess-pool of slime'.[20] Lady Ottoline is supposed to have modelled the Garsington layout with its evergreens, the sloping site and the presence of water on her aunt's Villa Capponi outside Florence.[21] Her diary for June 1915 records the progress and intended features: 'We hope in time to terrace the slope down from the house … We have made one terrace and a walk round the pond, and in the autumn we are arranging to plant yew hedges that will grow like a tall, dark wall round the water'.[22]

Working from left to right comes some intricate garden geography. From the Manor's narrow east front a terrace branches out with Sir Philip and the architect Philip Tilden's skilfully arched Loggia, modelled on the south loggia to Cranborne Manor in Dorset. The cost of it almost bankrupted the Morrells. Down from the terrace between towering twin piers – more Morrell constructs – comes Garsington's most sensational garden impact. The Morrells turned the old kitchen garden into a rectangular enclosure of blazing flower colour (*colour plate 19*), but with the flowers confined within 24 box-edged beds enlivened by 96 thin pyramids of Irish yew, corseted with wire for six months each year to preserve their waistlines. Aldous Huxley called it 'a great tank of warmth and perfume and colour … The place was shadeless and one breathed hot, dry perfume instead of air'.[23] Here there are no Italian austerities but a blast of zinnias, dahlias, sunflowers, phlox and delphiniums. Ottoline's favourites were zinnias, red-hot pokers, monbretia and marigolds, all planted together with snapdragons and poppies. Standard fruit trees flanked seats where guests could sit for tea against the brick walls of the enclosure, and a grass path terminating in a statue divides the space into two equal halves.

Below the Flower Garden is a Heaton-designed territory of small flowery terraces leading to a rose-covered 1714 Dovecote, a mulberry of 1930s planting and the croquet and tennis lawn. The late Queen Mother planted the big magnolia for the Wheeler-Bennetts and they brought in John Prior, then 15, to work in the garden; he is still at Garsington today. On the far side of the pool a second yew hedge was planted, creating a dark walk for Ottoline to parade along. D.H. Lawrence helped to plant this and together they would walk there 'in moonlight, reciting Verlaine, or in the afternoons, locked in *tête-à-tête*'.[24] Lawrence was fonder of the aristocracy than he pretended, but then aristocratic gardens are seductive forces. Below the yews is an orchard and then steep fields. Garsington is not a large garden but it is an intense one and it is that Ottoline-inspired intensity of flower colour that distinguishes it from the typical traditional Edwardian layout.

After so much floral effusion it is a distinct change in aesthetic register to turn to Geoffrey Jellicoe's 1936-8 garden at Ditchley Park. This was created for the Americans, Ronald and Nancy Tree. More English than the English, the Trees had required Jellicoe to work within the existing garden framework. Gibbs' great terrace was re-instated and a small Doric Temple down by the lake was rebuilt to stand, concentrating views from the house, at the north-west end of the new terrace, on the edge of a ha-ha on the line of the Grim's Ditch. Despite the constraints, Jellicoe could never be dull and the Sunken Garden he laid out on the old north-west lawn is one of his best. It was inspired, or so he claims, by the Villa Piccolomini at Frascati[25], and perhaps also by the south garden at the Villa Gamberaia with its terminal pool.[26] Whatever the source, Jellicoe contrived a most ingenious paradox: a sunken and enclosed garden room (*74*) that, nevertheless, seems to go on for ever. It is ideal for intimate entertainments as an extension to the house, yet it moves on to a swimming pool that can be screened, temporarily, by raising a curtain of fountain jets.[27] The jets played along the straight edge of the pool, and further jets spouted from lion masks set into the pedestals of urns that were placed along the top semicircular step of the pool. After the pool the vista continues beyond the Doric temple on the ha-ha to a distant horizon in the park.[28] This was real garden design, with flowers playing a very minor role.

A huge bronze bust of Winston Churchill, looking like a Frink but by Angela Conner (1994), presides over the parterre next to the house. Twin knots of box flank the brooding statesman, each centred on a small pool. These were originally cut-work grass parterres like huge curly monograms. The central stone-edged, four-part parterre was brought from the classical garden at Wrest Park when its furnishings were sold off; the parterre was later returned to Wrest and the space laid to lawn. Raised up on a higher level at each side of the central lawn is a miniature allée of ruthlessly pleached lime trees.

74 Geoffrey Jellicoe's Sunken Garden at Ditchley Park once had a parterre bought from the Wrest Park sale and a curtain of water jets fronting its terminal pool, which protected bathers from prying eyes in the house

Each allée concludes in a typical Jellicoe mischief with small, yew-hedged exedras. They are pebble paved and have semicircular stone seats backed by statues from Wrest of naked children frolicking with a dog. The twentieth-century statuary of Ditchley, via Wrest, always set against perfectly trimmed beech or yew hedges, tends to a vaguely suggestive nudity. But then the Trees' famous parties had daring decorations with negroes' heads by Oliver Messel, so the mood of the 1930s gardens reflected that louche decadence. It is interesting to note how, during the 1930s, swimming pools were becoming garden structures of sensuously overstated symbolism, as here, where naked bodies might be viewed from a drawing room window tastefully revealed through a veil of spouting water. Jellicoe's paving on the house side of the pool is exquisitely measured and recessed by rounded pebbles.

In contrast, Jellicoe's reshaping of the terrace at Pusey House is disappointing: just a terrace with Art Deco-style tripod urns. More recently a row of sphinx-like monsters and an open metalwork hound have been added to liven it up. But Jellicoe probably and rightly thought it was such a brilliantly theatrical garden that all it needed was this audience area. The house has quadrant arms fore and aft; the entrance quadrant faces a dull park with elegant horses posing as if for Stubbs; the south-facing garden front gives a visitor everything in one amazing, crowded panorama. Jellicoe also prepared a plan in 1954 for re-ordering the approaches and making a new, axial, tree-lined drive at Bletchingdon Park when the Astors owned the estate, but this was not carried out.[29]

The gardens at Tusmore House, north of Bicester and close to the Northamptonshire border, preceded Jellicoe's Pusey work, dating partly to 1929, and the modern additions to Middleton Park at Middleton Stoney are almost contemporary with it, dating to 1934-8. But these two very private gardens are linked together by their modern garden pavilions. The four at Tusmore by Imrie and Angell are of a harshly angular classicism, overtly twentieth century in feeling.[30] The two at the rear descended geometrically into sunken gardens. The pavilions and their parent house of 1766-79, by Robert Mylne, have been demolished, but an eighteenth-century Temple of Peace survives, rebuilt, at one end of the lake.[31] Middleton's four forecourt pavilions, by Edwin Lutyens for Lord Jersey, are self-effacingly correct and conventionally seventeenth-century French in their classicism, enhancing an unremarkable main house.[32] The angularity and severity of the layout at Tusmore is similar in style to the Water Garden at the south end of the ha-ha terrace at Cornbury Park, which must be contemporary. There, a narrow, stone-edged canal has a blockish fountain like a miniature version of Lutyens' great memorial arch at Tiepval.

To turn from Lutyens' creative work at Middleton Park to the Astors' roughly contemporary reshaping of their garden at Bruern Abbey, south of Chipping Norton, makes the point of how hit-or-miss was the historicism of these early to mid-twentieth-century years. The Astors must have felt trapped into a strictly formal layout by the sheer Baroque severity of their house. One can sense them struggling for a little interest by topping their gatepiers with carved ducks, one of which has caught a frog; and their broad, stone-flagged terrace is attractively unkempt with spurge, marjoram and valerian allowed to flourish in the cracks. But basically what is first seen is all there is: the giant regularity of twelve Irish yews in three sets of four and a rectangular Canal pointing to a goose-foot of avenues cut into the wooded slopes a quarter of a mile away. There are no ingenious groves or garden buildings to explore; there is a boat on the Canal, but no island to visit, only a duo of naked boys lolling back-to-back at the far end to focus the axis.

Cornwell Manor has the most imaginative garden of this early-century cluster and, with at least nine garden enclosures set around the 1750s and earlier house, the richest display. Across the stable yard with its tricked-up Dovecote is an immense, billowing yew hedge and, hidden behind it, yet another swimming pool, virulently tiled and with a trim, four-bay Pavilion. Leading away beyond it is a vast Kitchen Garden with an apple avenue and, in angles of the house itself, a Maid's Garden, a Fiddler's Garden with an eponymous lead statue, a courtyard garden, a Wild Garden and a Ballroom Garden; all essentially Edwardian garden rooms. But what matters at Cornwell is the Corn Well brook and what Clough Williams-Ellis, the genius of Portmeirion, made of it when the American wife of the new owner, Anthony Gillson, brought him in to reshape the village in 1939.[33] Nikolaus Pevsner disliked Clough's work, which from that inveterate Bauhaus fancier is a recommendation. With gables, buttresses and round windows, Clough enlivened virtually every cottage in Cornwell. 'Stagey', 'self-conscious', 'sadly dated', and 'beautifications' were Pevsner and Sherwood's verdicts.[34] Even the air-raid siren got its gable; but with the Corn Well brook canalised to trickle down the green main street under stone slab bridges the impact is bewitchingly arch. The village is an integral part of the garden, but then the stream really gets active around the lawns of the house.

75 Clough Williams-Ellis' archly clever canalisation of the Corn Well brook, carried out after 1939, threads through the village and grounds at Cornwell Manor to end in a wild garden

In the valley below the house the widened brook runs under Clough's grand classical bridge for the drive, falls out of this tunnel down a cascade and then fills a rectangular basin with rounded corners and a central fountain with two dolphins supporting a cherub (75). It then runs into wilder territory down a rock garden. Woods close in and above a bog garden of gloomy gunnera a copper beech and acers make bright splashes of colour. Lastly, as the ground falls away, the brook cascades in a musical waterfall over rocks to feed a long, willow-marshalled pool, as woodland Oxfordshire succeeds the park. When I visited in Spring the gardens billowed with white cherry blossom and white tulips fringed with purple. White hydrangeas climbed the courtyard garden's walls and the Venetian wellhead at its centre had a five-pointed star of clipped yew around it. Only the leaden fiddler, with roses, lilies and lavender in formal box beds struck a conventional note. Fiercely as the privacy of the estate village is guarded, there are generous *clairvoyées* cut from the public lane to the very best vistas of this, the very last of Oxfordshire's inter-war gardens.

Clough and Mrs Gillson made the gardens of Cornwell, but who, Lord Berners or his live-in lover, Robert Heber Percy, made the gardens of Faringdon House and conceived their happily intrusive follies, one of 1935, one of the 1960s? Follies are a mysterious garden phenomenon. What motivated their builders? Now here at Faringdon the spirit of the follies and the motivation behind them seems to be graspable, which makes it not only a most enjoyable garden, but for psychological insights an important one.

The approach is directly from the bucolic textures and crooked street vistas of rough-trade, peasant Faringdon. A short, well-wooded drive leads past the long, low church and a Palladian-style lodge with a recessed arch and an enormous lion head mask on its door. On one of its windows Roy Hobdell painted the image of a fox reading the local *Faringdon Gazette*. That was done for Robert Heber Percy, not for Lord Berners, so it is the first pointer as to who was the insipration behind the follies and the tension between the house and the town so closely tied up against its garden. When the neat, snug manor house comes into view it is easy to understand what a devastating put-down it must have been for Berners when one of his combative chums remarked: 'I suppose this must have been the vicarage'.[35] After all, it does face the church down a wide plane and beech avenue, and it is quite a modest house with its fussy recessed arch like an attempt by Robert Adam to re-interpret the Palladian. John Wood the Younger has been suggested as the architect, but nothing is proven, and Faringdon is more likely to have been designed by John Sanderson.[36] Attractive little pavilions stand at the end of exedral arms, niched with alternate red begonias and white lilies; but a note of defiant perversity dangles over the entrance door: a crystal chandelier clearly intended to light an indoor dining room. Berners hung that whimsicality, not Heber Percy. Down the wide tree avenue stands a noble statue of a crowned goddess, Athene and Greece, or Europe, interpretations vary. Together with its sinister cowled twin – Egypt or Africa – which stands threateningly in the park overlooking a public road (*76*), it was brought from the Crystal Palace Gardens by Heber Percy in 1966. Lord Berners had died in 1950 leaving almost everything: house, estate and investments, to Heber Percy, so there the decorative garden drive was clearly coming from the younger man.

In 1932, the year after he had moved into Faringdon House following the death of his mother in 1931, Berners fell in love with 'the Mad Boy', or 'Madders', as the Mitford girls called him. Robert Heber Percy was 20 years old to Berners' 48; he was a big, hard-riding, handsome lad from a Shropshire county family, the youngest son of four boys. He was inclined to knock things over, to climb over a taxi in order to get into it, and prone to the sort of wild antics that Lord Berners appreciated but could never act out himself. On one occasion he rode naked on his hunter right into the house. On another occasion Heber Percy punched Cecil Beaton on the jaw, knocking him down in the street for an insult. He was bisexual, twice married with a child. Berners played a vague grandfatherly role to this menage and left everything in his will to Heber Percy except for £2,000 to William Crack, his violet-eyed 'Adonis' of a chauffeur. So is a certain sexual apartness another element of the folly drive, an expression of defiant difference from society?

Berners had begun talking of building a folly tower in the middle of that grove of pine and beech on the hill above the town from about 1933. Local opposition was strong, which appealed to Berners' sense of humour. As he said, 'The great point of the Tower is that it will be entirely useless'.[37] Lord Gerald Wellesley, later 7th Duke of Wellington, was his architect and he was constructing a very dull, square brick erection until Berners returned from France and insisted on a Gothic top (*colour plate 20*). Wooden stairs lead up to two viewing rooms and a platform. Berners' notice at the foot of the stairs reads: 'Members of the Public committing suicide from this tower do so at their

76 A refugee from the Crystal Palace Gardens at Sydenham – Robert Heber Percy's 1966 purchase, representing Egypt or Africa, stands in brooding isolation in the park at Faringdon House

own risk'.[38] Another notice in the park read: 'Trespassers will be prosecuted, dogs shot, cats whipped'.[39] Berners kept a dachshund with a pearl necklace; Heber Percy had a retriever, no necklace.

The two men represented a perfect attraction of opposites. Lord Berners was a fastidious composer of frail, airy ballet music; he was notably undistinguished in looks, and bald with a small moustache. He had inherited Faringdon in 1918, and was possessed of a sharp wit and known as a confirmed bachelor, that is, homosexual. Picasso, Diaghilev, Cocteau and Gide were among his foreign acquaintance and he lured to Faringdon English friends such as the Sitwells, Rex Whistler, Cecil Beaton, Siegfried Sassoon, Harold Nicholson, Evelyn Waugh and the Betjemans, all drawn by the excellent food he offered at weekend parties and by his dry, often cruel, wit. He claimed, for instance, that one heavily made-up lady friend had caused a visiting admiral to reconsider his whole programme for camouflaging the Mediterranean fleet. Is such malicious apartness one element of the folly building drive?

On its bland garden face Faringdon House looks out across a honeysuckle-smothered terrace to a vast, undramatic view of the level half of Oxfordshire, yet the landscape is only the merest backcloth to Dionysus (*colour plate 21*), a naked young boy holding a shell that sprays water. Sculpted in 1991 for Sofia Zinovieff by Nicholas Dimbleby as a memorial to her grandfather Heber Percy, he stands there, muscular in a Donatelline fashion and overtly sexual, poised in the middle of a small, round pool and flaunting his beauty to the windows of the house. At the corners of the lawn are ambos of balustrading. Down in the woods to the left the lake, enlarged from a fishpond by William Hallett in the 1820s, shows up with a three-arched bridge and a boathouse. Because one arm of the lake has silted up, the bridge crosses a weedy marsh, so a pond has been created on its house side in order to give a Stourhead impression. This fails. Hallett bought Faringdon after the death in 1813 of its builder, Henry Jones Pye, who was possibly England's limpest Poet Laureate.

The real folly treasure of Faringdon has been reserved for the end of this account because it was the latest of the garden's several exercises in the genre and it was certainly Heber Percy's inspired creation. It owed nothing to Berners' wit, but everything to Heber Percy's bisexual flamboyance and confidence, a true late twentieth-century folly, yet entirely historicist in its Gothick and heraldic forms. It lies behind the Edwardian shrubbery to the left of the entrance drive and it literally hangs over, not just the Kitchen Garden, but also many of the red-tiled roofs of the market town. A path through the hollies and laurels leads into a clearing in front of the Halletts' plain but handsome golden stone Orangery. In the centre of the clearing is a circular pool where the bust of General Havelock in full military uniform stands with delicious absurdity, veiled partly by reeds and lilies. This sector of the grounds was not cleared out until the 1960s, so the General seems to have been Heber Percy's invention. Does he perhaps count as a folly?

On either side of the pool semicircular Pompeian stone benches set a scene as if for one of Alma-Tadema's frolicsome Roman revelries. The Orangery is a most civilised room, stuffed with semi-tropical plants in pots, pelargoniums, pandanus and thin bamboos. Anyone sitting there faces out across General Havelock to a solemn flight of 22 steps which climb a ziggurat mount and are lined with low clipped yew. This is Heber Percy's gloriously overt gesture to nudity, raised up defiantly in the very eye of Heaven, for at the top of the steps is a deep, square swimming pool (*77*), presided over on its further edge by two enormous stone wyverns. Berners had always claimed that swimming pools were the height of vulgarity.[40] To complete the Gothicity there is, on the left of the pool, a round, embattled Gothick tower to serve as a changing room with coloured glass in its arrow-slit windows. Its floor is entirely covered with inset concentric circles of pre-decimalisation pennies. It is not easy to convey the surprise element of this tower-pool. It commands a wide view of Faringdon, and beyond the wyverns is a sheer drop to the garden service areas.

So who really decided on a Gothic crown for Berners' Folly Tower? Was it Berners or Heber Percy? Water is at the essence of most gardens, but it is hard to think of any genius who has ever used it with such challenging imagination. It will remain one of my treasured Oxfordshire garden memories, alongside those watery caves at Friar Park,

77 Lord Berners thought that swimming pools were vulgar, but his live-in lover, Robert Heber Percy's riposte was to create, after Berner's death, the most astonishing pool in the country with its stone wyverns and Gothick changing tower

and I will forever regret not using that changing room tower and diving into the clear deep water to try it out. Heber Percy and Berners complemented each other, but the true genius behind the folly building was the poetic Heber Percy, not the wry, nervously critical Berners. In Heber Percy's life we have defining clues as to what makes a folly builder: a confident outsider, half poet, half bruiser. Lastly we have the celebrated white fan-tailed doves of Faringdon, the birds that so delighted the Mitford girls, Nancy and Diana, on their visits. They too were Heber Percy's creation. He tracked down a harmless Indian vegetable dye and so they flew, emerald green, cochineal pink and Wedgwood blue, about the house in an inspired gesture of high campery. On my visit just one of that flock survived, half pink, but still wholly enchanting.

NOTES

1 See back cover of this book. It is also reproduced in John Harris, *The Artist and the Country House*, 1979, plate 139, and in the current guide to the house and park.

2 See Sam Smiles, *The Image of Antiquity: Ancient Britain and the Romantic Imagination* (New Haven & London), 1994. There are statues of Druids at Erddig Park in North Wales, Shugborough in Staffordshire and Croome Park, Wiltshire.

3 For Buscot see two *Country Life* articles: 21 October 1916 and 18 May 1940, the latter by Christopher Hussey; see also the excellent National Trust guidebook, *Buscot Park & The Faringdon Collection*, published for the Trustees of the Faringdon Collection, 2004.

4   The west pavilion was for servants, that to the east housed a squash court and a miniature theatre.

5   Hastings, then Lord Huntingdon, studied under Diego Rivera.

6   These seats are discussed by Whalley, *Garden History*, 33, no.2 (Autumn, 2005), pp.256-73.

7   Internally, of course, it has the somnolently beautiful Briar Rose series by Burne Jones of 1890 and some rare Egyptian-style Regency furniture by Thomas Hope.

8   Created in the 1860s by Robert Campbell for his industrial farm.

9   This dates from the 1860s and was moved here from the eastern pleasure grounds.

10 W.R. Lethaby, *Architecture Mysticism and Myth*, 1891 (Architectural Press facsimile edition, 1974), p.8.

11 Ibid.

12 Ibid.

13 See Lawrence Weaver, 'High Wall, Oxford', *Country Life*, 10 & 17 November 1917. The articles appear in the 'Lesser Country Houses of To-Day' section appended to the main magazine. I am indebted to Arpad Turmezei, son-in-law of the owners, Brian and Reinhild Lloyd, for his observations on the symbolic planning of the house. Cave also designed Ewelme Down in Oxfordshire where there are similar balustraded terraces and semicircular steps. I was not allowed access to Ewelme.

14 Quoted by Godfrey Rubens in his introduction to *Architecture Mysticism and Myth*, p.xviii.

15 The 'F' in Feilden is carved oddly to approximate the symbol for Pi. Further initials on the rainwater heads are in ordinary lettering.

16 A full account of these axial orientations and mathematical synergies awaits publication and will not, therefore, be expanded upon here.

17 Percy Cane, *Modern Gardens, British and Foreign*, 1927, pp.26-8.

18 Ibid., p.7.

19 This year's festival was a sad occasion as it was the last to be devised by Leonard Ingrams before his death in July 2005. I am most gratreful to his wife, Rosalind, for her kindness on my visit to Garsington.

20 Deborah Kellaway, 'Pugs, Peacocks and Pekinese: The Garden at Garsington Manor', *Hortus*, no.25 (Spring, 1993), pp.15-28; p.19.

21 Ibid., p.17.

22 Ibid.

23 Ibid., p.22; quoted from Huxley's *Antic Hay*.

24 Ibid., p.19.

25 Geoffrey Jellicoe, 'Ronald Tree and the Gardens of Ditchley Park: The Human Face of History', *Garden History*, vol.10, no.1 (Spring,1982), pp.80-91. See also Michael Spens, *Gardens of the Mind: The Genius of Geoffrey Jellicoe*, 1992, pp.56-60.

26 Spens, *Gardens of the Mind*, p.56, plate on p.58.

27 This effect is shown in a 1936 *Country Life* illustration reproduced in Spens, *Gardens of the Mind*, p.59, and also in Jellicoe's *Garden History* article, figure 5. The central parterre, which is now laid to lawn, is also illustrated by Jellicoe, figure 4.

28 There was originally a low yew hedge on the ha-ha, but this was subsequently removed. Jellicoe records that this was the source of the only disagreement he had with his clients.

29 The plan survives at Bletchingdon. I am grateful to Michael Peagram for showing me this and other maps of the estate.

30 See Arthur Oswald, 'Tusmore – I, Oxfordshire', *Country Life*, 30 July 1938.

31 I was not allowed access to the site, but should like to thank Sarah Frost for her help and advice.

32 See Christopher Hussey, 'Middleton Park, Oxfordshire I & II', *Country Life*, 5 & 12, July 1946.

33 See Christopher Hussey, 'Cornwell Manor, Oxfordshire I & II', *Country Life*, 24 & 31 May 1941; also George Plumptre, 'Fitting it all in', *Country Life*, 7 July 1988.

34 Sherwood & Pevsner, *Oxfordshire*, p.557.

35   For a richly entrertaining account of Berners' life see Mark Amory, *Lord Berners: The Last Eccentric*, 1998.

36   See Gervase Jackson-Stops, *Country Life*, 23 December 1976, where he also attributes Pusey House to Sanderson, who died in 1774.

37   Amory, *Lord Berners*, p.149.

38   Ibid., p.150.

39   Ibid., pp.137-8.

40   Of the two *Country Life* articles on Faringdon, Mark Girouard's is faintly disapproving. He shared Sacheverell Sitwell's view that Berners' Faringdon was 'like a perpetual April Fool's Day'; Tony Venison's account is warm and positive.

10

FEY SCULPTURE AND TENTATIVE EXPERIMENT IN THE LATER TWENTIETH CENTURY

To suggest that the majority of twentieth-century gardens of a whole county were cautious and conservative is perhaps a dangerous generalisation. But the point of this series is that each English county is a miniature horticultural kingdom with a distinctive life and pattern of its own. Both Dorest and Wiltshire inclined in the modern period to garden experiments: heads by Elisabeth Frink, bronze-twisted into aggressive sexual shapes, even an entire tribe of prehistoric men sculptued in life-like metal. But genteel Oxfordshire inclined to the figurative fey, as in Raymond Blanc's Manoir aux Quat' Saisons. Robert Heber Percy's garden pool at Faringdon House was sited daringly, but with those wyverns and Gothick changing room tower its forms were safely historicist and conservative.

Most moves towards a full-bloodied modernism in any county usually begin with abstract sculpture. Inspired by the Berners Folly Tower, The Vale of White Horse District Council has recently turned the southern slopes of Jasper's Hill into 'Folly Park', a pleasant country park leading up, past solid wooden picnic tables and a fishing pond, to the Tower; so far, so traditonal. But then the Arts Department of the Council commissioned in 2005 a group of four cement-clad resin shapes, abstract in style (78), from Michie Herbert, a local artist, and set them up in the park. The menhirs are entitled 'As Old As The Hills' and are based on wind-eroded megaliths, responding to the prehistoric associations of the Vale, which the group overlooks. The sculpture is set in a circle of Cotswold stone paving and benches surrounded by carved inscriptions like 'Hope Conversation Family Laughter' and 'Beyond sky and clouds undulating tender solitude'. When I visited the Park I found that one of the standing menhirs had been brutally shattered, leaving a hollow shell, and some of the engraved stones had been smashed. Abstract sculpture is still seen as provocative and is, therefore, unsafe, whereas figurative statues can usually stand unharmed by paint or axe. It was saddening to see what a town as outwardly idyllic as Faringdon had suffered when it presented its wilder element with an aesthetic challenge. I hope that Faringdon can move on and that Michie Herbert can feel that she has been part of a battle worth winning.

Not that the well-heeled of Oxfordshire are averse to garden sculpture. While it is unsurprising that a lavish nursery garden like that at Waterperry should have a wide influence, pressing the case for flowers, it is remarkable that a restaurant should have set

78 Michie Herbert's 'As Old As The Hills' group of menhirs, inspired by the prehistoric associations of the Vale of the White Horse, was set up in Folly Park, Faringdon in 2005

the mood for seductive wit in garden bronze. The first indication of the atmosphere of high-spirited frivolity which infuses Raymond Blanc's gardens will come in the visitor's car-park. Towering above the attractive shrubbery on its island roundabout is a group of much larger-than-life bronze artichokes. The great metal flowers rear up against the sky, warning those intent upon merely feasting in the celebrated restaurant that this is primarily a garden with a restaurant attached, a notably characterful garden, possibly even a great garden in a style of modern eclecticism, but never a deeply serious garden.

Walking in alongside the Croquet Lawn with a cluster on the left of vaguely French round towers, conically capped, there is another warning to the right where a bronze gardener crouching permanently at work on the flower border turns out, on closer inspection, to be a young cricket wicketkeeper. An eighteenth-century Rococo Arcadian garden, like Rousham in the north of the county, will present classical statues of nude young men and women, satyrs, the rural god Pan. Here at Great Milton, in Raymond Blanc's stimulating entertainment for the anticipatory or replete diners at his tables, the bronze statues by Lloyd le Blanc and Judith Holmes Drewry are mostly studies of modern young women (*colour plate 22*) in various stages of dress or undress with a scattering of bronze birds as a leavening. In that sense this is a truly modern garden with no classical hangovers. There are rich eclectic elements – Japanese and Malaysian, not Greek, Roman or Gothic – but the real heart of the garden circuit is Le Potager, no ordinary kitchen garden, but a formidable ranking of exotic vegetables crisply waiting to be arranged in subtle salads, a place where an exedra of banana plants confronts an army of red chard.

Everything in these grounds is so successful, whether it is the Cloche Tunnels, Herb Garden or cloistered courts for overnight guests, that it is some relief to notice a rare flaw. The 1995 Japanese Tea Garden claims to be a fusion of Buddhist, Taoist and Shinto influences, a sixteenth-century Chaniwa or Roji, a Dewy Path Tea Garden, but it has strong English influences. Mature oak trees exert a decisive presence and the monumental rocks have a water-worn smoothness more Cornish than sharply Japanese. Flower colours are out, everything is green upon green, with not an azalea in sight, and the feeling consequently is English, though the Tea House (79) itself is entirely authentic with four tatomi mats on my count. There are Viewing Stones at appropriate points and the pace of the garden is, by its stepping-stones, slow and deep. But the pools are gently stagnating: they are brown and muddy coloured when with recycling they should and could be clear or mysteriously dark. Japanese waters should reflect light, not hint at the farmyard.

After this Sabi and Yugen (rustic transcendent detachment) Le Potager is splendidly down-to-earth and a wonderful blowsy woman, all bronze, with a wide-brimmed hat and a basket of produce presides at one end while a bronze scarecrow holds court in the middle. The statuary is a constant and delightful distraction from the plants. In the Herb Garden next to this area four tall bay bushes each shelter a woman – perhaps representative of the four stages of womanhood – in contemporary dress and nudity (80), making it difficult to concentrate on the herbs. At every point young gardeners are at work, always smiling and helpful, ready to open a gate or explain a strange plant. The Manoir must be a valuable source of employment in the area and an education for its employees. Raymond Blanc is doing us a real service in demonstrating how easy it is to grow apparent tropical exotics like lemon grass and ginger in our mild climate.

I did not eat at the restaurant that is a treat for the affluent but it was apparent, walking the grounds, how perfectly these incident-packed areas complement the pleasure of those who dine there. It is hard to walk more than ten steps before being confronted with either a horticultural or a sculptural surprise, like the trademark giant pestle-and-mortar set on a wall and framed by fragrant lavender in the main axis from the car-park to the Manoir. On the way out there was still one more sheltered courtyard with a bronze peacock caught in the spray of a fountain. Thinking the visit over, it was interesting that not a single one of many visual memories related strongly to flowers. The grounds of the Manoir are essentially hard, so their landscape and ornamental features are likely to last as long as the best Tudor gardens. M. Blanc could teach us as much about successful gardening as about inspired cuisine.

A more orthodox influence on garden design, not just in Oxfordshire, but over the whole country, has been Brenda Colvin, the apostle of the suburban garden with ease of upkeep. She appears in the county at Sutton Courtenay Manor where David Astor, who bought the house in 1945, despaired of tending the multiple topiary spires and flowery borders that he had inherited from Norah Lindsay's Long and Persian Gardens.[1] Lindsay wrote evocatively of the garden that Colvin and Astor were to simplify:

> The tremendous solemn trees, the smooth green lawns which one remembers holding long evening shadows on their laps, the beguiling wild flowers which give and give, rushing in and out of the real garden with a reckless joy and a dancing grace.[2]

79 Raymond Blanc's
authentic, four-tatomi mat
Japanese Tea House for
replete diners in the garden
of his restaurant at the
Manoir aux Quat' Saisons

David Astor was the son of one of Norah's friends, Nancy Astor, and had often helped Norah at weekends when he was up at Balliol. Therefore he knew the garden well, but realised that he needed professional help. He brought in Brenda Colvin in 1948 to advise on clean lines and tree patterns along the riverbanks.

Colvin replaced the former gravel forecourt to the south-east of the Manor with a paved terrace edged by curved hedges of lavender, its clean lines running out towards the informal garden beyond. The Long Garden had been swept away before she arrived so she kept the space open with a fine lawn, and the Persian Garden was redesigned, to reduce its long and narrow proportions, with box-hedged beds filled with lavender. To set off the open vistas Colvin planted 'lengths of dense and bosky shade where thickets of bamboo and *Cornus siberica alba*, growing under willows and poplars emphasise the contrast of light and shadow'.[3] Her 'intention of seeking to 'unite the old and the new' in her treatment of the whole garden was and remains successful. The more formal areas

80 Judith Homes Drewry's gently erotic sculpture distracts attention from the plants in Raymond Blanc's Herb Garden at the Manoir

close to the house retained a degree of their former exuberance in planting yet suited the new owner's need for lower maintenance'.[4]

It is always interesting to beard a garden designer in his or her own garden to see where their taste in design really runs. Colvin's 1947 *Land and Landscape* was intended as her personal testament to what works and does not work when gardens are being created, urban environments re-adjusted or natural landscapes assessed. Her own house at Little Peacocks, Filkins, on the Gloucestershire border, remains the base for her firm of garden and landscape designers. They look after the garden, carrying on more or less in her tradition, tending the layout which she created around the house to keep it in the spirit in which it was left and as Colvin described it in an undated *Countryman* article written somewhere between 1955, when her house is mentioned, and 1965 when her new office, which does not feature in the article, was built.[5] At that time she was still experimenting with colour planting and using the Little Peacocks garden as her laboratory. 'My aim', she wrote, 'is eventually to make a labour-saving garden, its progress in that direction may be of interest to others who, like myself, have more enthusiasm than time at their disposal'. So she had the average middle class suburban gardener in her sights and was moving shrewdly in upon a promising market.

The garden is modest in size, no more than half an acre. The front garden to the Cotswold classical vernacular house is narrow and conventional with a thin show of flowers, two large clipped yews and a low stone wall. Unconventionally the Kitchen Garden lies next to it across the drive at the front of the house, creating an earthy cottagey impact even though it is half-concealed within its own stone-walled enclosure. Curiously Colvin never attempts to excuse its siting, but it is recorded on the plan of the grounds (*81*) in her article about the garden. All the rest of the garden flows around a large horse chestnut at the back, bouncing off the walls of the cottages that hem it in next door. That figures. Colvin liked the world around her; she writes analytically, but rarely critically: an environment is to be enjoyed, not concealed. Her garden does, however, create surprises. She had made changes in what had originally been an old farmyard on hard core to open up sight lines and to increase the sense of space and movement within the boundaries. It flows in a series of garden rooms, all shadowed by that horse chestnut and shaped at every turn by lesser overhanging trees and bushes. There are lilies and she was fond of the scruffy *rubrifolia* roses: 'Pride of place goes to *lilium regale*, generously planted where its pink buds are seen with the rose at that wonderful moment when the expanding foliage gives a haze of bluish grey-green so inadequately described as *rubrifolia*'. This is clear evidence that, for all her concentration upon labour-saving bushes, Colvin was sensitively aware of flower colours as well as leaves. The impression is, however, not one of flowers, but of shrubs, underplanted with good ground-cover and these elbow visitors from one garden room to another. She allows no straight lines, only rounded outlines.

From her article we can sense Colvin's delight in interconnected spaces, yet there are none of the hard landscaping features present in her other commissions, particularly the stone edging to the borders at Sutton Courtenay Manor. At Little Peacocks her intention seems to have been to blur the edges and keep the foliage visually on the move. One connecting tunnel of shade, in a passage between a stone outhouse and overhanging branches, leads from the casual main lawn, bordered by fig trees, apple trees, philyrea and rue, to a walled enclosure with a wooden table. In Colvin's 1955 article this is called the 'paved sitting-out place'. Next to it was originally the Bee Garden where she kept hives, but this is now given over to compost and is walled by the next-door cottage. Being able to create garden incidents unpretentiously and with minimal upkeep in a limited space accounts for her popularity. She relied heavily on hellebores of the *orientalis* hybrids for ground cover. Other designers like John Brookes, who worked for Colvin in the 1950s and early 1960s, learnt the idea of the outdoor room from her, and began to advocate such solutions for medium and small areas. Colvin seems to have developed the perfect template for the suburban garden.

With Colvin's sensitive handling of shades of green and silhouettes of leaf the wild garden, another area of relatively easy upkeep, was infiltrating garden forms. Oxfordshire has its own centrally-sited wild garden, the Jarn Mound and Wild Garden of British Plants, up on Boars Hill. This was raised, 50ft high, like a burial mound for a Saxon

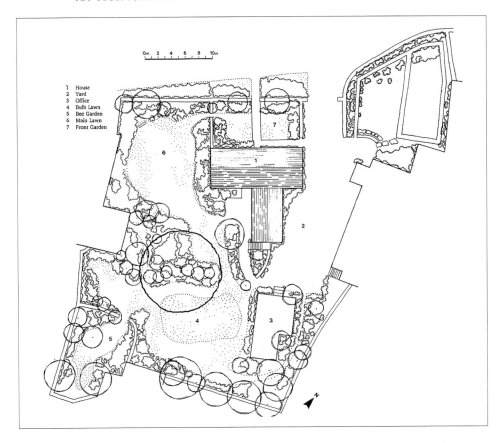

0m 2 4 6 8 10m

1 House
2 Yard
3 Office
4 Bulb Lawn
5 Bee Garden
6 Main Lawn
7 Front Garden

81 Brenda Colvin's plan of her own layout at Little Peacocks, Filkins illustrates, better than photographs of the garden, her aim of making garden areas flow effortlessly into one another

king, between 1929 and 1933, in response to an early conservationist appeal by the archaeologist, Sir Arthur Evans, to protect the area where he had built a large house, Youlbury, from suburbanisation. Sir Arthur hoped for 'a mound, in a plot set apart for it, that would open out a view, much more comprehensive than any yet attainable, over the whole surrounding country'[6], to preserve, in fact, the famous view that Turner had painted of Oxford's dreaming spires. He intended that, 'overcome with gorse and heather it might, in time, almost become a part of Nature'.[7] He believed that the site had strong spiritual associations because of Matthew Arnold's poem, *The Scholar-Gipsy*.

After a collapse of its clay base the Mound was constructed of local greensand, a concrete flight of steps was built and an indication plate of engraved copper covered by a sheet of glass was set up on top, recording the various topographical features that could be seen around it. The Wild Garden at its base was to be 'a kind of naturalistic Botanic Garden … representative of the flora from all parts of the British Islands'.[8] This was laid out between 1931 and 1933 to include chalk areas, woodlands, rocky sections, a bog garden and a pool. Native species planted included those flowers mentioned by name in Arnold's poems, *Thyrsis* and *The Scholar-Gipsy* and plants from the more temperate parts of the British Isles: Dorset, Cornwall and Killarney. 'Alternating patches of snowdrops and primroses, bluebells and the rarer grape hyacinths, foxgloves, cornflowers and poppies were set along the paths and thickets formed from the principal kinds of British roses, while Guelder Rose was introduced from neighbouring woods. In its formative period, the garden attracted the support of the University's Botanic Garden, with the Superintendent W.G. Baker supplying a number of wild species'.[9] Little remains of this early idealism for things natural. Trees have grown up to obscure most of the features indicated on the information plate. The plate itself, like Michie Herbert's menhirs at Faringdon's Folly Park, has been frequently vandalised, and bracken has taken over most of the Wild Garden. But it was the germ of an idea which would become popular: a self-deception that can only be maintained by very careful planting and nurture, but an approach to gardening that was not far removed from Brenda Colvin's handling of bushes and trees.

While Colvin's contrived simplicities were making some way in the 1930s, the Second World War, with all its upheavals and ruin, seems to have introduced another wave of nostalgia for the past and for a conservative revival. Greys Court has an interesting garden which reflects the taste of the British upper classes in the post-Second World War years, but it is not a notably beautiful or successful garden, more a group of disconnected garden rooms of varying charm jumbled together in the spaces around an ugly square tower. The aesthetic merits of the five principal gardens at Greys: Kitchen, Commonwealth, Rose, White and Cherry, are minor and they lie against a large, semi-vacant area of grass and a few good trees enclosed within its ha-ha. Consequently there is no strong feeling of togetherness or much of sequence. What will become more valuable about the Greys Court gardens, after some passage of time, will be their collection of artistic furnishings: benches, fountains, wood carvings and ironwork, as representative of those stylistically aimless years between 1937, when Sir Felix Brunner, who made his money in chemicals, bought it, and 2003, when Lady Brunner died.[10]

Nothing expresses the mood, the whimsicality and the hopeful high-mindedness of that period better than the Maze. Archbishop Robert Runcie in his enthronement sermon at Canterbury on 25 March 1980 had expressed a vague longing that Christians and non-Christians would help each other to reach the rewarding centre point of 'the maze of life'.[11] Lady Brunner, who had been an actress before her marriage, promptly decided to create a brick and grass 'maze of life' near the visitors' car-park, and persuaded Dr Runcie to bless and open it, wearing episcopal purple. There is something of a delayed action Arts & Crafts feeling about every addition that Lady Brunner made to the grounds. A minor, but known and approved, artist had to have designed it, which is why the garden might well gain in respect as it ages, but then again it might not; commissioning artists is always a brave gamble, though one the Brunners were always ready to take. Alec Peever carved the inscribed stone in the Cherry garden; John Hill, a smith living in an estate cottage, created the trellis that marked the Brunners' Golden Wedding in 1976; Andrew Shelton designed the Arbour and Seat to celebrate Lady Brunner's ninetieth birthday in 1984; Michael Harvey, who had worked in close association with Ian Hamilton Finlay on the lettering of Finlay's garden at Little Sparta,

82 Jacqueline Geldart's 1988 yew statue of Charles Taylor, the Head Gardener at Greys Court, expresses the homely atmosphere of the Brunners' garden complex

lettered another inscription, and Philip Jebb designed the plinth for the one undoubted masterpiece in all the list of commissions. This is the wooden, 1988 English yew statue of the Head Gardener, Charles Taylor (*82*) which broods over a spade at the end of one axial walk in the Kitchen Garden. With a wooden robin perched on his wooden shoulder and a quotation from that most acceptably 1920s poet, Walter de la Mare, carved into it, Jacqueline Geldart's statue perfectly expresses the homely safeness and sentimentality of the patrons and their 'Georgian' era background: de la Mare, not T.S. Eliot or Auden.

Two questions have to be asked: what was the result of all this patronage and advice, and what were the Brunners aiming at? When Sir Felix and Lady Elizabeth bought Greys Court in 1937 and moved in with their four sons and one adopted daughter, they believed that 'Places like this have got to be shared'.[12] Lady Brunner insisted that the

Greys ticket office should be painted scarlet and look welcoming. She decreed that on open days for the Court neither cauliflowers nor fish should be cooked because they create unwelcoming smells. She made a point herself on such days of making jam, for obvious reasons. Sir Felix, a patron of the Open Spaces Society[13], laid out a 'Gentle Walk' around the Court and, like William Shenstone in the eighteenth century at his The Leasowes[14], openly celebrated his own personal affections by dedicating each gate and stile along its route to one of his children, to daughters-in-law and 'Good Companions' (a very J.B. Priestley gesture). So there are 'Johnnie's Gate', 'Dan's Gate', 'Hugo's Gate', and, as a climax, 'The Gate of the Adopted Daughter', which is a Moon Gate designed by Francis Pollen to cross the ha-ha. Family nicknames are carved on them in a warm openness; and they add to that quality of movement and performance which the Brunners saw as an important educational aspect to a garden.

So what is there to share? Lady Brunner and her two male mentors went, not for history, the ugliness of the Tower must have been off-putting, but for horticultural beauty: the Sissinghurst experience as demonstrated by the Nicolsons at their garden in Kent. Paths and walks in the rough multicolour of flint, staring white chalk and warm brick create some connections. Humphrey Waterfield's 1947 Cherry Garden, asymmetrically planted, stone flagged and set with round topiary balls is one strong link. The Wisteria Tunnel is another. Behind the Bachelor's Hall and around the Commonwealth Building the garden rooms do hold together. Neither the Rose Garden nor the White Garden are remarkable, but against those rough, colourful walls the wisteria and the cherry trees create some feeling of unity. The so-called Commonwealth Garden, pent in by buildings, is in no way Commonwealth in style, but authentically Tudor with its box parterre and warmly textured paths of brick and flint. Roses had failed to flourish in this limited environment and on the thin chalk soil; the new planting is a great success, possibly the most memorable in the grounds.

On occasions in a twentieth-century garden the wild and the Rococo-style eclectic can co-exist. At Prue Leith's Chastleton Glebe, a Tudor-style Edwardian house of dark golden stone, nothing in the grounds is conventional. A vast Kitchen Garden with a most generous potager, initially laid out to service her restaurants, fronts the house and, far from being concealed, it is focused on the view through a crisply chiselled opening in the garden wall. To the side of the house a hellebore Mount is topped by the statue of a working lad taking a break from his chores, while a bronze boy wearing just a skimpy loincloth tries to extract a thorn from his foot in the centre of a lawn flanked by flowery borders and a rose and clematis pergola. The Glebe's main garden attraction lies on the far, south-western side of the house, beyond a deep ha-ha. A long sloping hay field alive with cowslips and green winged orchids, a true Wild Garden, though clearly marked by the ridges and furrows of a medieval field system, ends improbably on the shores of a lake inspired by a willow pattern plate. The trees on its far side are silvery willows and silver pears, the Chinese Bridge to its island is brilliantly scarlet and a large flock of geese have turned the actual waters a murky khaki green. A brightly-painted Chinese Pavilion on the island is guarded by rust-coloured lions. The complex makes no effort either to surprise, as would a real Rococo-style Chinoiserie incident, or to fit in with the garden as a whole, but the contrast between that very English meadow and the Chinese island is oddly memorable.

The equally open grounds of Chiselhampton House, close to Nuneham Courtenay, are also a surprise, but for a different reason. I was privileged there to experience a Capability Brown-style reshaping actually in progress: a whole parkland being stripped bare of turf and ambitiously re-contoured as a setting for a vastly improved lake.[15] Everything was brown earth with tractors and movers. The house, designed by a London builder, Samuel Dowbiggin, stands brashly, high up above the park.[16] Built in 1766-8, it is smartly distinguished by having, instead of a gate lodge, a handsome 1763 chapel-like Georgian parish church as the sentinel at its gate, from which a short drive sweeps briskly up to a brick façade with a Regency Ionic porch. The large boulder sculpture, suggestive of a crouching bull or bear, that stands to the right of the porch was the first indication of modern patronage. It is by Bridget McCrum, a fortieth birthday present from Sally Rowlands to her husband who works in the City of London. On the south side of the house Dowbiggin added two canted bays for the enjoyment of the wide, rather dull prospect, much in need of landscape enlivening, which is what the park is now getting. Prominent in the middle distance are the shining waters of a new lake with a penninsula of land jetting into it and crying out for a Claude Lorrain-style temple to focus the eye.[17] What is so valuable in being able to experience the first stages of a watery dramatisation is the realisation that mature trees are desperately needed on the farther shores of the lake to frame the vista.

The battered and broken walls of the old Kitchen Garden down by the new lake survive neglected, but used for pony exercising and jumping, and a piece of tortured modern aluminium sculpture by Austin Wright stands assertively by the drive, the twenty-first-century equivalent of a garden urn for punctuation. Trees begin to close in as the circuit drive climbs back towards the house, and there are relics of a half-lost chain of ponds and canals. Then a clean, stone-paved contemporary garden on a Regency site takes over to support the lofty façade of the villa. This enclosure concentrates dramatically on a white-painted iron and glass Vinery of 1790, meticulously renovated, its dome rising bubble-like above its skeletal form. Yet another big blue swimming pool fronts it, and whatever is not covered by pale cream paving stones is densely planted with billowing beds of flowery herbs with an urn or two added for distraction when modern sculpture would have been more interesting. This may be remedied soon as one of the major pieces in the 'on form o6' sculpture show at Asthall Manor, 'Leaning Orator' by Paul Vanstone, was awaiting placement on my visit.

The biennial show at Asthall is hosted by Rosie Pearson, who throws a month-long garden party for modern stone sculpture in the grounds of the Manor, a seductively picturesque house of 1620, built by Sir William Jones, a Welsh lawyer made good, in a style more Elizabethan-conservative than the Jacobean of its date. It is set low among the willows of the Windrush water meadows near Burford, though the land rises steeply behind it, and Asthall is yet another of those twentieth-century gardens with old bones. Between 1919 and 1926 it was the home of the 2nd Lord Redesdale, father of the formidable Mitford girls: Nancy, Pamela, Diana, Unity, Decca and Debo. The girls loved the place and hated leaving it for their father's new house at nearby Swinbrook. Asthall was where their Hons Society had its Hons Cupboard for meetings. In their time the house was actively haunted, by footsteps on the paving stones of the terrace and by the drip of non-existent water.[18]

Its cheerful gardens still feel faintly haunted by their boisterous presence, though the Bannermans, Isabel and Julian, have since transformed the planting, notably the terracing behind the house with its tight, low criss-cross of clipped box hedges. On my visit to view the 2006 sculpture exhibition this area was backed, on the grass terrace above, by a huge translucent disk of chalcedony quartz, crafted by Emily Young (*colour plate 23*).

Anyone with any doubts about modern abstract sculpture should visit next June-July 2008 to experience the amazing mutual flattery of stone and flowers. In June 2006 the sculpture contrasted with and complemented the courageous vulgarity of the Bannermans' 1998 planting. A gateway with bulbous modern finials to the gatepiers leads driectly in from the lane to a stone-walled enclosed, chestnut tree-shadowed space, enlivened by blue flowers. This afforded a pause before the shape and colour storm of the Church Terrace. An 8ft spike, Luke Dickinson's 'Summi Lust', looking more belemnite than phallus, jostled for attention with the mulleins. With fellow, eye-catching silver thistles and parsley the mulleins towered above an herbaceous blaze of phlox and the polished swirls of grey, silvery and golden limestone. In the back garden six male faces stared hypnotically out of rough stone blocks, all by women sculptors. There was a tug of war going on in the garden. Male sculptors like Dominic Welch and Anthony Turner extracted abstract forms from their stone, while women sculptors, particularly Emily Young and Emma Maiden, pulled evocative figurative parts, limbs and enigmatic heads of men, from their material. Jon Edgar straddled the two approaches, coaxing his stone into semi-figurative forms of brooding power, as in his 'Wight Man' and 'Arch' (*83*).

Then come three whirpools of Wild Garden colour, bordering an entirely plain lawned area. The Bannermans have crammed in marguerites, poppies and corn marigolds. As if the flowers had obliged the stones to compete, Richard Aumonier's multi-coloured granite and marble slices were bonded with resin and punctuate this area. Here the paths are only trails cut through tall hay, merging into the water meadows. Up on the hill behind the Manor there is a darker garden with mature trees, and a smooth green earthwork, a mini version of the Jenks' Garden of Cosmic Speculation, where the matching granite halves of Peter Randall-Page's 'Secret Life VI' were sited. Paths wind casually down to a brown pond with a boat much too large for it and a rustic summerhouse that looks Regency in date. One of the skills of this garden is how quickly, from every direction, after 100 yards' walk, the Manor can be forgotten and the Windrush valley allowed to take over.

At Pusey House, mentioned earlier as a landscape untouched by the Capability Brown treatment, and left to open up a wide, uncluttered view, the Hornbys and later, the Loudons have scorned abstract sculpture.[19] Instead an astonishing naked gold nymph (*84*) is diving out of, not into, the lake waters, suspended in mid-air from slim silver poles, and on the other side of the lake, near a dark cedar, a ghostly group of stone statues of monks and friars are in religious colloquy, animating the path to the church in the wood, a brilliantly imaginative stroke. Diana's statue lurks almost hidden in the trees. Yet the rest of Pusey's garden is so conventionally lovely, particularly Lady Emily's Garden in its formal walled enclosure with Portuguese laurels and Winchester Cathedral roses, a Victorian memorial Temple with a near-Hindu dome, and the swimming pool garden with its modern Gothick sitting area, that these quite daring experimental ventures go almost unnoticed.

Above: 83 Jon Edgar's 'Arch' crouches like a medieval gargoyle on top of the well at Asthall Manor – one exhibit in the 'on form 06' sculpture show at this former home of the Mitfords

Right: 84 Abstract sculpture is absent at Pusey House where this golden nymph dives dramatically out of the waters of the lake

To continue the theme of richly ornamented swimming pools, the modern Oxford speciality, Britwell House has one pool enclosure in its garden to the rear, while the symmetrical garden front of the house is charmingly over-balanced by a second blue tiled pool tucked away at the side. In such a Palladian-style formal garden the two pools make a very confident modern statement. Garden temples are out, changing rooms, Gothick or classical, are in. Britwell's entrance front looks out, conventionally Palladian, to a tall pilastered Column carrying an urn, erected in 1764 by the bachelor recusant, Sir Edward Simeon, to his parents' memory as a substitute for a crucifix at a time when such a symbol would have been frowned upon.[20] Another of his obelisks is designed to be visible, at the end of an axial ride through a Wilderness of stunted trees, as a visitor approaches the house from the rear. On this garden side, though David Hicks, the previous owner[21], has planted correctly Baroque formal avenues of pollarded limes to accord with the neat early eighteenth-century house, the other swimming pool boldly asserts the twentieth century with a cosily domestic pavilion and an unexpectedly complex double maze of beech and yew hedges. It has spiral box sculptures and at least eight cabinets of no obvious function unless they are also changing rooms. Nearby, under the skirts of the house, is a circular slate installation by Richard Long aligned on yet another pollarded lime avenue. Add to these garden enrichments a Butterfly Garden of buddleia, a tree house, an orchard with very old pollarded limes and a large Walled Garden with a vine arbour and herbal cross paths leading to a duckery, and this is a hyperactive garden, its Edwardian-style garden rooms set out on a Baroque frame; but all carried out in a self-conscious historicism with just a leavening, by the Akerman-Kressners, of modern sculpture.

Broughton Grange, in the north of the county near Broughton Castle, will demand as much time as the grounds of Britwell House to explore, as its garden is slung out along the slope of a shallow valley with the house half-way down. But whereas Britwell is a traditional-modern construct upon old Baroque-Palladian bones, Broughton Grange's gardens have only very recently been completed, and its ambitious Arboretum, a large wilderness in the making, still looks like a field of spindly young trees.

Broughton is so ambitious that it demands a detailed overview. On the left-hand side of the entrance drive, largely hidden by trees, is a substantial garden walled in contrasting brick and ironstone. Then comes the pleasant, but unremarkable house in the midst of such garden projects. Just below the house lies a rectangular formal terraced Parterre, heavily flowered and cut level into the slope. This leads into a new linear avenue of the Long Borders flanked by herbaceous beds limited to lilac, pale blue and white set at right angles and running parallel to an existing grove of mature trees. A paddock for horses and an orchard is to the left. Then, at the bottom of the valley, after the Sunken Garden, there is a savage Stumpery, and lastly the open fields of the Arboretum.

This is a major modern garden and Tom Stuart-Smith, the designer, was obviously working to the positive and ambitious tastes of the owner, a landowner in the eighteenth-century tradition, shaping the future beauty of a whole swathe of Oxfordshire, like the present owners of Chiselhampton.[22] The design for the Walled Garden was based on a rough sketch by the owner of a three-part terraced garden inspired by Villandry in

France.[23] But the place is a world apart, adapted by Stuart-Smith from the sketch and working in conjunction with the architect, Ptolemy Dean, who was responsible for the walls, it is only connected to the rest of the grounds by one long allée immediately to the right at its entrance. The top terrace contains Mediterranean and prairie plants such as warm-coloured salvias, *phlomis* and tall grasses puctuated by spires of Irish yew. The use of grasses is an acknowledgement of the influence of Piet Oudolf, with whom Stuart-Smith has been working at Trentham Gardens in Staffordshire.

The second terrace level has a big rectangular pool with the most spectacular shoal of variegated carp in my experience. The grasses and the fish are a delight, but the machine-cut Rockingstone York of the paths that cross the pool in over-scaled stepping-stones and line its sides are municipal in feeling and a disappointment. Stuart-Smith remarks that this stonework is 'cool and precise, emphasising the grid layout of the garden, and reminding you that this is design on the edge'.[24] One central stream falls noisily over the harsh geometric edge of these units into the fishpond. Here there are vertical accents of beech topiary (85) clipped into abstract shapes to accord with the modern design of the pool. The third terrace is an ingenious take on the formal seventeenth-century *parterres de broderie*, but executed in an, initially obscure, interweaving of abstract shapes. Stuart-Smith explains that 'we took leaves from the principal trees in the area [oak, beech and ash] and magnified them 6,000 times under a lens. Their cells and veins then provided the motif, the layout for the parterre's box hedging'.[25] Such biomorphic shapes are evident in the work of several landscape designers such as Robert Burle Marx and Patricia Johanson. Broughton Grange promises to be an important historic garden of the future, traditional in its lower reaches with the Long Borders, the Stumpery and the vast Arboretum, and tentatively modern in its walled sector.

One key to the informed use of plants in twentieth-century layouts has been the success of nursery gardens like Waterperry, cunningly isolated in a maze of lanes a few miles due east of Oxford and Shotover. Waterperry Gardens is not simply an excellent commerical nursery, it is a dynamic horticultural training school, turning out skilled and enthusiastic gardeners every year to influence amateurs across the county. It has, furthermore, been active as an influence for 70 years. Founded in March 1932 by Miss Beatrix Havergal, it moved to Waterperry in that next September and has gone from strength to strength, not just selling plants, bulbs, bushes, trees and garden implements, but ideas in exciting, copyable garden design. What aristocratic houses like Stowe in Buckinghamshire or Holkham Hall in Norfolk did for their counties in the past, Waterperry has been doing for Oxfordshire for over 70 years; never more so than now under its design consultant, Mary Spiller.[26]

We need to look no further than Waterperry for the inspiration behind the persistent formal features of Oxfordshire gardens, their themed garden rooms, whimsical statuary and an attractive fey feminism of floral display. There is a Virgin's Walk with the statue of a thoughtful girl, the Mary Rose Gardens hidden away behind yew hedges and blowsy with scentless single roses, climbing up five wooden obelisks, a Long Walk of endless herbaceous perfection leading to a Lily Canal, immaculately green, and the glowing horseshoe of Miranda's Border with its radiance of concentrated monbretia and a burning, almost brown, dahlia. Add a Tudor-style *hortus conculsus* with herbs and knots, in a secret square

85 The middle terrace of Tom Stuart-Smith's Walled Garden at Broughton Grange has a harshly angular modern pool flanked by abstract shapes of beech topiary, but softened by a feathery mass of wafting grasses

of castellated yews, where scent hangs in the air, and Nathan David's statue of a young girl who guards the flame in her lamp with the inscription: 'Out of mere compassion for them, I abiding their self destroy the darkness born of ignorance by the luminous lamp of wisdom', and Oxfordshire gardens' inclination to figurative rather than abstract sculpture is at least partly explained.[27] Everything is overwhelmingly professional and helpful, the only weakness in a wealth of garden events is that there is no real sequence; they do not lead anywhere except back to the shop.

Then, worryingly for anyone looking for a distinctive native theme of modern garden design, comes by far and away the most ravishing and memorable garden of the twentieth century in Oxfordshire: the Japanese Garden at New House, Shipton-under-Wychwood. This is not precisely at New House, but actually contains, encloses, conceals and magically elevates New House, completely hiding the building from the outside world.

That great, though not prolific, seventeenth-century poet, Andrew Marvell, described, in his poem *The Garden*, how a truly well-tended plot of land could work upon a man's consciousness: 'Annihilating all that's made/To a green Thought in a green Shade'.[28] What Marvell conceived, two architects, Stout and Litchfield, together with artist-designer, Viacheslav Atroshenko, have created at New House for Milton Grundy: a house and garden, both of innovative complexity, but perfectly complementing each other, the house entirely modern, the garden entirely traditional and Japanese in inspiration.[29] It is of its nature that this 1963 creation has no defining name; it is simply 'New', and has no outward image. The only sign that there is a dwelling place set back among high hedges and trees is a white post by the roadside, and even when the car has driven up a rough track into a parking clearing there is still no house in sight, only an angled stone wall with the garden door hidden to deceive malcious spirits that might want to enter.

But then the angle turns, the garden door opens and the green visual magic sets in (*colour plate 24*). From the vantage point of a tiled seat with a lean-to roof that acts like a rustic tea house the whole garden can be enjoyed. The sky is obscured by overhanging branches, one boldly shaped horse chestnut towering above all the rest; the ground is not so much hidden as dramatised and made delicately precious by an enveloping covering, not of grass, but of moss that contours each and every mound and undulation. Stepping-stone paths lead across this to preserve it from footfalls so that, as visitors must take off their shoes before entering a Japanese house, so here even the garden ground is a carpet to be treated with reverence.

Only the pools of water that surround the five blocks of the house offer a level surface and the house itself is entirely irregular and unpredicatable, the linked sections rising like abstract sculptural monoliths, each with three external limestone walls and the fourth side mostly window.[30] As the garden gate was concealed so is the entrance door to the house, reached by a narrow bridge across the moat-pool, on the right of a small three-sided gravel court, 'all in *Katsura Rikyu* style'.[31] Yet one section can be reached directly by its own individual zig-zag bridge over the water, designed again to prevent evil spirits from entering the house. Those are the basic units, though there is the external courtyard to the side of the house of glittering white gravel raked into wave-like patterns about a memorable island rock. A covered verandah commands this exquisitely modelled area that 'gives strong hints of *Ryoan-ji*'.[32] Other rock islands rise at odd angles from the sea of moss and are framed by carefully sited stands of bamboo. The power of the garden is that it makes every item in its green and watery expanses seem significant. There is no attempt to create visual escape vistas. Leaves and branches hide the sky and its clouds, filtering the light into a verdant gloom. In places the rivulet that runs in and out from the moat-pool has beaches of large rounded pebbles from the east or Portland end of Chesil Beach. Nothing, not a single step, can be taken for granted; the stepping-stones are slippery and the murky water is not guarded by a fence. On that moss lawn the conkers fallen from the great chestnut lie like shiny brown pearls, each one a visual event in a garden without flowers, though one frail autumn crocus had contrived to intrude.

Along the courtyard side of the garden space (*86*) a wall has been painted with a representation of Night and Day by Paul Atroshenko, brother to Viacheslav; but the prevailing moisture has blurred all the painted outlines and the mural is now just one element of the all encompassing green shade. A mere yard or two outside the thicket of slender young trees, in the more natural garden on the far side of the house, is a full-sized river, the Evenlode, but it can only be seen in small water reflections glimpsed through leaves in that area where the rivulet trickles away through shallow pools and small

86 The gravel raked courtyard in *Katsura Rikyu* style in Milton Grundy's atmospheric green shade of an enclosure at New House – the most authentic Japanese Garden in the country and Oxfordshire's greatest garden

waterfalls. Here there are iris, cotoneasters, arundinarias, rhododendrons, acers, fern, pine, azaleas, chaenomeles and junipers. The main garden relies upon the significance and proper placing of every item, whether it is a rock formation, a bridge, a solitary acer or a lantern. When the usual moss cover turns to an exquisite fern moss or to that serviceable ground-cover known whimsically as 'Mind your business', it is automatically registered, and if the slightest divot of moss covering is displaced then the two gardeners, Rodney Wilkinson and John Burgess, who tend the place, put it back solemnly into place, devoted to perfection.

Other so-called Japanese gardens, like that at Friar Park or that at the Manoir aux Quat' Saisons, gain their effects with jolly picturesque structures: curved bridges laquered scarlet, or bamboo tea houses. As Robert Saunders writes: 'All of the materials in the garden come from the UK. There are no imports. There are no gimmicks. This is a Japanese garden in a seemingly natural setting. Tranquility abounds'.[33] The garden does have one or two small stone lanterns; otherwise it works entirely by a disciplined drama of exaggerated perfection: leaves, stones, water, mosses, very little else. It creates a visual cleansing; after experiencing it every other garden, however successful and beautiful, seems to be trying too hard. Nature alone, it suggests, once carefully presented and enjoyed, should be enough. The garden is not regularly open, though specialist groups do sometimes gain access and, in any case, visitors should be wary as it will make them into visual snobs. It has featured most dramatically at twilight as a precursor to one extra-violent scene in Stanley Kubrick's 'A Clockwork Orange'. Sherwood and Pevsner describe the site, evasively, as 'one of the most outstanding modern private houses in the country … set in a Japanese water garden'[34] and do not go into detail about the setting. What they were probably expressing was the absolute unity of the garden with the house.

NOTES

1 For Lindsay see Jane Brown, *Eminent Gardeners: Some people of influence and their gardens 1880-1980*, 1990, pp.60-76; also her *The English Garden through the 20th Century*, 1999, pp.178-81. Illustrations of Lindsay's garden are given in her *Country Life* article: 'The Garden of the Manor House, Sutton Courtenay', 16 May 1931. I am grateful to Trish Gibson for her insights into both Lindsay's and Colvin's work at Sutton Courtenay.

2 Brown, *The English Garden*, pp.179-80.

3 Brenda Colvin, 'Sutton Courtenay Manor, Berkshire', *Journal of the Institute of Landscape Architects*, November, 1953, pp.5-8.

4 Trish Gibson, unpublished notes, 2 April 2003.

5 I am grateful to Trish Gibson for this article and for her insight into Colvin's design aesthetic at Little Peacocks. We await her forthcoming biography of Colvin, due out in early 2008.

6 Arthur Evans, *Jarn Mound: With its Panorama and Wild Garden of British Plants* (Oxford, 1933), p.10; quoted in Sheila Ottway, 'Conservation Statement: Jarn Mound, Boars Hill, Oxfordshire', unpublished report for MA Garden History, Bristol, 2003, to which I am indebted. I have also consulted David Lambert's excellent report on the site for the Oxford Preservation Trust (hereafter OPT), July 2004, 21pp.

7 Evans, *Jarn Mound*, p.10.

8 Ibid., p.36.

9 Lambert, OPT report, p.10.

10 I am most indebted to Francesca Fraser-Darling's informed dissertation on Greys Court for biographical background on the Brunners and for her sensitive interpretation of the grounds: 'Subverting the Hortus Conclusus: The Brunners at Greys Court, Oxfordshire', MA, University of Bristol, 2005.

11 The text of his sermon was printed in *The Times* for 26 March 1980.

12 Quoted in Mary Keen, 'A Spirit of Place', *Perspectives*, August, 1995, p.52.

13 He was also, post-1954, Chair of Henley-on-Thames Rural District Council.

14 The modern influence may well have been Ian Hamilton Finlay's garden of inscriptions.

15 The owners have been advised on the new landscaping around the house by Barbara Simms and John Brookes.

16 *VCH*, vol.7, 1962, pp.6-8.

17 The new lake is being constructed on the site of the old house and alongside the original Kitchen Garden. The owners await an archaeological survey by John Moore on this historically important area of the grounds.

18 Mary S. Lovell, *The Mitford Girls*, 2001, pp.44-5.

19 I am grateful to Leonard Rwodzi for a most enthusiastic and informed tour of the grounds.

20 See Gervase Jackson-Stops, 'Britwell Salome, Oxfordshire – I', *Country Life*, 5 October 1972.

21 The house is now owned by the Akerman-Kressners. I am grateful to Trudy Akerman-Kressner for allowing me access to these private grounds.

22 I am indebted to Valerie Ferguson's Bristol MA Garden History report (2006) on the garden for much of my information. Tom Stuart-Smith and the then Head Gardener, Iain Davies, were most helpful in providing her with comment on the design. The present Head Gardener, Andrew Woodall, gave me an excellent tour of the Walled Garden.

23 The owner has asked that I do not name him.

24 Quoted in Galiena Hitchman, 'A Winter's Tale', *Gardens Illustrated*, March 2004; taken from the Ferguson report, p.5.

25 Quoted in Mark Griffiths, 'Through a Glass Brightly', *Country Life*, 12 May 2005; taken from the Ferguson report, p.6.

26 See Mary Spiller, *Waterperry Gardens* (Norwich, 1998).

27 Nathan David sculpted the Virgin; the Mary Rose Gardens were started in 1991; the Formal Garden (*hortus conclusus*) was designed in 1986 by Bernard Saunders and Mary Spiller; the Canal has a statue of Miranda from Shakespeare's *The Tempest* sculpted by Tanya Russel.

28 Lines 47-8.

29 I am most grateful to Milton Grundy for allowing me access to the garden and to David Clark for bringing to my attention the article on the house in the Journal of the Japanese Garden Society by Robert Saunders: 'The New House, Shipton-under-Wychwood', *Shakkei*, vol.4, no.4 (Winter, 1997), no pagination. The Saunders article states that Alex Rota designed the garden, though Milton Grundy says that he contrived it together with his partner, Viacheslav Atroshenko.

30 See Michael Webb, 'A House where East meets West', *Country Life*, 3 November 1966.

31 Saunders, *Shakkei*.

32 Ibid.

33 Ibid.

34 Jennifer Sherwood & Nikolaus Pevsner, *The Buildings of England: Oxfordshire*, 1974, p.760.

GAZETTEER

The following is a list of gardens of significant historic importance, which are covered in this book and are open to the public.

Abbreviations

NT   National Trust
EH   English Heritage
P   Privately owned but open regularly
NGS   Privately owned but open occasionally as part of the National Gardens Scheme
H/CC   Hotel/Conference Centre
GC/N   Garden Centre/Nursery
EX   Exhibition Venue
O   Setting for Opera

Asthall Manor House	(EX/NGS)	Kelmscott Manor	(P)
Blenheim Palace	(P)	Kingston Bagpuize House	(P)
Broughton Castle	(P)	Nuneham Park	(CC)
Broughton Grange	(NGS)	Oxford Botanic Garden	(P)
Buckland House	(NGS)	Oxford College Gardens	(P)
Buscot Manor	(NT)	Rousham	(P)
Chastleton Glebe	(NGS)	Shotover Park	(NGS)
Chastleton House	(NT)	Stonor Park	(P)
Ditchley Park	(CC)	Sutton Courtenay Manor	(NGS)
Eynsham Park	(H/CC)	Tackley Water Gardens	(NGS)
Garsington Manor	(O/NGS)	Waterperry Gardens	(GC/N)
Greys Court	(NT)	Wroxton Abbey	(P)
Harcourt Arboretum	(P)		
Heythrop House	(H/CC)		

INDEX